DATE DUE

~~JE 4 '03~~			

DEMCO 38-296

Internet Security Protocols

ISBN 0-13-014249-2

90000

9 780130 142498

Prentice Hall Series In
Advanced Communications Technologies

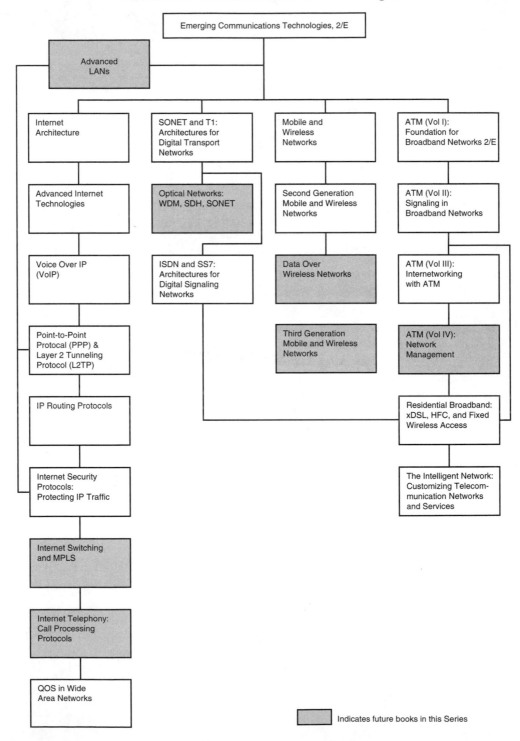

Emerging Communications Technologies, 2/E

Advanced LANs

Internet Architecture

SONET and T1: Architectures for Digital Transport Networks

Mobile and Wireless Networks

ATM (Vol I): Foundation for Broadband Networks 2/E

Advanced Internet Technologies

Optical Networks: WDM, SDH, SONET

Second Generation Mobile and Wireless Networks

ATM (Vol II): Signaling in Broadband Networks

Voice Over IP (VoIP)

ISDN and SS7: Architectures for Digital Signaling Networks

Data Over Wireless Networks

ATM (Vol III): Internetworking with ATM

Point-to-Point Protocal (PPP) & Layer 2 Tunneling Protocol (L2TP)

Third Generation Mobile and Wireless Networks

ATM (Vol IV): Network Management

IP Routing Protocols

Residential Broadband: xDSL, HFC, and Fixed Wireless Access

Internet Security Protocols: Protecting IP Traffic

The Intelligent Network: Customizing Telecommunication Networks and Services

Internet Switching and MPLS

Internet Telephony: Call Processing Protocols

QOS in Wide Area Networks

Indicates future books in this Series

Internet Security Protocols
Protecting IP Traffic

UYLESS BLACK

PH
PTR

Prentice Hall PTR
Upper Saddle River, New Jersey 07458
www.phptr.com

n-Publication Data

Acquisitions editor: *Mary Franz*
Editorial assistant: *Noreen Regina*
Cover designer: *Anthony Gemmellaro*
Cover design director: *Jerry Votta*
Buyer: *Maura Goldstaub*
Marketing manager: *Bryan Gambrel*
Project coordinator: *Anne Trowbridge*
Compositor/Production services: *Pine Tree Composition, Inc.*

 © 2000 by Uyless Black
Published by Prentice Hall PTR
Prentice-Hall, Inc.
Upper Saddle River, New Jersey 07458

Prentice Hall books are widely used by corporations and government agencies for training, marketing, and resale.

The publisher offers discounts on this book when ordered in bulk quantities. For more information contact:

Corporate Sales Department
Phone: 800–382–3419
Fax: 201–236–7141
E-mail: corpsales@prenhall.com

Or write:

Prentice Hall PTR
Corp. Sales Dept.
One Lake Street
Upper Saddle River, New Jersey 07458

Printed in the United States of America
10 9 8 7 6 5 4 3 2

ISBN: 0-13-014249-2

Prentice-Hall International (UK) Limited, *London*
Prentice-Hall of Australia Pty. Limited, *Sydney*
Prentice-Hall Canada Inc., *Toronto*
Prentice-Hall Hispanoamericana, S.A., *Mexico*
Prentice-Hall of India Private Limited, *New Delhi*
Prentice-Hall of Japan, Inc., *Tokyo*
Pearson Education Asia Pte. Ltd.
Editora Prentice-Hall do Brasil, Ltda., *Rio de Janeiro*

This book is dedicated to Lt. Ron Wolfe USNR, a shipmate, fellow crypto officer, and a fine friend.

In my youth I read the *Mad* comic magazine. Two characters that I remember from *Mad* were the security spies. The "good" spy was dressed in white (and wore a white hat of course). This character is called Ted in this book. The "bad" spy was dressed in black, and wore a black hat. He is called Mallory.

Earlier in my career, and many years ago, I served as a Communications Officer on several ships in the South China Sea (and I also wore a white hat ... that of the U.S. Navy). During this time, I spent many hours on these ships setting up the (now defunct) "post-Enigma crypto machines." I say post-Enigma, because during the early 1960s, many of the U.S. Navy's crypto capabilities were off-shoots of the "ancient" crypto devices that were designed before the World War II era.

Anyway, back to the Ted and Mallory story. These two spies spent most of their time trying to do each other in. I don't recall who won, Ted or Mallory. But their battles were always in a humorous vein, and intended to be taken lightly.

Unfortunately, the same cannot be said for the Internet security battles of today. As indicated by articles in mass-media magazines, and the evening news reports, the Mallories of the Internet world are creating serious problems for any Internet user. The costs of a single security breach, such as a virus, are staggering, amounting to billions of dollars in lost revenue and productivity.

Who is winning the Internet security wars, Ted or Mallory? I think it is accurate to say that Mallory is ahead now, at least in regard to the non-business users of the Internet. But Ted is gaining. Eventually, revamped operating systems and supporting security protocols will be in place to reduce the damage of these Internet security attacks.

But I doubt that in the near future we will see an impregnable security wall that defeats Mallory's ploys, and his thrusts into our information systems.

So, in the meantime, keep your security software versions up-to-date, back up your resources often, and don't open those loving attachments.

Contents

CHAPTER 3   **Basic Security Concepts**   **25**

CHAPTER 10   The Internet Key Distribution, Certification, and Management   183

Preface

This book is one in a series of books called "Advanced Communications Technologies." As the name of the book implies, the focus is on Internet security and the principal protocols that contribute to Internet security services. The book is an expansion of *Advanced Features of the Internet,* also part of this series.

Due to the breadth of the subject of Internet Security, and in keeping with the focus of the Advanced Communications Technologies Series, the focus in this book is on the protocols that operate between Internet nodes, such as routers, servers, and hosts.

The book has been written for this series to act as an introduction to the subject of Internet security. As such, it is written for the person who is new to the subject. It assumes the reader is versed in Internet Architecture, and TCP/IP.

I hope you find this book a valuable addition to your library.

ACKNOWLEDGMENTS

In many of my explanations of Internet security operations, I have relied on the Internet Request for Comments (RFCs) and draft standards published by the Internet Society, and I thank this organization for making the RFCs available to the public. The draft standards are "works in progress," and usually change as they wind their way to an RFC (if indeed they become an RFC). A work in progress cannot be considered final, but many vendors use them in creating products for the marketplace. Notwithstanding, they are subject to change.

For all the Internet standards and draft standards the following applies:

1

Introduction

T his chapter describes the nature of the security problem in the Internet, and the types of security services that are available to solve or alleviate these problems. Security policies are explained, as well as risk management. The Virtual Private Network (VPN) is also introduced. The chapter concludes with a discussion of privacy issues in an automated society.

SECURITY PROBLEMS

Since the inception of the computer and computer networks, a very small number of people in the telecommunications community have existed who have wished to demonstrate their intellectual prowess by attacking computer systems and networks. On other occasions, the attacks have come from those who wished financial gain, or to seek revenge for a wrong, either real or imagined.

The attacks have consisted of devising ways to damage others' information systems, sometimes with rather innocuous consequences, but at other times with severe results.

On a rather pathetic note, these individuals have often exposed their intellectual ineptitude. Their successes are owed more to the openness and exposure of the systems that they have attacked than anything else. But, not in all cases. There are documented instances of attacks that indicate facile minds with high intellects and a profound knowledge of communications networks and computer operating systems.

In a Catch-22 situation, these individuals are also subject to attack from others of their ilk.

HOW PERVASIVE ARE SECURITY ATTACKS?

It is impossible to know how often an information system is (a) attacked and (b) penetrated. A security breech to your PC, or to a small business, etc. is not known to the world. Indeed, most companies do not release information about their security problems, because of the commonsense belief that the mere discussion of the problem leaves them open to further attacks (not to mention the problems that arise from their stockholders at the annual meeting).

But many of you who are reading this paragraph have been the victims of some type of security breech on your computer or your company's computer. Sometimes this breech is only mildly irritating, or it may even be amusing. Other times, it can be disastrous, resulting in the destruction of programs and data files. More often than not, it results in the loss of many hours of productive work.

To gain a sense of the scope of the problem, the FBI operates a special organization devoted to computer network security. This organization, located in San Francisco, reported in 1998 that 60% of the companies in the Fortune 1000 reported security breeches to their systems; and this means successful penetration into their systems. In all likelihood, most of these companies experienced attempts of penetration [ZIMI98].[1] The FBI further reports that each incident wherein the loss was caused by insider access (a so-called trusted person) cost a company $2.8 million to recover! That amount of money might appear too large, but consider that a security breech might lead to thousands of employees, contractors, and customers being denied access to automated resources.

---

[1][ZIMI98]. Zimits, Eric C, and Montaño, Christopher. "Public Key Infrastructure: Unlocking the Internet's Economic Potential," *Istory,* Volume 3, Issue 2, April, 1998. Go to *szmits@hamquist.com* or *amontano@hamquist.com* for more information.

It does not take many hours of service denial to tabulate into a very large loss.

The types of losses and the costs to recover from those losses depend on the type of attack. [ZIMI98] offers a summary of the FBI study, as shown in Table 1–1.

IBM maintains the Anti-Virus Center at its Hawthorne, New York, facility. At this site, IBM has battled over 20,000 separate security invaders. Today, it is processing and analyzing six to ten new viruses a day [BUDE99].[2]

The well-known "Melissa" virus that disrupted email systems throughout the world in March 1999 is estimated to have done more than $80 million in damage [GOLD99].[3] David Smith, a computer programmer, pleaded guilty to creating and distributing Melissa (reportedly named after a topless dancer Smith once knew). Under a plea bargain, Smith could face five to ten years in state prison, and up to five years in a federal prison. Rounding it to ten years, the damage comes to about $8 million for each of Smith's prison years. Smith is going to have to make a lot of license plates to make up for the damage he did.

In February 2000 several Internet sites were attacked by individuals (whom I will call Mallory in this book—no offense if your name is Mallory) who saturated the sites' computers with a spate of traffic, rendering the machines incapable of servicing legitimate customers' needs. These attacks made the covers of the weekly newsmagazines—a sure in-

Table 1–1 The Average Loss of Various Security Attacks

Type of Attack	Average Financial Loss ($)
Unauthorized Insider Access	$2,809,000
Theft of Proprietary Information	1,677,000
Telecom Fraud	539,000
Financial Fraud	388,000
Sabotage	86,000
System Penetration by Outsider	86,000

---

[2][BUDE99]. Buderi, Robert. "The Virus Wars," *Scientific American,* April, 1999.
[3][GOLD99]. Gold, Jeffery. Associated Press dispatch, December 10, 1999, published in *USA Today.*

dication that security problems have entered the mainstream of our lives. Suspects have been arrested, and are awaiting trial.

Obviously, Internet security is a big problem. Let us take a look at several services that are available to combat this problem.

TYPES OF SECURITY SERVICES

When the term Internet security is mentioned to some people, and they are asked what it means, a common response is, "It means encrypting the traffic that flows through the Internet." Another is, "Keeping those cookies off my computer!"

Yes, but it means more. Internet security means employing security operations to achieve these major goals (and summarized in Table 1–2):

- *Privacy/Secrecy/Confidentiality:* The assurance that an Internet user's traffic is not examined by non-authorized parties. In so many words, it is an assurance that no one "reads your mail."
- *Authentication:* The assurance that the traffic you receive (email, files, Web pages, etc.) is sent by the legitimate party or parties. For example, if you receive a legal document from your attorney through the Internet, you are confident that your attorney sent it—not someone else. This idea is also called data origin authentication.
- *Integrity*: The assurance that the traffic you receive has not been modified after it was sent by the proper party. This service includes anti-replay defenses. That is, operations that prevent someone from reinjecting previously authenticated packets into a traffic stream. Because of its anti-injecting operations, this service offers sequence integrity, which means "rogue" packets may be rejected

Table 1–2   Different Types of Internet Security Services

Privacy/Secrecy/Confidentiality	Assurance that user's traffic is not examined by non-authorized parties
Authentication	Assurance that traffic is sent by legitimate party or parties
Integrity	Assurance that received traffic has not been modified. Integrity includes anti-replay defenses
Access control	Prevention of unauthorized use of a resource
Non-repudiation	Inability to disavow a transaction

if they do not meet certain rules for their arrival at a receiver.[4] For IP networks, this idea is also called connectionless integrity.

- *Access control:* The prevention of an unauthorized use of a resource, including the prevention of the use of a resource in an unauthorized manner. This service might prevent someone from monopolizing resources, or deny the use of the resource entirely. Resource monopolization is a common security attack and leads to the denial of service to legitimate users.

- *Non-repudiation:* Inability to deny or disavow a transaction. This service is part of the authentication service described above. An example of this feature is an option in the X.400 personal message service. An email recipient is not allowed to examine the contents of the message body of the email until this recipient has acknowledged that the email was indeed received. It is like a certified letter at the post office. You can look at the envelope, and sign-off that you received it, but you cannot look inside the envelope before signing the receipt.

These security services employ mechanisms that are independent of the encryption/decryption algorithms. It would be foolish to impose specific algorithms on a security protocol, since various coding/decoding disciplines come and go.

Furthermore, these security services need not be invoked for each piece of traffic sent through an internet. For example, a user (say, Ted) may not care if someone reads Ted's mail; Ted may only care that the receiver (say Carol) has confidence that the mail indeed came from Ted. Of course, Carol also cares about the authenticity of Ted. In this example, Ted and Carol are concerned with authentication, but not privacy.

The manner in which an organization or person decides on the combinations of these security services is the subject of later discussions.

INTRODUCTION TO THE FIREWALL

We need to introduce the security firewall before proceeding further (it is explained in more detail in Chapter 4). A firewall is a system (often a router or a PC) that is used to enforce an access control policy within

---

[4]A rogue packet is an illegal or untrusted packet, usually one with suspicious origins or one that is destined to be used on applications that are known to be vulnerable to attack.

an organization or between organizations. The firewall allows or forbids traffic to pass from one side to the other of the firewall. Any authorized traffic that is allowed to pass through this firewall from one network to another or from one host to another host, must be defined by the security policy established in the access control plans of the organization.

THE SECURITY POLICY

One of the biggest challenges involved in developing an effective security system for an organization is to determine who should be given access to the organization's information and who should not. The actual tools that will place these decisions into effect (cryptography, firewalls, etc.) will prove to be suboptimal if an organization has not given considerable thought to its security policy. Moreover, these thoughts must be placed into action with a cohesive implementation plan. In a nutshell, the deployment tools, such as a firewall, may not solve an organization's security problems. Indeed, firewalls can create almost as many problems as they solve if they are not implemented properly.

To gain an idea of the challenge, consider a private company with private internets. Typically, employees are continuously leaving the company, and are being hired. Ongoing employees move from one project to another. Moreover, many companies are involved in acquisitions, reorganizations, and mergers, all of which entail the use of information—in many instances, the use of confidential information. This complex and dynamic environment must be able to react to changes to allow access to resources of information and yet be secure enough to guard against unwanted intrusions.

The problem is compounded considerably if an organization must interact with public networks such as the Internet. As new networks and new hosts are made known to the Internet, as new servers are added, as new products are made available, an organization is challenged to find a means to safely integrate these services and make them available to the employees of the organization.

Trusted and Untrusted Networks

In order to implement a security program, an organization must first develop an access control policy for its internal and external networks and resources. Some organizations consider that their internal networks (those they control, such as local area networks inside their buildings) are trusted networks. Those networks external to the organization are untrusted. The firewall is meant to isolate the trusted networks from the untrusted networks.

It is important to remember that internal networks must be thought of as exhibiting some level of untrustworthiness. The statistics in Table 1–1 show why. Yet, the security policies of these internal networks can be different from those for external networks. For example, individual workgroups inside the organization may be identified, and traffic flowing *within* the workgroup may be treated differently than traffic flowing *between* workgroups. This level of detail would not be visible to external network users on the "other" side of the firewall. This aspect of security is revisited in later chapters.

SECURITY AND RISK MANAGEMENT

In establishing the security policy guidelines, an organization must identify those entities that are considered valuable enough to warrant security measures. Within these entities, it is likely that certain resources will be considered more valuable than others in relation to the damage done if security breaches occur. For example, in an electronic funds transfer system (such as at a bank or the Federal Reserve), the exposure of financial transactions likely will have much more severe impact than the exposure of a personnel record. Moreover, assessing the risks and potential damages allows an organization to make rational cost/performance decisions pertaining to the degree and expense taken to protect the resources.

Some institutions will benefit from implementing the security measures and prototyping them for a while to evaluate them. This period of designing, coding, and testing a security system may take a considerable length of time. Some organizations have taken over a year to formulate the plan, implement it, and test it. Therefore, patience is the key word, as is developing a coherent cost-effective plan from which to build a security policy.

VIRTUAL PRIVATE NETWORKS (VPNs)

The term Virtual Private Network (VPN) has been in the industry for many years. It was first used in X.25-based public packet networks in the mid-1970s to describe a data network that was available to the public, much like the public telephone network being available to voice customers. Figure 1–1 shows the layout for this early VPN. For the data VPN, the idea was to provide data communication services to the customer such that the customer perceived that the service was provided by a private network, one tailored to the customer's needs, when in fact the network was used by many other customers.

The earlier VPNs did not provide much in the way of tailored services. Part of their attraction was the ability to reduce a customer's long-distance phone charges by using the public data network and obtaining economies of scale by accessing the data network. A customer would dial into a local access device for a local call (called a packet assembler/disassembler [PAD]), and the PAD would act as a gateway to the X.25 network. The PAD was designed to support asynchronous start-stop protocols, so it was a fairly simple task to get the customer connected to the VPN (the public data network).

The Modern VPN

In today's environment, a modern VPN still provides the services of the older VPN, plus other features. The layout for the new VPN is shown in Figure 1–2. The additional characteristics of this VPN are as follows:

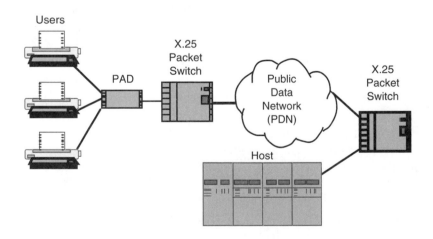

Where:
  PAD   Packet assembler/disassembler

Figure 1–1   The original VPN concept: X.25 and PADs

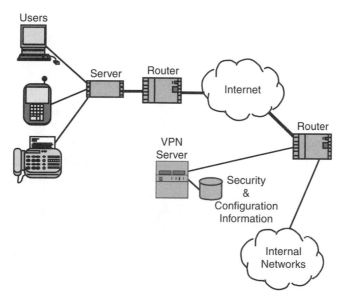

Figure 1–2   Today's VPN

- The VPN user is not aware of the VPN bearer services, such as the Internet.
- The VPN user is provided extensive security services, including privacy and authentication operations.
- The employees or customers of an organization can dial-in to the bearer network, and obtain automatic configuration services from remote servers.
- Usually, the users dial-in to a local server, with the operations taking place through the Internet to remote servers (say, a VPN server as shown in Figure 1–2). Users can reduce substantially dial-up expenses by using the Internet instead of long-distance toll lines.
- PPP, remote RADIUS servers, and IPSec become very important tools to support this type of environment (discussed later).

I emphasize once again that significant cost advantages can result in using secure connections across the Internet between the user's devices, instead of using private lines, or a public Frame Relay service.

Figure 1–3 shows the VPN topology in more detail. This topology is an example; there is no one topology that is required. But this example is a practical one, and it will be used to make several points about VPNs.

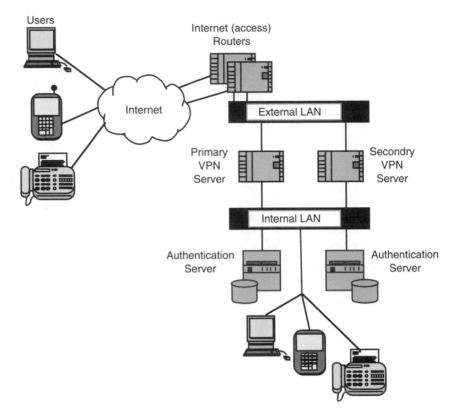

Figure 1–3   A VPN Topology

The Internet acts as the VPN bearer service. Remote users dial-in to an ISP, which relays the traffic to an external Internet router (and backups). This device is sometimes configured to be an "access firewall." If it is so-used, its main job is to check IP addresses in the incoming traffic to determine if they are valid. The VPN server functions may be located at this machine. If so, its job is to perform decryption of the traffic that was encrypted at the source.

The VPN server may also operate behind the access firewall (the "Internet Router" in this example) and reside on an internal LAN (as shown in Figure 1–3). If so, the access router (or a server in the Internet, not shown here) must pass the incoming traffic to the VPN server for the decryption functions. If this traffic is an initial session set up, it is sent to an authentication server to validate the dial-in user. The authentication server often also provides configuration services to the dial-in user.

Figure 1–3 shows several nodes; some participate in VPN operations, and others do not. It may be more convenient and cost-effective to place the functions of the VPN server and the authentication server in one machine, because the authentication and privacy functions may best be performed in one function (and therefore the same machine). Therefore, it is not unusual to see authentication, traffic encryption, and configuration operations placed into the VPN gateway. Also, this figure shows that the critical machines are backed up with secondary machines.

Notwithstanding the position of the VPN gateway, the main task is to support secure logical connections (called IPSec [IP Security] tunnels) through the Internet.

The remote users in this figure are connected in one of two ways. With the first, the security tunnels are set up and remain static. This approach is used between sites that are not mobile, for example between branch offices and headquarters. The second approach supports the mobile user, one who dials-in from a mobile phone, a hotel room, etc.

This VPN operation is examined in considerable detail in this book.

VPNs AND SLAs

Wide area networks (WANs) that offer VPN may offer quality of service (QOS) features. Throughput and delay are examples of these features. Others are traffic loss guarantees. The service level agreement (SLA) contract—the contract between the customer and the service provider—is used to codify the VPN's "commitment" to its customer.

In a large customer internet, there may be hundreds of connections and services with different network providers. SLA contracts have been signed, and the SLAs should be supported.

In a public data network (such as a Frame Relay network), a customer enterprise is often billed based on its bandwidth usage on each permanent virtual circuit (PVC). It is important for the customer to be able to know how the service provider has billed for the PVC and the traffic across the PVC. In the past, software was not readily available to monitor these circuits and provide meaningful information to the customer. This situation is changing, and a number of vendors now have products that enable Frame Relay customers to gather information for monitoring their SLAs.

Figure 1–4 shows the topology for implementing an SLA monitor. The enhanced channel service unit/data service unit (CSU/DSU) collects performance data by monitoring the traffic passing through it. The data

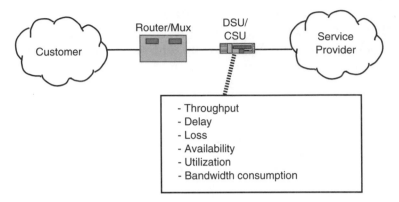

Figure 1-4   Service Level Agreements (SLAs) and SLA Monitoring Tools

are passed to software that generates reports on key QOS operations: (a) availability, (b) delay, (c) throughput by PVC or physical port, (d) traffic discards, (e) port utilization over time, and (f) percentage of bandwidth being used by a protocol (SNA, IP, etc.).

The price for these enhanced CSU/DSUs range from $1000 to $4000. They are available from a number of vendors [TAYL98][5] and [JAND99].[6]

THE DEBATE OF PRIVACY VS. LAW ENFORCEMENT

The debate about the right to privacy of an individual vs. the need-to-know of the law enforcement or defense community about an individual's activities has been with us for many years. But with the wide use of computer networks, and the emergence of inexpensive commercial cryptographic (crypto) systems, the debate is taking on a different context. The good news is that more people are becoming aware of the issues.

It is an irony that these new crypto systems can give a citizen more privacy, but these systems are the very tools that some believe should be denied to a citizen for the good of a nation to fight crime, and to provide for effective defense measures.

---

[5][TAYL98]. Taylor, Steven and Wexler, Joanie, "Maturing Frame Relay Makes New Demands," *Business Communications Review,* July, 1998.

[6][JAND99]. Jander, Mary, "SLA Monitoring Tools," *Data Communications,* February, 1999.

I have great empathy for those parties that espouse the right to be able tap into a "consumer" security system, if there is a sound legal reason to do so, because of a serious crime or serious national security problem. Earlier in my career as a US Navy Communications Officer, I had a tour in cryptography, and later a tour with the Defense Intelligence Agency (DIA), where I was custodian of the NSA security intelligence estimates documents. I understand how valuable it is to be able to gather intelligence information.

Now that you know my credentials as one who recognizes the "need to know" of certain government bodies, you also can know that I am "partisan for privacy."

I am because the right to privacy is one of the most fundamental aspects of a free society. With the respect for privacy comes the respect for the individual. One flows from the other. My concern is that a freedom, once denied, is very difficult to retrieve. Give a little here, and a little there, and it is gone.

And there is probably no better example than the US social security number (SSN). The intent of the SSN was for keeping records for the social security program, so it followed that the SSN could be used for payroll and tax records. As late as the 1970s, that was how the SSN was used (early 1970s). In fact, those who had access to SSNs (comptrollers, payroll managers) often viewed the SSN as sacrosanct, and did not allow it to be used for any other purpose.

During those days, I made a faulty assumption. I assumed the US government would protect the SSN and would not allow its use for commercial purposes. Why did this not happen? For one thing, it was too easy to use, it was too cost-effective for an ID. And there was no citizen group that was watching over its "integrity."

Today, the SSN is certainly an efficient ID. Several years ago, I received a citation from a state policeman for speeding. A few days later (not weeks, not months), I received a notice from my car insurance company that my insurance rates were raised because of this ticket.

Efficient? Absolutely. Disturbing? For me, yes. It was not the fact that my rates were raised, it was the fact that a state government agency was sharing (perhaps selling) information with a commercial enterprise. And this trend is accelerating. Privacy is becoming obsolete.

Some of my colleagues in telecommunications have said, "What do you have to hide? If you have nothing to hide, then you should not be concerned." My answer is, "I have nothing left to hide because of the very efficiency of our 'information society.'" So perhaps all this is a feigned exposition! Maybe it's too late!

Anyway, assuming that a person who knows all about someone else is a benevolent person, then my colleagues have a beguiling argument. But are all persons benevolent? I rest my case on this matter.

On another level, the issue also comes down to mundane yet exasperating day-to-day experiences. I receive calls almost every night (around dinner time) from marketing firms who know my buying profiles (they have yet to learn my eating habits). This intrusion violates what was once was considered a tool for private communications, the telephone. My point about the marketing calls is a serious one: An important aspect of the right to privacy is simply the right to be left alone.

We could go on and on about this subject. I will conclude this brief diatribe by saying that the erosion of privacy in the United States is astounding. Furthermore, the tools to erode it even further are in place and being exploited every day. Some of the culprits are cookies, discussed in the next chapter.

But I am (and just recently) becoming optimistic. What has been lacking in the United States is a discussion (on a mass scale, beyond the specialists) about the issue. This discussion is starting to reach heretofore unreachable parts of the population because of the presence of the Internet in their lives. From these debates, I am hopeful that this country will develop a workable compromise between the "need-to-know" and the right to privacy.

This is a technical book and not one on social or political policy. Hereafter, the focus of the book is on Internet security problems and the tools to attack those problems.

2

Types of Security Violations

T his chapter describes the types of the security attacks that may take place in an internet.[1] Security violations, such as the virus and the worm, are explained. The chapter concludes with a discussion of cookies, and how they can be both beneficial and harmful.

TYPES OF SECURITY PROBLEMS

What types of security problems should an organization protect against? Most security issues are associated with catchy names, such as a virus, a worm, and so on. This part of the book provides a review of these problems.

Denial of Service: Attacks and Counter-attacks

Several of the security violations explained in this chapter lead to a denial of service to the users of the attacked resource. The resource may be disabled by rogue code, or it may be simply saturated by an excessive

---

[1]Hereafter, the term Internet (upper case I) refers to the public Internet. The term internet (lower case i) refers to a private network.

workload as the attacker sends spurious traffic into the resource. This problem is called a denial of service attack. The service denial is to the legitimate users of the resource.

The counter-attack is to take preventive measures against the attack. In so doing, the system denies service to the attacker, for example, checking addresses in the incoming packets and discarding suspicious source addresses. This is called a denial of service counter-attack, and the service denial is to the attacker.

VIRUS

Typically, a virus is a piece of code that copies itself into a program, and executes when the program runs. It then may infect other programs. The infection may not occur immediately. It might not manifest itself until it is triggered by some kind of an event; as examples, a date, the detection of an event, such as a person's name being removed from a database, etc. A virus may also modify other programs. A graphical representation of the operation of a virus is shown in Figure 2–1.

The damage of a virus may only be irritating, such as the execution of a lot of superfluous code that degrades a system's performance. But a virus can do considerable damage. Indeed, some people define a virus as a program that causes the loss or contamination of data, or a program.

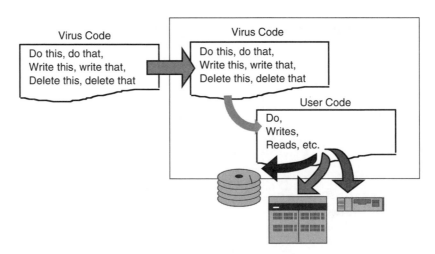

Figure 2–1   View of a virus operation

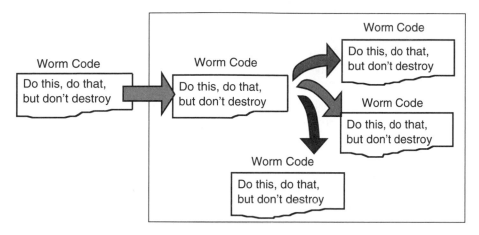

Figure 2–2   View of a worm operation

A virus may be difficult to detect or find. The virus may even get rid of itself at some point. That is, it may execute and then eradicate itself.

WORM

A worm is sometimes confused with a virus (see Figure 2–2). They have some similarities; the worm is code. However, it is an independent program that does not modify other programs, but reproduces itself over and over again until it slows down or shuts down a computer system or a network. One reason a worm is called a worm is because of two PARC researchers, John Schoch and Jon Hupp, who described a worm as code that existed in a machine. The worm segment on the machine can join or leave the computation.[2] A segment was likened to the segment of a worm—able to stay alive on its own.

---

[2]John F. Shoch and Jon A. Hupp. "The Worm Programs—Early Experience with a Distributed Computation," *Communications of the ACM,* Vol. 25, Number 3. Also, Deborah Russel and G.T. Gangemi Sr. [RUSS91] provide an interesting history of early viruses and worms. See *Computer Security Basics,* by these authors, O'Reilly & Associates, Inc., 1991. I am using their taxonomy for the description of the types of security violations.

CLOGGING OR FLOODING

Clogging or flooding is a form of worm. It entails sending a very large amount of bogus traffic to a node, such as a server or a router. The receiving node becomes clogged and is unable to service legitimate users, because of the excessive workload on the computing resources. Obviously, this fits the description of a denial of service attack, described earlier.

TROJAN HORSE

A Trojan horse is also a piece of code, and a worm or virus may be classified as a Trojan horse. It is so-named because it hides itself (inside another program) like the old story of the Greek soldiers. They hid inside a large hollow horse that was pulled by unwary Troy citizens into the city of Troy. Later, once inside the fortress of Troy, the soldiers came out of the horse and opened the city's gates to let in the rest of the soldiers.

In Figure 2–3, a piece of code is hidden inside a login program. A legitimate user logs on to a system in which the Trojan horse is hidden in the login program. The user's login IDs are intercepted by the Trojan horse and made available to the Trojan horse "soldier." Thereafter, the user's logon is compromised, and the Trojan horse interloper can use the ID to access the user's resources. It is possible that the Trojan horse may not be found because, after finding desired information, it exits the system and leaves no trace of itself.

BOMB

The bomb is yet another security-compromise instrument. It may take the form of a Trojan horse, and may do the harm of a virus or a worm. Its signature is that it is actuated by either a *time* trigger or a

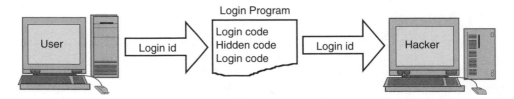

Figure 2–3   Trojan horse

logic trigger. The time trigger, introduced earlier, activates the bomb. One date-triggered bomb comes to mind; after a date is passed, the bomb prevents a program from executing further. The Y2K situation is an example of an inadvertent bomb, now diffused with the passing of midnight, December 31 to the year 2000.

The logic trigger is based on the bomb examining an event captured in the legitimate software's normal execution. Once again, an example is the deletion of a record from a database. For example, an employee is dismissed and the employee record is removed from the personnel file. It so happens that this former employee was the programmer for the personnel system. So, the disgruntled programmer disables the system the programmer created.[3] The trigger is a software routine that, upon detecting the absence of the rogue programmer's record, initiates actions to damage the system.

TRAP DOOR

A trap door is a mechanism to get into a system. It occurs due to faulty security measures, allowing Mallory to penetrate a system. However, this "door" may be programmed in the code by the code's programmer. I have found them useful in my past work because they allowed me to access a software system that had become a production system, but still needed my intervention on special occasions. In some applications, once the system is in production, its access may be restricted.[4]

---

[3]In an earlier part of my career, I was a partner in a communications consulting firm. One of our partners wrote the code for our accounting and billing system. Later, as this company devolved, bombs were inserted into the software. Thereafter, in subsequent entrepreneurial activities, I have either written critical code myself or established a means to make certain the code will not place me in jeopardy. The cliché, "Trust but verify," is an aphorism that is applicable to arms control as well as information systems security.

[4]In one of my programming jobs many years ago, I was the lead programmer for a Federal Reserve Board money supply simulation program. It was used for the Federal Reserve Open Market Committee (FOMC) operations. Obviously, this system and its database was very secret, since it was used as an information source to determine the creation or destruction of the US money supply. Since deadlines were critical and the FOMC often asked for some "tweaking" of the model, my trap door was an effective and productive tool to get into an otherwise secure system. Note to the Fed: I removed the trap door when I left the project.

As a good security practice, trap doors are removed from the code once it is debugged and given to the customer. If the trap doors are maintained (which is not uncommon), their entry should be very difficult. One approach is that the calculated or inadvertent entry into the trap door requires the entrant to go through another more discerning trap door, say one with encryption requirements. This operation is not as easy as it seems, since the code may be taken out of the hands of the original designer.

SALAMI

Another security violation merits our attention here. It is called the salami, and I ran across it during my programming days with the banking industry. It involves the small alteration of numbers in a file (a small piece of an eventual large salami). For example, the rounding-up or rounding-down of decimal places in a bank account, or the small, incremental shaving of a number in an inventory system to distort the goods in the inventory.

REPLAY VIOLATIONS

A replay violation is an active attack on a resource, in that it entails capturing data, perhaps modifying it, and resending it. An example of a replay attack is applying a transaction to a database more than one time, when it is supposed to a one-time application. The transaction, say to a financial accrual account, may or may not be altered, but the effect is to distort the accuracy of the accrual data, to the benefit of replay perpetrator, and to the detriment of the accrual account victim. Replay can be used in conjunction with the salami attack.

COOKIES

This part of the chapter describes cookies, and how they can create privacy problems. Parts of this general discussion are sourced from [SCHO99],[5] and I recommend you read Mayer-Schönberger's full paper.

---

[5][SCHO99] *http://www.wvjolt.wvu.edu/wvjolt/current/issue1/article*, a paper by Mayer-Schönberger.

A cookie is a piece of information sent by a Web server to store on a Web browser so it can later be read back from that browser. This practice saves time and reduces overhead by allowing the browser to store specific information about a session between a server and a client.

But this feature also allows a system that uses cookies to store information about the cookie's user, and that is the crux of the debate today about cookies. Cookies are restricted as to what they can do in a user's computer, so they are not considered dangerous from the standpoint of corrupting code or data. Of course, this statement is correct now; it may not be tomorrow.

The Web is built on a very simple, but powerful premise. All material on the Web is formatted in a uniform format called HTML (Hypertext Markup Language), and all information requests and responses conform to a standard protocol, the Hypertext Transfer Protocol (HTTP). This idea has become so popular and pervasive that other technologies are adapting the use of HTML and HTTP in order to be able to "gracefully" integrate with the Web. HTTP is used to transfer information between Web sites and clients, and emerging technologies such as voice over IP (VoIP), make use of HTML and HTTP.

Cookies are generated by a Web server and stored in the user's computer, ready for future access. Cookies are embedded in the HTML/HTTP information flowing back and forth between the user's computer and the servers.

In most cases, not only does the storage of personal information into a cookie go unnoticed, so does access to it. Web servers automatically gain access to relevant cookies whenever the user establishes a connection to them, usually in the form of Web requests.

Cookies operate with a two-stage process. First, the cookie is stored in the user's computer. For example, with customizable Web search engines like My Yahoo!, a user selects categories of interest from the Web page. The Web server then creates a specific cookie, which is a tagged string of text containing the user's preferences, and it transmits this cookie to the user's computer. The user's Web browser, if so-configured, receives the cookie and stores it in a special file called a cookie list. Once again, these operations occur without any notification to the user, or user consent. As a result, personal information (in this case, the user's category preferences) is formatted by the Web server, transmitted, and saved by the user's computer.

During the second stage, the cookie is automatically transferred from the user's machine to a Web server through HTTP, without the user's knowledge. Whenever a user directs the Web browser to display a certain Web page from the server, the browser will, without the user's knowledge, transmit the cookie containing personal information to the Web server.

For example, when you enter your password and user ID, say to access your account at a stock brokerage, a cookie stores your preferences for your browsing of the site, say which report you access at the site. Another example is the ability to customize what you see at a site. Perhaps you don't want to be bothered with the weather news, and so forth. Cookies can be used to filter what you see or do not see. A cookie can also be stored for a long time, such that if you log on to a site after a long absence, that site might still have information about you (say credit information), thus reducing your hassle of inputting information again.

All these operations are mutually beneficial to the clients and their browsers. However, there is a downside to all this information collection. The way cookies operate, an HTTP cookie can be used to track where an Internet user browses, considered by some (count me in) as an invasion of privacy. Of course, any intelligent protocol analysis package (a sniffer) can track your activities through IP addresses, and domain names, but tracking your Web activities is much easier to do with cookies.

[COOK00] provides the following guidance of getting rid of cookies:[6]

> If you want to disallow cookies you can do so with version 3.0 or greater of Netscape. Go to the Options Menu. Select the Network Preferences Menu Item. From the window that appears select Protocols. Locate the section Show an Alert Before. Check the box labeled Accepting a Cookie. From now on you will get an Alert box telling you that a server is trying to set a cookie at your browser. It will tell you what the cookie value is and how long it will last before it is deleted.

Box 2–1 provides guidance on setting up cookies in a browser, and you can perform reverse operations to forbid their use.

APPLETS AND SANDBOXES

During the past few years, Java has become a popular programming language used on many Internet applications. It is the language of choice for writing small pieces of code, called applets. The applets are designed to be downline loaded to a user computer from another machine, such as

---

[6][COOK00]. CookieCentral has some excellent material on its Web site about cookies. Go to *www.cookiecentral.com*.

Box 2–1   Enabling Cookies (do the opposite to disable them)

To enable cookies in **Netscape Navigator 3.x:**
–Click on the "Options" menu and select Network/Preferences.
–Uncheck the box that says, "Accepting Cookies."

To enable cookies in **Netscape Navigator 4.x:**
–Click on the "Edit" menu and select Preferences/Advanced.
–Click on the radio button that says, "Accept all cookies."
–Uncheck the box that says, "Warn me before accepting a cookie" to disable the warning, if you choose.

To enable cookies in **Internet Explorer 3.x:**
–Click on the "View" menu and select Options/Advanced.
–Uncheck the box that says, "Warn me before selecting a cookie," if you choose.
–Click "Apply" and then "OK."

To enable cookies in **Internet Explorer 4.x:**
–Click on the "View" and select Options/Advanced.
–Select "Accept all cookies."
–Click "Apply" and then "OK."

To enable cookies in **Internet Explorer 5.x:**
–Click on "Tools" and select Internet Options/Security.
–Click on "Custom Level."
–Select "Enable" from both "Cookies" entries.
–Click "OK" and then "Apply."

a server. The operation provides opportunities for security breaches; a tamperer could potentially design the applet to interfere with the user's computer system, doing damage to files and programs.

To combat against this situation, Sun Microsystems has developed software called the Java Virtual Machine. Any applet that is to run on a machine must rely on this software. When the applet is downloaded, it initially is not allowed to access the computer's vital resources, such as hard drives, device drivers, etc. This part of the operation is known as the Java sandbox, something like a child that is placed in a sandbox: safe, and at the same time guarded from pillaging the surroundings outside the sandbox.

The applet is allowed to move from the sandbox and access the computer's resources, but only if the virtual machine verifies that the applet came from a known and trusted party.

The Java Virtual Machine is embedded in the user's browser software, and allows the applet to reside in RAM, but limits its access to interfaces.

The virtual machine performs two major functions: (a) first, it checks the code of the applet to make sure that the code is proper (legitimate), (b) second, it examines a Digital Signature that is attached to the applet, which will reveal the source of the program, and if a third party has changed the applet.

If these checks are passed, the applet is allowed to access the user computer's interfaces (for example, the disk drives). The virtual machine can determine how much access the applet is to be given as well; perhaps only part of a disk can be accessed.

If the checks are not passed, the applet may still execute, depending on what it is designed to do. But it must remain in the sandbox.

OTHER PROBLEMS

There are other forms of security problems, and many are variations of the systems described here. Many commercial software applications have measures to protect themselves against these intruders. But others do not. To be safe, it is a good idea to review the features of any code that is placed on a system critical to the enterprise. If you do not have a security mechanism, and you are on the Internet, it is only a matter of time until your system is penetrated, perhaps with unfortunate consequences.

SUMMARY

The intent of security attacks in a computer network is the denial of service to the users of a resource, such as software, data, or even a machine. Most attacks take the form of a virus or worm, with variations such as the Trojan horse. Cookies are making the news, because of their potential to compromise a user's privacy, but they are not intrusive into a user's automated resources.

3

Basic Security Concepts

This chapter introduces the methods used to protect a user's information that is transported across a communications link. We start with defining several key terms and follow with a brief discourse on some early encryption and decryption methods. Private and public key operations are explained, as are hash functions. Digital Signatures are examined as well. Several examples of privacy and authentication operations are provided in the chapter, with one example showing how a mobile phone user is authenticated by the mobile network, then how the mobile traffic is encrypted and decrypted. Also provided is a bit of history about some of these operations.

If you have experience with security operations, such as a hash, a one-way function, public keys, and session keys, you need not read this chapter. If you are not familiar with these topics, they are important prerequisites to the other chapters in this book. For example, you will not be able to follow our discussions on key exchange protocols explained in later chapters if you do not understand the concept of public (asymmetric) keys.

HOW SECURE IS SECURE?

Sensitive information, such as a "secure" software library, a "secure" message, or a "secure" database may be secure against some forms of security attacks, and vulnerable to others. The level of security exhibited by a system is a function of what security measures are taken to make the system secure. There is no such thing as a completely secure system because the system may exhibit overly simplistic security operations. It may be subject to human frailties and possible bureaucratic bungling. Indeed, newspapers contain articles on a daily basis of security breaches brought about by human error.

Notwithstanding the personal failings, a system can be made computationally secure. This term means that the user information (software, message, or a database) can have a very complex set of security operations applied to it. These operations make it unfeasible, even with the use of high-speed computers, to try to penetrate these operations and compromise the protected system, at least not in any reasonable time.

In addition, we will see in this chapter that more than one security operation can be applied to a system; for example, one to support authentication and another to protect the privacy of the traffic.

DEFINITIONS

Before we proceed into the subject matter, a few definitions are needed. For this introduction, these definitions will be kept at a general level in order to move into the gist of the chapter. They are explained later in more detail.

Encryption and Decryption

The first term is *encryption*. It means the changing of the syntax of a message (cleartext), making it unintelligible to the casual observer; it appears as a bunch of gibberish. This altered data is often called ciphertext. *Decryption* is the opposite of encryption. It means changing the ciphertext back to the original intelligible format—back to cleartext.

Encryption and decryption are performed with one of two methods, and often a combination of them. The first method is known by three names: *private, symmetrical,* or *conventional*. Whatever the name used, this method uses the same key for encryption and decryption. This key is a secret key, and it is shared between the sender and receiver of the message; that is, it is called a shared secret key. The sender uses the key to encrypt the cleartext into ciphertext, and the receiver uses the same key to decrypt the ciphertext into cleartext.

The second method is known by two names: *public* or *asymmetric*. This method uses two different keys (actually key sets); one is used for encryption and the other is used for decryption. One key is called the public key and the other is called a private key, and we will have much to say about these keys later.

Another term we need to introduce is the *Digital Signature*. It describes an authentication procedure to verify that the party who supposedly sent a message to another party is indeed the legitimate party. The best way to think of this operation is that it is like someone's signature; it verifies that someone's authenticity. Later discussions will show how public key encryption methods are used to support the Digital Signature.

The final introductory term is called the *hash, hash function, hash code,* or a message *digest* (MD). This operation performs a calculation (mapping) on a message of any length to produce a fixed-length value. When protected with encryption, it used to authenticate a sender of a message.

Let us now move into more detail about the operations just introduced.

BASIC ENCRYPTION AND DECRYPTION METHODS

Encryption and decryption are performed by transposing/altering the cleartext through an algorithm (a cryptographic function) into ciphertext. There are two inputs into this function: (a) the cleartext, and (b) a special value called the *key*.

The cryptographic function might be available to anyone; it may not be a secret function. On the other hand, the key must not be made available to everyone. If one has this key, and the function is known, then it is an easy procedure to decrypt the ciphertext to reveal the cleartext. Thus, the term key is aptly named, for it provides the "key" to unlock the "chest of ciphertext" to find out what is inside.

My first encounter with a secret key was in my youth in a drug store many years ago. I happened to know the owner of the store. I was looking around at all the goods on the shelves, and on every package there was a group of characters under the price for the product, like this: $4.95/RSM.

It was a *substitution* cipher, and the owner of the store used it to note the price he paid for it. He told me the practice was useful when selling vitamins (his big income product), because it would allow him to see this price, and easily mark down the listed price during a sale. Anyway, can you figure out the key to his cipher system? Take a look at footnote 1 for the answer.[1]

Here is another example of a simple encryption and decryption operation. The key is a 26-digit key, (not recommended for your funds transfer to Geneva, but more on that topic later). The key (in this example, it is a cipher alphabet) is repeated across the 26-character alphabet as follows (I have simply reversed the letter order for this basic example):

Key: Z Y X W V U T S R Q P O N M L K J I H G F E D C B A
Alphabet: a b c d e f g h i j k l m n o p q r s t u v w x y z

Like my pharmacist friend, anyone who uses this arrangement would simply substitute some cleartext, using the key for the resulting ciphertext.

An example of this system is encrypting the phrase: show me the money! It would appear as (the ! has no cipher key in this simple example):

HSLDNVGSVNLMVB!

Another example of a simple (and ancient) encryption method is known as the Caesar shift cipher or the Caesar cipher. It is so-named because its first known use was during Julius Caesar's time. Using the example above, the plain alphabet is shifted five places as shown:

Alphabet: a b c d e f g h i j k l m n o p q r s t u v w x y z
Cipher: F G H I J K L M N O P Q R S T U V W X Y Z A B C D E

The examples shown here are important to the idea of how many ciphers can be created in the process. In this simple example, restricting the shift to *five* places, would make it possible for someone to find the shift, and break the cipher. However, if the shifting possibilities allow *any* arrangement of the alphabet, there would be over 400,000,000,000,

---

[1]The druggist's cipher system was the character set of PHARMOCIST, where each successive letter represents the numbers 1, 2, 3 … to 0.

000,000,000,000,000 possible arrangements [SING99].[2] The person trying to break this cipher has a very big job.

This idea is the essence of decryption: (a) knowing the "cipher alphabet," which is key in this example, or (b) being able to try various combinations of the key, *applying it to the ciphertext, and seeing if the resulting cleartext makes sense.* It follows that a large range of potential keys makes the task of finding the right key more difficult; that is, it is more computationally infeasible.

One can understand why our ISP, stock/bond account representative, etc., advises the use of a password with many digits. The password is part (or all) of the encryption key, and a key of few variations is not a "strong" key. In this context, the term strong means a security system that is difficult to break.

The German Enigma Machine

As another example, the famous Enigma ciphering machine, built (in the 1930s) and used by the Germans in World War II, was designed with a keyboard input, and each time a key was pressed, a cylindrical wheel moved on one of its 26 positions, thus introducing a new circuit for each letter entered. After 26 keystrokes, a middle wheel moved around one position, and after 26 more keystrokes had been entered, a third and final wheel moved one position. The machine was designed for 60 possible orders for the wheels to be placed in the machine, with a total of 17,576 different position settings for each wheel. A plug board, when used with the system, allowed 150 million million changes of the circuit. The total number of possible settings for the Enigma was 159 million million million [SMIT98].[3]

The Germans thought their system impregnable, and for a while, so did everyone else. Overconfidence in any security system is not a good idea. A poor encryption method is worse than no method at all. The Germans thought that the Enigma's ability to assure that no original letter was ever represented by the same encrypted letter would prevent a code breaker from building up any body of knowledge about the system.

---

[2][SING99]. Singh, Simon. *The Code Book,* Fourth Estate Limited, 6 Salem Road, London W24BU, 1999. Without question, this book is one of the very best written on cryptography.

[3][SMIT98]. Smith, Michael. *Station X, The Codebreakers of Bletchley Park,* Channel 4 Books of Macmillan Publishers, Ltd., London, 1998. This is another excellent book, with the focus on the British security operations during World War II.

At that time (before the war), the many possible settings for the Enigma did appear to make it impenetrable, Yet, the British were able to break the Enigma system early in the war, due to some fine sleuthing on the part of the British, and some egregious errors on the part of the Germans, a story told in the section in this chapter titled, "Randomness of Keys."

SUBSTITUTION AND TRANSPOSITION

As mentioned, the examples just shown are known as cryptographic substitution, which is so-named because a specific value is substituted for another specific value. In contrast, with transposition, the letters in the message are rearranged. Once again, the fashion in which the transposition occurs must be known by the sender and the receiver. An age-old example of transposition is the rail fence transposition in which the characters in the message are written on two lines. The sequence of letters on the lower line is tagged on at the end of the sequence on the upper line to create the final encrypted message. For example (again from Singh):

THY SECRET IS THY PRISONER; IF THOU LET IT GO, THOU ART A
    PRISONER TO IT

    T Y E R T S H P I O E I T O L T T O H U R A R S N R O T
    H S C E I T Y R S N R F H U E I G T O A T P I O E T I

TYERTSHPIOEITOLTTOHURARSNROTHSCEITYRSNRFHUEIGTOATPIOETI

ONE-WAY FUNCTIONS AND MODULAR ARITHMETIC

Many modern security systems, using asymmetric/public operations, are built on one-way functions. A one-way function is one that is easy to compute in one direction (easy to do), but very difficult to compute in the other direction (not easy to undo). An example of a two-way function is exponentiation: it is easy to compute $2^3 = 8$, and almost as easy to compute $8 = 2^3$. Many of the older cryptographic systems were made up of two-way functions: easy to do and easy to undo.

Modern security systems take advantage of one-way functions by the use of modular arithmetic. It is likely you have used modular arithmetic if you have worked with computers. Even if you have no direct knowledge of the subject, it is likely you have used systems that employ this arithmetic method.

The reason modular arithmetic is used in security algorithms is because it helps create one-way functions. Take a look at Figure 3–1. (I extracted this example from a data link protocol example, which uses what some people call clock arithmetic, or a wrap-around counter). There are eight numbers on this circle, 0 to 7. This example is called modular 8 (or mod 8). Let's assume we wish to compute 2 + 1. Starting at 2, we move 1 place to 3, which is the answer in normal and modular arithmetic, 3. Let us compute 2 + 8. In normal arithmetic the answer is 10, but in mod 8, it is 2, and is expressed as: 2 + 8 = 2 (mod 8), executed by simply rotating around the "wall clock."

As you can see from the mod 8 function, the answer is not intuitively obvious. Well, perhaps this simple example is, but consider another comparison between normal arithmetic and modular arithmetic [SING99]. Consider the function 3^x, with $x = 2$. The answer is $3^2 = 3 \times 3 = 9$. If $x = 3$, and so on, as x increases so does the result. Therefore, it is a relatively easy task to work backwards and deduce x. For small values of x, we even have the "deductions" memorized, and $3^x = 243$ can be deduced (if not memorized) fairly easily to be 5.

But consider the function $3^x = 1$ (mod 7). I use a different mod in this example. Now it is not so easy to reverse the function to get the value of x. In other words, modular arithmetic leads to one-way functions. By the way, the correct answer is 6.

One could certainly argue that a high-speed processor can solve this kind of function due to its ability to check many possible answers in a short time. But the problem is that the function in modular arithmetic behaves erratically. Table 3–1 shows a very simple example of how inconsistent the behavior is of modular arithmetic.

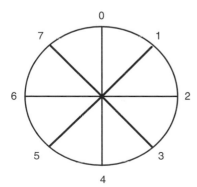

Figure 3–1   Modular arithmetic

Table 3–1   Comparison of Normal and Modular Arithmetic

x	1	2	3	4	5	6
3^x	3	8	27	81	243	729
$3^x \pmod 7$	3	2	6	4	5	1

[SING99]

A function of $543^x \pmod{21{,}997}$ is easy to compute if I am given x. But if I am given (say) 5,787 and asked to reverse the function and arrive at x, it becomes computationally infeasible to arrive at a solution. This is especially evident if we apply other algorithms, discussed in Chapter 5.

Example of a One-way Function

An example of a one-way function is the discrete logarithm problem:

$$g^x = y \pmod p$$

and stated as: with a large prime p, and a generator g, for a particular value y, find x. This example is introduced here, in order to expand our discussion on one-way functions and prime numbers.

The Diffie-Hellman Idea Using Modular Arithmetic

Chapter 5 includes a description of RFC 2362, the Internet standard for implementing the ideas discussed in this part of the chapter. Chapter 5 also provides a brief history of how Winfield Diffie and Martin Hellman came up with some revolutionary concepts about keys. Much of it is based on modular arithmetic. The idea described in the next paragraph was developed by Hellman.

Hellman's idea revolves around a one-way function of $Y^x \pmod P$. It also entails two parties, say Alice and Bob, agreeing on the values of P and Y to use for their mutual ciphering operations. As we will see shortly in this chapter and in Chapter 5, Hellman's formula set the stage for solving one of the most intractable problems in the security industry: the exchange of keys between Alice and Bob without their meeting, or the use of a secure communications channel for the key exchange.

But I am getting ahead of the story. We need to turn to some more detailed descriptions of the definitions introduced at the beginning of this chapter, then we can return to the subject of keys, and key distribution.

THE HASH FUNCTION

This part of the chapter provides more information on the coding and computational mechanisms for providing security. We start with a very basic and important process called the hash, or hashing function. This function condenses the user information (say, a packet) into a *digest,* also known as a digital fingerprint, or message digest (MD). It is called Digital Signature because it can be used to detect forgeries, or the tampering of the document.

The hash operates as follows, and as shown in Figure 3–2. In Figures 3–2(a) and 3–2(c), the same input to the hash function yields the same output. In Figure 3–2(b), the different inputs yield different outputs.

The text of the message is converted into binary numbers and segmented into equal size blocks. These blocks are then input into a ciphering algorithm, which produces an output called the digest or hash. Keep in mind that the digest is based on a computation on the original user message.

For most hashing operations employed today, the digest is a fixed size regardless of the length of the user information. A common convention is to produce a hash code of 128 bits, often represented as a string of 32 hex digits.

An example of how the hash function operates can be explained by using a function employed in the financial industry (and simplified to show the steps) [WRIX92].[4] Assume a value of 4392072 is to be protected from alteration. The sending site multiplies each number in the value in turn (except 0), and the last digit. The first digit in the multiplied product is dropped. The computation proceeds as follows:

Operation:	*Result*
• Multiply 4 by 3	12
• Drop first digit	2
• Multiply 2 by next numeral (9)	18
• Drop first digit	8
• Multiply 8 by 2	16
• Drop first digit	6

---

[4][WRIX92]. Wrixon, Fred B. *Codes, Ciphers, and Other Cryptic and Clandestine Communication.* Black Dog & Leventhal Publishers, 1992, New York. Mr. Wrixon has many interesting examples of codes and ciphers by many industries and hobbyists.

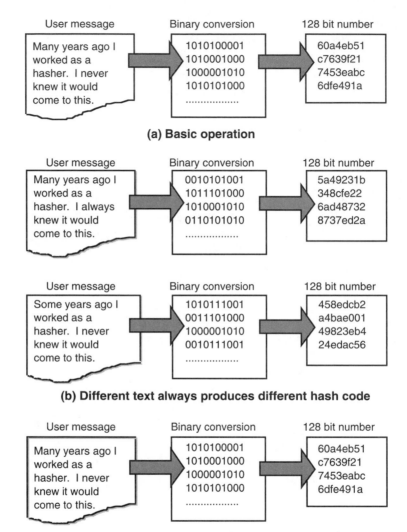

(a) Basic operation

(b) Different text always produces different hash code

(c) And, same text always produces same hash code

Figure 3–2   Examples of the hash function

- Exclude the 0   6
- Multiply 6 by 7   42
- Drop the first digit   2

The hash value (in this simple example, it is called a check digit) is 2. At the receiver the computation is performed on the data value, and if the hash result is the same, the data value has not been altered.

Of course, this example is presented because you can follow the execution quite easily. For a more challenging example, take a look at the Message Digest 5 function, presented in Appendix A.

USE OF A ONE-WAY HASH FUNCTION

The hash algorithm is established so that no two messages will yield the same hash (at least not within any reasonable statistical bound). This fact means that it is not possible within any reasonable number of calculations to produce a message that reveals the same hash as another (different) message.

Because of this operation, the digest can serve as a fingerprint for its message [ZIMM98].[5] In addition, the hash function can be used to detect the tampering of a message. Therefore, it provides a tool to support two aspects of security: (a) authentication, and (b) integrity. Examples of hashing and message digests are provided later in this chapter.

RANDOMNESS OF KEYS

One method cryptanalysts (codebreakers) use to break an encryption system is to examine the key to determine if it has recurring attributes; that is, if its values are not random. For example, a five-digit key necessarily repeats itself when applied against the plaintext to create the ciphertext. If a cryptanalyst can discover the length of the key, the ciphertext is viewed as a series of five cipher values. Problems with an encryption/decryption key occur if: (a) the key is too short, and (b) the key is not random, or not sufficiently random-like (an attribute called pseudo-random).

Ideally, one would have a wide number and range of keys from which to draw. The simple key used in our substitution example earlier in this chapter is a very poor key. In the Caesar shift cipher example, there are 1 to 25 possible shifts to create 25 keys, and a potential adversary, say Mallory, can easily check the 25 possible keys against the ci-

---

[5][ZIMM98]. Zimmerman, Philip R. "Cryptography for the Internet," *Scientific American,* October 1998.

pher text to find one that decodes the message. However, if the alphabet were scrambled randomly, it would be computationally impossible task.

Randomness or Lack Thereof Equals the Demise of a Crypto System

An example of a system that was broken, partially because of the lack of sufficient randomness, was the Enigma machine, introduced earlier. Recall that this German system was the state-of-the-art in the early 1940s, and no one was able to compromise its security in any systematic way. That is, until a Polish mathematician and codebreaker, Marian Rejewski, began working on the problem.

Fortunately for the Allies, Rejewski had been trying to decipher Enigma messages since the early 1930s, and during those days, the Germans did not change the Enigma wheel order settings very often, sometimes every three months!

During the war, they were changed every day, but by this time Rejewski had learned much about the Enigma operations. To make this analysis even easier (relatively speaking), the first six letters of any Enigma message were the three-wheel settings, the starting position for that message, repeated twice. This information allowed Rejewski to hack various combinations to come up with sequence and repetition relationships. He eventually built an Enigma clone, an almost unfathomable accomplishment. Well ... perhaps, this job was greatly aided by the recruiting of a spy, who furnished over 300 documents on the machine.

The British used this information and the discovery that parts of many German messages had the same syntax. For example, the beginning of a message often had *An die Gruppe* (To the Group), and some messages from specific locations read only as *Keine besondere ereignisse* (No special occurrences). The accumulation of this information led to the loss of randomness: the death knell of a security system.

As a result of these happenings, and of course because of a lot of brilliant analysis, Enigma lost its random key capability; it was broken. The Germans continued to think their messages secure. As the Allied leadership developed more confidence in the code breakers' extraordinary accomplishments, they began to rely heavily on the German's messages for their tactical and strategic actions and plans. The breaking of the Enigma system had a profound impact on the war.

We must leave this fascinating story, and return to the matter of exchanging keys in a secure manner. I refer you to [SMIT98] for a fine account of the Enigma story.

KEY PROBLEM: EXCHANGING KEYS

Public keys were introduced earlier in this chapter. Public keys have been used to encrypt data in communications networks for a number of years. The public key concept rests on the idea of establishing two keys (actually sets of keys) from one function. One key is called the public key and the other key is called the private key. They are so-named because the public key can be disseminated to a body-at-large, whereas the private key is not disseminated. This method is also called asymmetric keys, which means the encryption and decryption keys are not the same.

The idea of a public key system is to realize an asymmetric cipher. Let's review some of the important aspects of a secure public key system between Alice and Bob:

- Alice creates a public key that she can disseminate to anyone (including Bob).
- Bob can use this key to encrypt messages to send to Alice.
- Alice's key system must be a one-way function, making it computationally infeasible for anyone else to deduce the key, and decrypt the messages sent from Bob to Alice.
- Alice has a private key to decrypt the message from Bob, which does indeed reverse the effect of the public key used by Bob.
- The two keys are derived from the same function, which among other features, are designed to allow Alice to decrypt her message from Bob, by using the Hellman function described earlier: Y^x (mod P), where X is the secret key, one for Alice and one for Bob.

These events represent the basic idea. In hindsight, they make sense, but they were revolutionary to the security industry. These ideas can be summarized as follows [SING99], see Figure 3–3. In event 1, Alice and Bob both choose the same values for Y and P. There are some rules on how these values are chosen, and they are discussed later. For this example, it is only important to note that the values can be exchanged in a nonsecure manner, even over the telephone. Alice chooses the values, and Bob agrees to their use.

In event 2, both parties choose a secret value. The value is known only to Alice and to Bob, but not to each other. In this example, the values are 3 for Alice, and 6 for Bob. They are labeled A and B, respectively, in this example. Next, in event 3, Alice and Bob use their secret keys to compute a and b, respectively. These values are sent to the other party

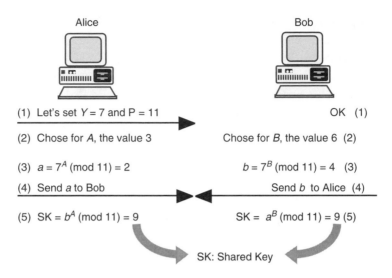

Alice   Bob

(1) Let's set $Y = 7$ and $P = 11$ OK   (1)

(2) Chose for A, the value 3   Chose for B, the value 6 (2)

(3) $a = 7^A \pmod{11} = 2$ $b = 7^B \pmod{11} = 4$ (3)

(4) Send a to Bob   Send b to Alice (4)

(5) SK $= b^A \pmod{11} = 9$ SK $= a^B \pmod{11} = 9$ (5)

SK: Shared Key

Figure 3–3   Example of $Y^X \pmod{P}$ [SING99]

(in event 4). Next, in event 5, Alice and Bob use their secret keys and their partner's public key to derive a shared (secret) key, the value of 9 in this example.

These ideas, shown in the protocol flow in Figure 3–3, changed in a profound way the view of secure communications.

The operation thus far has not yet yielded asymmetric keys, since the key is the same at both parties. But the first step has been made toward the asymmetric key method. And besides, symmetric keys are "not bad." In fact, they may be preferable to asymmetric keys due to their computational efficiency (explained later).

Also, notice that Alice and Bob did not exchange their secret values, only the result of the mod function, which makes it quite difficult to reverse the process to obtain the secret key. Therefore, one of the attractive aspects of the operations shown thus far is that it is very easy for Alice and Bob to compute a and b, but it is very difficult for Mallory to discover these values and the final shared key. This is the basic idea behind the revolutionary ideas of Hellman.

Awkwardness of Key Distribution

However, as seen in Figure 3–3, the key exchange between the two parties is awkward. Alice and Bob must be "synchronized" with each other in order to agree to a key. So, as great as the Hellman idea is, it needs refinement. It would be much better if either party could set up their association at any time, and when the need arises, simply find out about the other's a or b. That is, they would not have to be on-line to each other to obtain each other's key.

THE ASYMMETRIC KEY

This problem was solved by Diffie, and published in 1975. He came up (as did others independently of Diffie) with the concept of the asymmetric key. The basic idea is that the two parties, Alice and Bob, independently create their own pair of keys, one for encryption and one for decryption, with the keys having different values, but derived from the same function.

What follows is (in retrospect) the commonsense idea that these public keys can be made available to anyone, perhaps in a public directory such as X.509. When Alice wishes to send secure information to Bob, she merely goes to an X.509 information repository to find Bob's public key, and uses it to encrypt her message, and vice versa. Consequently, the parties do not have to synchronize with each other as depicted in Figure 3–3. In fact, they can be off-line, and the parties can send email at any time. When the other party logs-on to the net, the stored email can be decrypted with the correct private key.

Fine, but there still exist some problems. The first problem is: How do Bob and Alice know that their supposedly valid pubic keys are actually valid? One could answer that it does not matter. If an incorrect public key is used to encrypt traffic, the correct private key cannot decrypt it. So, no harm done, but a nuisance factor has been introduced. It is a nuisance this far in this discussion, but this situation can create serious problems, which we address shortly.

The second problem is: Diffie laid the conceptual ground work for the asymmetric key, but there was not yet a specific example and implementation of one, nor (obviously) its mathematical proof.

The solutions to both problems are discussed later in this chapter. For the present, we now have enough information to show how asymmetric keys can be used to (a) provide privacy/confidentiality, and (b) provide authentication.

USE OF THE ASYMMETRIC KEYS IN REVERSE ORDER

Let's summarize briefly the concepts introduced so far. Alice is the creator of the private key and keeps this key in a secure manner. Bob does the same with his private key. The idea of the asymmetric key arrangement is to keep the private key close-to-the-vest, and not reveal its contents to anyone but the creator and those approved by the creator, but to allow the public key to be just that: public.

There are two operations for asymmetric keys. In one operation, the public key is used for encrypting, and the private key is used for decrypting. But what happens in a different operation if the process is reversed? What if the private key is used for encrypting, and the public key for decrypting? This operation can serve a very useful purpose: authentication. We examine these operations in the next two sections in this chapter, which once again reinforce the idea of why asymmetric keys are so valuable.

ASYMMETRIC KEYS FOR PRIVACY

Figure 3–4 shows an example of how asymmetric keys are used to support privacy/confidentiality services. The sender (say, Alice) uses the receiver's public key (say, Bob) to encrypt the clear text of a message into the ciphered message. The process is reversed at the receiver, where the receiver (Bob) uses his private key to decrypt the ciphered message into the clear text. This operation provides privacy/confidentiality of the user traffic. Mallory would have to gain access to Bob's private key in order to penetrate this system.

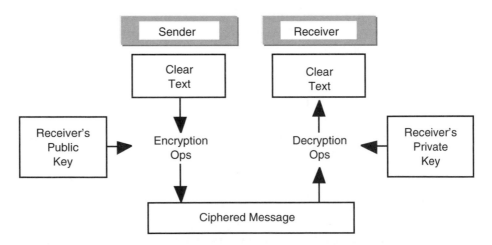

Figure 3–4   Public keys for encryption

ASYMMETRIC KEYS FOR AUTHENTICATION: THE DIGITAL SIGNATURE

In addition to the use of public keys for supporting privacy services, they are widely used for authentication procedures, as shown in Figure 3–5. They are also used for integrity checks and proof of delivery, discussed later.

In this example, the sender (Alice) uses Alice's private key to encrypt a known value into the *Digital Signature*. The purpose of the Digital Signature is to validate the authenticity of the sender. Consequently, through other measures, the sender has sent or otherwise made available to the receiver the sender's public key. This key is applied (with an algorithm) to the incoming Digital Signature. If the resulting decryption operations result in the computation of the known value that was encrypted by the sender, then the sender is considered to be the legitimate sender (that is, the sender is authentic).

In summary, if the computed known value at the receiver is equal to the expected value, then the sender has been authenticated. If the computation is not equal, then the sender is not authentic or an error has occurred in the processing. Whatever the case may be, the sender is likely not allowed any further privileges at the receiver's system.

The Digital Signature is like a handwritten signature. It should be difficult for the sender to forge and difficult for the receiver to repudiate. However, authentication on a Digital Signature alone presents these problems:

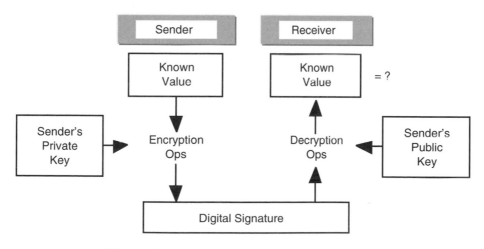

Figure 3–5   Public keys for authentication

- The valid Digital Signature does not assure that the document associated with the signature is valid. Mallory may intercept the document and add or delete text to it, giving the receiver the impression that the signer of the document validates the text. This problem is not just for traffic being transmitted at the moment in an internet; it pertains to archived documents that are stored electronically. One can see this situation as being a very big problem for (say) legal documents that are altered to favor one party over another.

- Executing a simple hash operation on a block of data does not provide authentication of the document and the signature, because an attacker can alter a document, and execute the hash function over the changed data.

To handle these problems, a Digital Signature uses a one-way hash function to reduce a piece of information (the entire message, for example) to a message digest. Then, for protection, the *message digest is encrypted*. With this approach, it is assured that the Digital Signature is associated with the document, and it provides integrity on the signed document.

A few problems remain. Digital Signatures and public keys take a lot of resources to compute, and the entire document must be used for the signature generation. The solutions to these problems are explained later in this chapter.

But we can now pick up once again on the asymmetric key subject. Recall that Figures 3–4 and 3–5 show the two important aspects of the idea. The next section explains how it is implemented.

THE NEXT STEP: RSA

In order to provide a logical sequence of events in explaining security concepts, I have mentioned some of the ideas of RSA earlier. This section will now focus on the RSA concepts in more detail. RSA are the initials of the last names of Ron Rivest, Adi Shamir, and Len Adleman, three individuals who took the ideas of Diffie-Hellman to the next level: the creation of a workable asymmetric key system.

RSA still uses mod arithmetic, and adds the use of prime numbers (a number that has no remainder when divided by itself or 1). In the RSA Algorithm, two prime numbers p and q are multiplied together to equal N, which becomes a public key.

Returning to Alice and Bob, their computed Ns can be made available to the public. If Alice wants to send a secure message to Bob, she uses Bob's N as part of a one-way function (the math is explained along with the RSA operation defined by RFC 1321 in Chapter 5 and Appendix A). The result is Bob's tailored one-way function that is used to secure Alice's message to Bob.

However, the one-way operation is not one-way to the party that knows p and q. So, Alice can use p and q to decrypt her traffic from Bob, since Bob is using N, which is derived from p and q. The beauty of the RSA idea is that if N is a very big number, it is computationally infeasible (with what we know today, let's say impossible) to reverse the process to discover p and q.

By multiplying p and q to create N, RSA's ideas make N a one-way function. To see why, let's look briefly at prime number multiplication. It is very difficult to find the prime numbers of a multiplication, given the answer. The effort to derive p and q is known as factoring, and it takes a lot of effort and considerable time to find N. The approach is to continue to pick prime numbers until one is found that divides perfectly into N; once that is done, the next prime number is found (and is easier to find).

To gain a sense of how effective the approach is, let's return to Singh's computations, updated with faster processors. Consider a prime of 10^{65} for p and q. Taken together, they result in a number of N^{130}. A 500-MHz processor would take about 10 years to factor the value for N. Of course, faster processors and parallel processing can factor to this answer much more quickly.

In 1977, a challenge was issued to the industry to break a 129-digit code [GARD77].[6] The expectation was that the code could not be broken for many years. In 1994, a task force organized by the former Bellcore broke the code. The team was able to find two prime numbers that when multiplied together, resulted in the factors for N. Today, a 129-digit code is not very large. Notwithstanding, choosing a large value for N makes RSA impregnable.

The RSA Key Pairs

Asymmetric keys actually use key pairs. They operate as follows. See Figure 3–6. In event 1, Alice selects two large prime numbers p and q and calculates $N = p \times q$. Next, Alice chooses a random integer e. (The

---

[6][GARD77]. Gardner, Martin. "Mathematical Games," *Scientific American,* January, 1977.

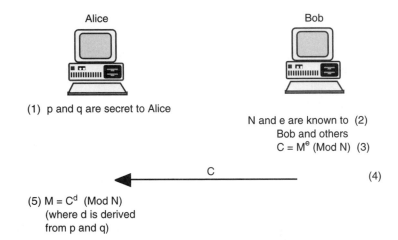

Figure 3–6   RSA operations

value e must have no integer divisors > 1 that are in common with $p - 1$ or $q - 1$.) Alice publishes the (N, e) pair (event 2), but not the (p, q) pair. Thus, (N, e) is the public key, and (p, q) is the private key. Bob can do the same at his site: He can calculate his own N.

We assume that Bob now has Alice's public key (N, e). In event 3, Bob encrypts a message M into a cipher C to send to Alice (event 4):

$$C = M^e \ (\text{mod } N)$$

In event 5, Alice decrypts the ciphered message C as follows:

$$M = C^d \ (\text{mod } N)$$

The value d is Alice's secret decryption exponent. The value d is computed correctly from e only if p and q are known:

$$e \times d = 1 \ (\text{mod } (p - 1) \times (q - 1))$$

Therefore, Bob's original message M is recovered.

So, one of our problems, a workable implementation of the asymmetric key concept, was solved by RSA. Another problem remains, the assurance that the public key from Bob, used by Alice, is really Bob's. This question moves us to the next subjects of this chapter, key generation and key transport, followed by the subject of certifying keys.

KEY TRANSPORT AND KEY GENERATION

Two methods are defined for using public key cryptography for key establishment: key transport and key generation [MAUG98].[7] An example of key transport is the use of the RSA algorithm to encrypt a randomly generated session key (also called a one-time symmetric key) with the receiver's public key. The encrypted session key is then sent to the recipient, who decrypts it using his/her private key. At this point both sides have the same session key (for encrypting subsequent communications), however the operation is based on input from only one side of the communications. The benefit of the key transport method is that it has less computational overhead than the use of the public key on the traffic itself.

The Diffie-Hellman (D-H) algorithm illustrates key generation using public key cryptography. The D-H algorithm begins by two users exchanging public information. Next, each user mathematically combines the other's public information along with their own secret information to compute a shared secret value. This secret value can be used as a session key or as a key encryption key for encrypting a randomly generated session key. This method generates a session key based on public and secret information held by both users. The benefit of the D-H algorithm is that the key used for encrypting messages is based on information held by both users and the independence of keys from one key exchange to another provides perfect forward secrecy. The parties can agree on a shared secret without requiring encryption, and the shared value is available immediately for encrypting traffic for privacy and/or authentication.

Detailed descriptions of these algorithms can be found in RFC 2412, and Chapter 5 explains the OAKLEY Key Determination Protocol, which is based on Diffie-Hellman.

MESSAGE AUTHENTICATION CODE (MAC) AND KEY HASHING

During the past few years, it has been recognized that some of the methods for supporting authentication services are subject to compromise. The message authentication code (MAC) is designed to provide a higher level of security to authentication services. It uses a single key to

---

[7][MAUG98]. Maughn, D., et. al. *Internet Security Association and Key Management Protocol* (ISAKMP), RFC 2408, November, 1998.

verify the authentication data, and a MAC also uses a hash function. Here is the way it works:

- The MAC is generated by hashing a shared secret key (symmetric cipher) and the message.
- This digest is attached to the message.
- At the receiver, the MAC is verified by hashing the shared secret key and the message to produce a temporary digest.
- The temporary digest is compared with the digest attached to the message. If they are equal, the message and the signature have been authenticated.

The technique just described is called key hashing, and it is quite important because non-keyed hashing is vulnerable to attack. Keyed hashing is used by IPSec to allow a block of traffic to be divided up into packets, with a MAC computed on each chunk. MAC is described in more detail in Chapter 5.

PUTTING TOGETHER THE SECURITY FUNCTIONS

We have learned that there are two main operations involved in the transport and support of secure data. The first operation is the encryption (at the sender) of the sender's message, and the complimentary decryption of this message at the receiver. The second operation is to assure that the proper sender sent the message and is not an imposter. That is to say, the sender of the message is authenticated. Other services are important, such as anti-replay, and we will not ignore them.

Several techniques are used to place these operations into effect, and we just learned about asymmetric key operations. An example is shown in Figure 3–7. It uses the public key cryptography just explained, and the hash functions described earlier. The figure shows a common procedure for using asymmetric keys to cipher, authenticate, and perform integrity checks. To ease the study of this figure, I explain six operations that are so-numbered in the figure. The notations in the boxes symbolize the input to and output from the six operations.

In event 1, the original message (clear text) is subjected to a one-way hash operation. The result of this operation is the message digest. In event 2, the message digest and the sender's private key are parameters into an encryption operation, which results in the Digital Signature. The

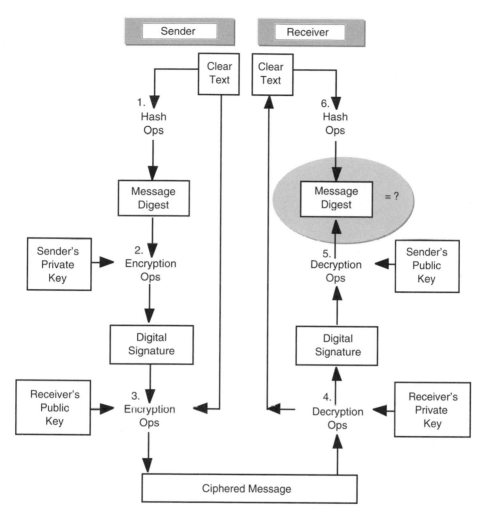

Figure 3–7   Public keys for ciphering, authentication, and integrity

Digital Signature is added to the original message (clear text) and this entire data unit is encrypted in event 3 with the receiver's public key. The result is the ciphered message.

The process is reversed at the receiver. In event 4, the ciphered message is decrypted with the receiver's private key resulting in (a) the original message (clear text) and (b) the Digital Signature. Event 4 is a critical aspect of public keying cryptography because only those who posses the receiver's private key can decrypt the ciphered message.

Next, the Digital Signature is decrypted with the sender's pubic key (in event 5) and the clear text (in event 6) is subjected to the identical one-way hash operation, which was performed at the sender. The receiver then compares the operations resulting in events 5 and 6, and if the resulting values are the same, the receiver can be certain that the sender is authentic. If the results are different, something is amiss, ei-

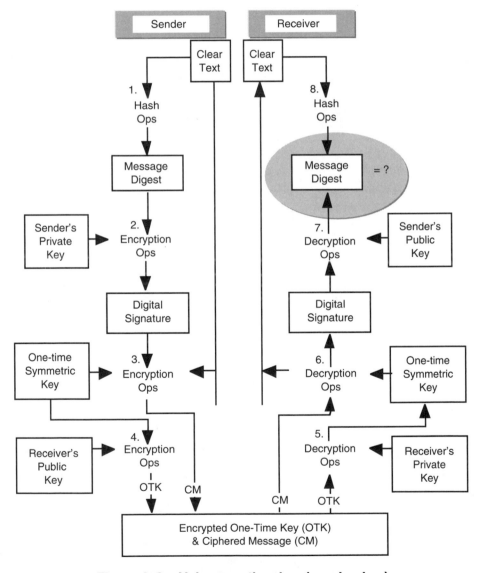

Figure 3–8   Using one-time key (session key)

ther the sender is a phony or an interloper has intercepted the sender's traffic and altered it. Or, perhaps the traffic has been damaged in transit, and the error was not detected by separate, independent error-detecting operations (highly unlikely).

Many implementations embed another operation into the operations just discussed. It is known by various names in the industry. Some people call the operation a session key, others call it a one-time key, and others call it a one-time symmetric key.

Figure 3–8 shows how this operation is combined with the operation just discussed. The difference in the operation is shown in events 3 and 6 of the figure. A one-time key symmetric is used to encrypt a Digital Signature and clear text in event 3 and to perform a complementary operation at the receiver in event 6.

In addition, the one-time key is encrypted at the sender by the receiver's public key to produce the encrypted one-time key (OTK). At the receiver, this protected key is decrypted by the receiver's private key. In turn, this key is used to decrypt the ciphered message (CM).

This key is known as the symmetric key because the same key is used to encrypt and decrypt the data. One of the advantages of this technique is that it can be implemented to perform operations quite quickly and obviously it adds yet another layer of security to the overall process.

PAUL ZIMMERMAN AND PRETTY GOOD PRIVACY (PGP)

The operations shown in the previous section demonstrate how the Pretty Good Privacy (PGP) protocol operates:

(a) PGP creates a session key.
(b) The session key is used with an encryption algorithm to encrypt the message.
(c) RSA is used to encrypt the session key (with the receiver's public key).
(d) The ciphertext and the encrypted session key are sent to the receiver, where the process is reversed.

Once again, the attractive aspect to PGP (and the session key) is that it speeds up the process considerably. And Paul Zimmerman, the author of PGP, came up with this novel idea. The end result is that the operations in Figure 3–8 provide an efficient method of obtaining both privacy and authenticity services.

PGP's Use of Key Certificates

PGP also supports a concept called key certificates. Each public key is associated with a key certificate that contains the key, an ID of its creator, the date created, and a list of Digital Signatures who vouch for the key's validity. Key certification is explained in more detail later in this chapter.

PGP is just that—pretty good. A detailed discussion of PGP is beyond the scope of this book. For more information, I refer you to [GARF95].[8]

Example of a PGP Public Key

Below is an example of a public key published by the IETF Registrar for the IETF meeting in Adelaide, Australia, 26–31 March 2000.

```
----BEGIN PGP PUBLIC KEY BLOCK----
Version: 2.6.2

mQCPAzF+LtIAAAEEAOR6J+TD0InYcfH5R40F4/+t0dZt02vljKi1ymMJqyVpUyWe
U4I6t/rFxkZntupxKOIJgNEC93W41XKSn4q9fUuviAduTzXR9ppBAxa1evJPSlnz
4OSzIoxC6k+VmtAyAbkEwDvgA9nyXTkK3weC4T8IMjle0ItEfwIhmzn+kqSBABEB
AAG0I01FVEYgUmVnaXN0cmFyIDxpZXRmLXJlZ2lzdHJhckBAWV0Zi5vcmc+iQCVAwUQMrAx
bvvCP42xMxQ5AQGUcwQAiB0v037y978B8cR0USMuQUvdnX7IXsLc+TogBf1HsDQP
Na/oYuzjD1qXtbQo/HKyj2rItWpcg4KrD6hJ9x2nYzZTOhjoFa8FI567PdUg7TfN
J4wjspCykAO0Egk0FXh9rMCRk14ac4qVdYY69Aii/p/i8thLb+ps8xDioRQAtiGJ
AHUDBRAyJMfkDHlcePGjdhEBASM7Av4yaX4eSIceiZnwpBepL0toiWpywUzm2P+u
9PFQ23ws/Crk1CvFfSL4MSg+wNj3jVeC52MZOep0E2m5PgFH590xTqqfRg4AxGnz
H5AHTCyjwD14ClXFhX2rYQ6xvE1GaRe0KGlldGYgcmVnaXN0cmFyIDxpZXRmLXJl
Z2lzdHJhckBpZXRmLm9yZz6JAJUDBRAzzfcRAiGbOf6SpIEBAXdsBADFu/qsRB7z
D//tDoDult1tOImS6WGecBDGmtyqURhtFuowPJrrn+WtBLTHI3hRLWOOob/gscfR
YJxCY+MaSUjvs3iwPIkUXjqUe3sZXFUINjcT9ELzpOPX15NIcGrWmQzHRlDrwQm+
zjcW7NmsDTQ+m0bYiiiXQZGtd1ANC5HfCokAlQMFEDPOJeOHG8BZjxsZpQEB3dsE
AKHdY4awpqPbbqG81B93vOzGnveQSI9AafpYbVkIXypoGvnRnnM70AP9zRaI8rur
YVwOzIk8jxCETgPziVHNEeEkRk9TAC3lbB985re5UH9i33Gajs/jc1n6dG25xj6C
PZSLcFLB7VhPFxXumUJuIf2/pYIXqvzioOebMCP01DaY
=CbD3
----END PGP PUBLIC KEY BLOCK----
```

---

[8][GARF95]. Garfinkel, Simson. *PGP: Pretty Good Privacy*. O'Reilly & Associates. 1995. Sebastapol, CA.

OpenPGP

OpenPGP [CALL99][9] is an Internet working draft that revises RFC 2440, "OpenPGP Message Format," and replaces RFC 1991, "PGP Message Exchange Formats." OpenPGP provides data integrity services for messages and data files by offering: (a) Digital Signatures, (b) privacy, (c) compression, (d) key management and certificate services. Other services are offered that are described in [CALL99].

OpenPGP uses symmetric and asymmetric key operations. With public-key encryption, the object is encrypted using a symmetric encryption algorithm. Each symmetric key is used only once. A new session key is generated as a random number for each message. Since it is used only once, the session key is bound to the message and transmitted with it. To protect the key, it is encrypted with the receiver's public key. The sequence is as follows:

- The sender creates a message.
- The sending OpenPGP generates a random number to be used as a session key for this message only.
- The session key is encrypted using each recipient's public key. These "encrypted session keys" start the message.
- The sending OpenPGP encrypts the message using the session key, which forms the remainder of the message.
- The receiving OpenPGP decrypts the session key using the recipient's private key.
- The receiving OpenPGP decrypts the message using the session key.

With symmetric-key encryption, an object may be encrypted with a symmetric key derived from a passphrase (or other shared secret), or a two-stage mechanism similar to the public-key method described above in which a session key is itself encrypted with a symmetric algorithm keyed from a shared secret.

Both Digital Signature and confidentiality services may be applied to the same message. First, a signature is generated for the message and attached to the message. Then, the message plus signature is encrypted using a symmetric session key. Finally, the session key is encrypted using public-key encryption and prefixed to the encrypted block.

---

[9][CALL99]. Callas, Jon, et al., draft-ietf-openpgp-rfc2440bis-00.txt.

The Digital Signature uses a hash code or message digest algorithm, and a public-key signature algorithm. The sequence is as follows:

- The sender creates a message.
- The sending software generates a hash code of the message.
- The sending software generates a signature from the hash code using the sender's private key.
- The binary signature is attached to the message.
- The receiving software keeps a copy of the message signature.
- The receiving software generates a new hash code for the received message and verifies it using the message's signature. If the verification is successful, the message is accepted as authentic.

PERFECT FORWARD SECRECY (PFS)

Let us pause here, and clarify a term. Many Internet security procedures use the term perfect forward security (PFS). Using RFC 2409 as the source, PFS refers to the idea that the compromise of a single key will permit access to only data protected by a single key. For PFS to exist, the key used to protect transmission of data must not be used to derive any additional keys, and if the key used to protect transmission of data was derived from some other keying material, that material must not be used to derive any more keys. PFS will be explained in more detail later, with examples provided.

MAN-IN-THE-MIDDLE ATTACK

Thus far, we have assumed that the receiver trusts the sender and the receiver believes that the sender's public key (which it has stored) is authentic. This situation may not be true. Public key cryptography is vulnerable to compromise with what is called the middle man attack (also called piggy-in-the-middle, or man-in-the-middle), shown in Figure 3–9.

A middleman, named Mallory, has fooled Carol and Ted by sending them false public keys. (What happened to Alice and Bob? They are still around, but I need to introduce other characters into our narrative for future examples. So Bob, Carol, Ted and Alice seem convenient.) Ted receives Mallory's public key (MPUB1) in event 1, and Mallory also generates another public key and sends it to Alice (MPUB2), in event 2.

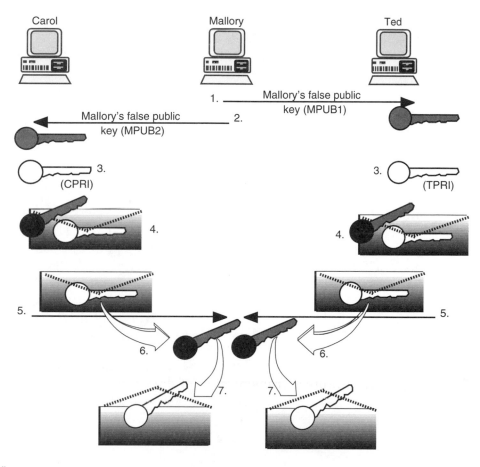

Where:
  MPUB: Mallory's public keys CPRI: Carol's private key TPRI: Ted's private key

Figure 3–9   The middleman attack

The false keys are shown in dark gray in the figure. At some other time (event 3), Carol and Ted generate legitimate private keys, shown as white keys in the figure for Carol (CPRI), and Ted (TPRI). We assume these keys are session keys (a one-time symmetric key), and are used to encrypt and decrypt the public keys (see Figure 3–9 for a review of this concept).

In event 4, Carol and Ted use what they think are each other's public key to encrypt their private session key. In fact, they are using Mallory's false public keys. The icons in event 4 imply that the session keys of Carol and Ted are in envelopes, coded by each other's public key and that can be "opened" only by each other's private key.

In event 5, the encrypted session keys are sent by Carol and Ted, but they are intercepted by Mallory, who (in event 6) uses his two public keys (MPUB1 and MPUB2) to decrypt the private keys.

Thus, in event 7, Mallory has captured Carol and Ted's private session keys, and can continue to play the middleman and intercept traffic.

CERTIFICATION

To deal with a middleman attack, most high-end security systems implement the digital certificate concept introduced earlier. This operation is used to ensure at the receiver that the sender's public key is valid. For this operation to be supported, the sender (Carol in Figure 3–10) must obtain a digital certificate from a trusted third party, known as the certification authority. Carol, in event 1, sends her public key to the certification authority along with information-specific identification and other information. The certification authority uses this information to

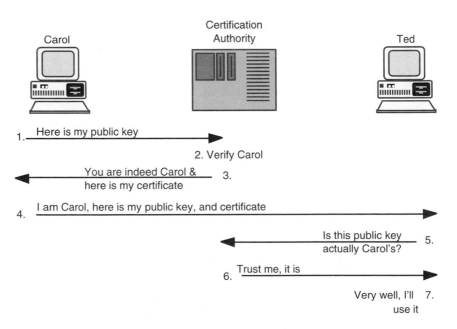

Figure 3–10   A trusted certification authority (CA)

verify Carol and her public key, shown in event 2. If Carol checks out satisfactorily, the certification authority returns to Carol a digital certificate that affirms the validity of Carol's private key, and states that the CA so-validates. This operation is shown in event 3 in the figure. In event 4, when Carol sends traffic to the receiver (Ted in this example), Carol executes all the operations discussed in our previous examples (that is to say, the hash functions, Digital Signature, etc.) and sends this information along with the digital certificate to Ted.

In previous operations, the certification authority's public key has been disseminated to other parties including Ted, consequently, in event 5, Ted uses the certification authority's public key to validate the certification authority's Digital Signature that is part of Carol's certificate. If all checks out, Ted is assured that Carol's public key (also part of the certificate) does indeed belong to Carol. Ted is so informed by the certification authority in event 6, which results in event 7 wherein Ted can use Carol's public key to decrypt the ciphered message.

THE CERTIFICATION PROCEDURE

The certification authority certifies a public key by digitally signing the certificate with the authority's private key. Any user who wishes to use someone's public key can verify its validity by applying the certification authority's public key to the certificate. If Mallory attempts to intercept the authority's certificate during its transmission to a user, it would be detected because the Digital Signature would not be correct.

Of course, we could get in a dog-chases-his-tail situation; obviously the user of the certificate authority must trust that authority to issue only valid certificates. If Mallory penetrates the certification mechanisms of the authority we are back to square one.

ANTI-REPLAY MEASURES

Recall from Chapter 2 that replay is an active attack on a resource, in that it entails capturing data, perhaps modifying it, and resending it. One method of protecting packets from a replay attack is to use a sequence number in the transmitted packet, and at the receiver: (a) check if the arriving packet contains a duplicate sequence number of a previously arrived packet, (b) make certain the sequence number is large enough that a wrap-around of the sequence number will not result in a

valid sequence number being rejected, and (c) implement a sliding window scheme to reject "aged" packets. Aged packets may have been captured, perhaps modified, and resent.

The idea of this anti-replay measure is shown in Figure 3–11. The
receive window is a length of 7, and sits at sequence numbers 1 through
7. This illustration is an example only. The window is small for purposes
of illustration, and the Internet standards state that its value must provide a large wrap-around counter for counting 2^{32} incoming packets.

In Figure 3–11(a), packets 0, 2, 3, 4, 6, and 7 have been received and
authenticated. Therefore, the right-side of the window reflects the
largest packet sequence number that has been received and authenticated. Packet 9 has been received but has not been authenticated, so the
window cannot slide over to 9, until the packet is authenticated. Notice
that packets are accepted (in regard to sequencing) if they fall within or
to the right-side of the window, and they need not arrive in order.

In Figure 3–11(b) packet 9 has now been authenticated, with the re-
sultant sliding of the window to encompass sequence numbers 3 through
9. Packet 1 now sits to the left-side of the window, and if it is received, it
must be rejected. Packets 5 and 8 have not arrived, and if they do arrive,
they are processed because they still sit within the receive window.

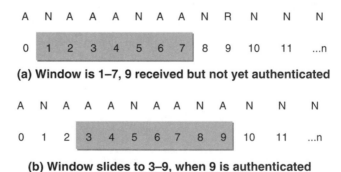

(a) Window is 1–7, 9 received but not yet authenticated

(b) Window slides to 3–9, when 9 is authenticated

Where:
  A   Received and authenticated
  N   Not received
  R   Received, but not yet authenticated

Figure 3–11   Anti-replay measures

SECURITY IN A MOBILE NETWORK

This part of the of our analysis shows an example of how the Global System for Mobile Communications system (GSM) uses keys for user authentication and the encryption/decryption of traffic.

Authentication

One of the most important operations in the handshake of any mobile system is the proper authentication of the user. GSM provides authentication by checking the validity of a subscriber's subscriber identity module (SIM) card located in the mobile phone. This authentication is based is based on the A3 algorithm, which is stored in both the SIM card and at a network authentication control center (AUC). It is also based on a private key Ki, which is also stored on the SIM and in the network AUC.

The AUC is responsible for the creation of the signed response (SRES). See Figure 3–12(a). A Ki value is associated with each IMSI. The mobile station is identified by (a) the international mobile equipment identity (IMEI), which is an identifier of the physical equipment, and the international mobile subscriber identity (IMSI), which is the identity of the user of the mobile station. The A3 algorithm uses Ki and a 128-bit random number (RAND) to produce the SRES.

In Figure 3–12(b), the AUC downline loads several sets of the RAND, SRES pairs to the HLR (which are also called challenge, response pairs). In turn, the HLR makes these values available to a VLR as needed. When the VLR exhausts the set (by using one set each time the MS registers in a cell for which the VLR is responsible), it can request more sets from the HLR.

To authenticate, the network sends to the subscriber a RAND in a message, shown in Figure 3–12(c). The message is a "challenge" to the user. The mobile station uses RAND as input to the A3 calculation along with the authentication key, Ki. Remember, this value is stored only on the SIM card and by the network. The input of Ki and RAND into the A3 algorithm produces the signed response (SRES). This value is returned to the VLR and checked to determine if it has been coded properly. In this manner, the network is able to verify the proper identity of the user. Obviously, if SRES does not equal the pre-computed value stored at the VLR, then the user is not authenticated.

Typically, a set of RAND and SRES values are stored by the network (at the HLR and VLR), and managed by the AUC. This approach al-

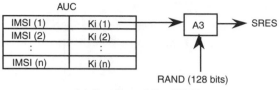

(a) Creation of the SRES

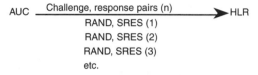

(b) Distribution of challenge, response pairs

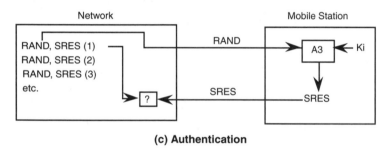

(c) Authentication

Where:
   RAND   Random number
   SRES   Signed response

Figure 3–12   GSM authentication

lows different values to be used with each authentication. If the HLR exhausts the list of numbers, additional values can be requested from the AUC. Under normal conditions, A3 and Ki are never sent across any of the communications channels.

Privacy Operations

In Figure 3–13(a), a ciphering key called Kc is created at the AUC using IMSI and Ki pairs. The A8 algorithm is used, along with RAND, to produce Kc.

In Figure 3–13(b), the AUC downline loads Kc to the HLR. Note in the figure that multiple installations (five is common) of RAND, SRES, and Kc are sent from the AUC to the HLR, and then to the relevant VLR.

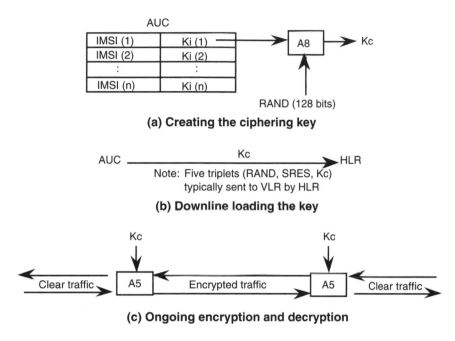

(a) Creating the ciphering key

(b) Downline loading the key

(c) Ongoing encryption and decryption

Figure 3–13   Encryption of user traffic

Finally, in Figure 3–13(c), Kc and A5 are used to encrypt and decrypt the user traffic.

The idea of these operations is to make the production of SRES an easy affair if Ki and RAND are known. In contrast, deriving Ki from RAND and SRES is quite complex, which is the essence of this approach.

SUMMARY

A wide variety of methods are used to protect user traffic in an internet and the Internet. Most of them involve some form of hashing function, modular arithmetic, large prime numbers, and asymmetric key usage. In addition, symmetric (session) key operations are often applied for the sake of efficiency.

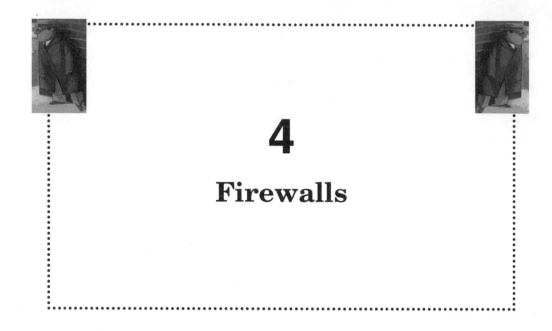

4

Firewalls

This chapter explains how firewalls operate, with emphasis on what a firewall can and cannot do. We examine internal firewalls and external firewalls, also called proxy and access firewalls, respectively. Filtering operations are analyzed, and examples are provided about how to set up firewalls in consonance with the security policies of an enterprise. A number of firms provide firewall services, and these operations are also examined.

WHAT IS A FIREWALL?

A firewall is a system that is used to enforce an access control policy within an organization or between organizations. A firewall need not be just a machine but can be a collection of machines and software that institutes the access control policy (a security association).

In its simplest terms, the firewall allows or forbids traffic to pass from one side to the other side of the firewall. Any authorized traffic that is allowed to pass through this firewall from one network to another or from one host to another host, must be defined by the security policy established in the access control plans of the organization. Another important attribute of the firewall is that it itself must be secure. Insofar as possible, it must also be immune to penetration.

Protection from Untrusted Networks

In its simplest terms, a firewall is a system that protects trusted networks from untrusted networks, a concept introduced in Chapter 1, and shown in Figure 4–1. The trusted networks could be the internal networks of an organization and untrusted networks could be the Internet. However, the concept of trusted and untrusted systems depends on an organization. In some situations within an organization, there could be trusted and untrusted networks depending on the need to know and the need to protect the resources. Indeed, the concept of internal firewalls (internal to the company) and external firewalls (standing between an internal network and external networks) is an important consideration in building security mechanisms. In fact, internal firewalls are quite important because it is well known that internal hacking and security breaches are more numerous than external hacking or external security breaches.

In summary, we can think of a firewall as a tool to help support an organization's security procedures, as a tool to support its access control policies. It is used to accomplish the actual procedures and, therefore, it represents both the security policy and the implementation decisions of the organization.

Since most organizations allow their employees to connect to the public Internet (an untrusted network), the firewall must be designed to take into account the organization's wishes for Internet (or other public networks) access. In essence, the organization may allow no access to the organization's sites *from* the Internet, but allow access from the organization *to* the Internet. As another alternative, filters may be applied that allow only selected systems into and out of the private systems across the firewall.

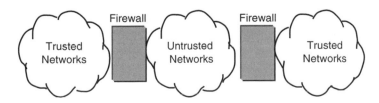

Figure 4–1   Firewall protection from untrusted networks

PERMITTING AND DENYING SERVICES

An organization's access policies may implement the firewall in two basic ways: (a) permit any service unless it is expressly denied, or (b) deny any service unless it is expressly permitted [NCSA96].[1] Option (a) offers considerable opportunity for security breaches. In most situations, option (b) is the service in which most access models are designed. The problem with option (a) is that it becomes an all-encompassing umbrella, which can be bypassed. For example, new services can be brought into play, which are not defined in the firewalls' filters, or defined by the organization's access plans. To take one simple illustration, denied services running in an internet architecture could be circumvented by using nonstandard internet ports, which were not defined (and denied) in the express policy.

One last point in this initial discussion on firewalls: In many situations, it makes sense to have different kinds of firewalls and to perform access analysis and filtering depending on the nature of the traffic and attributes such as addresses, port numbers, etc. This idea leads us to the concept of packet filtering, discussed shortly.

WHAT FIREWALLS CAN DO AND CANNOT DO

Firewalls are not the answer to all security problems an organization faces; Firewalls themselves are vulnerable to security violations. This section explains what firewalls can do and equally important, what they cannot do. First, what they can do:

- *Reflection of security policy:* The firewall's configurations reflect the enterprise's security policy. This policy has established what kinds of traffic can come into the trusted network from the untrusted network, and what traffic can go out into the untrusted network from the trusted network.
- *A concentration point for policy enforcement:* One of the tenets of many security experts is to provide as few access points as possible

---

[1][NCSA96]. National Computer Security Association, *NCSA Firewall Policy Guide,* Version 1.01. I recommend highly the information published by NCSA. This organization can be reached at *request@ncsa.com* or (717) 258–1816, ext. 250. My comments here are based on this reference.

for rogue packets to enter a trusted network. The firewall allows the enterprise to focus access to one (or a few) access point(s). This approach is more efficient than distributing efforts across multiple access points. Of course, the network manager and the security administrator must understand that one concentration point may create traffic congestion, and this potential problem must be weighed against one access point. In large networks, there will be of necessity multiple access points, but the idea is to control and contain their number.

- *Segmenting and isolation of problems:* We will see shortly that many companies install multiple firewalls, and some play different roles. One may sit in front of another, with each set up with different responsibilities. This being the case, it is convenient for the security administrator to isolate and analyze problems emanating from the different firewalls.

Next, here is what firewalls cannot do:

- *The enemy within:* No matter how effective the firewall is, it cannot protect the enterprise from the insider, and as mentioned before, the insider is one of the biggest security risks for a company. Proprietary information, for example, may be copied by an insider and given to potential competitors and adversaries. It is a common occurrence, with no absolute solution. Careful employee/contractor evaluation, with limited access to sensitive and vulnerable information is the practical approach to this problem.

- *Unforeseen penetration attempts:* It was stated in Chapter 1 that the IBM Virus Center discovers several new viruses each day, and the Mallories of the world are always devising new penetration methods. The firewall is not clairvoyant. Its effectiveness is directly associated with how it is configured to check for rogue packets. If Mallory has come up with an new method to bypass the firewall's screening programs (it is called a lazy firewall; actually, it is often a lazy security administrator), then a security violation has occurred.

- *Viruses are not detected:* Speaking of viruses, an access (external) firewall usually does not detect a virus. As discussed shortly, the firewall does not examine the user payload in the IP packet, and that is where the virus resides. Certainly, virus checks can be placed in a firewall, and is it possible to have a firewall that does nothing but check for viruses. But for the access firewall shown in Figure 4–1, the checking for the many viruses is often too big a job, and creates unacceptable performance problems. Increasingly, virus-detection programs are being installed in internal (proxy) firewalls.

PACKET FILTERING

One of the key operations performed by a firewall is packet filtering. This term describes the operation where certain packets (also called datagrams) are allowed to pass through the firewall and others are not. The filtering operations are based on a set of rules encoded in the software running in the firewall. The most common type of packet filtering from the standpoint of a traditional router is done on IP datagrams. Filtering may be done on (a) the source IP address, (b) the destination IP address, (c) the TCP or UDP source port number, (d) the TCP or UDP destination port number, and (e) the protocol number that resides in a field in the IP header (the IP Protocol ID).

While these criteria are used for most high-end routers, not all routers can filter on port numbers. Furthermore, other routers perform filtering based on outgoing network interfaces—to make decisions as to whether or not to pass the datagram forward across an input interface to an output interface.

Filtering also is dependent upon the specific operating systems. For example, some UNIX hosts have the ability to filter and others do not.

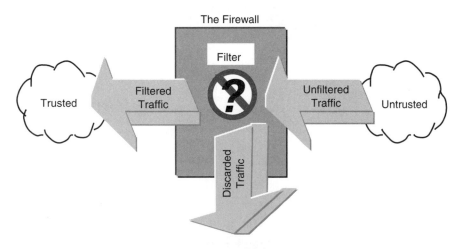

Figure 4–2   Packet filtering

Figure 4–2 shows an example of packet filtering at a firewall. The traffic is delivered to the firewall from an untrusted network. Before being processed by the firewall, the traffic is unfiltered.[2] Based on the security policy at the firewall, traffic will be passed to the trusted network(s), that is, it is filtered.[3] Otherwise, the traffic that does not pass the firewall's tests is discarded. In this situation, the traffic should be logged for further analysis, and important aspect of tracking down possible security problems.

PROXY OR APPLICATION FIREWALLS

Applying all the filtering rules at one router may be too complex a job. Even if it can be implemented, it may place an undue processing workload on the router. Another approach is to have more than one firewall in which some of the filtering operations are performed in what is referred to as a proxy firewall or an application gateway (as seen in Figure 4–3). For example, the NCSA paper states that a router might pass all TELNET and FTP packets to a specific host, which is designated as the TELNET/FTP application gateway. This gateway then makes further filtering operations.

A user who wishes to connect to a system site may be required to connect first to the application gateway, followed by the connection to a destination host. The user would first TELNET to the application gateway and enter the name of the internal host that wishes to use the system. The application gateway then checks the user's IP source address for validity. (At this juncture, the user may also have to authenticate to the application gateway.) Next, a TELNET connection is created between the gateway and the local internal host, followed by the passing of traffic between the two host machines.

In addition, application firewalls can be further configured to deny or admit certain specific transactions. One that comes to mind is to deny the use of some users to write to a server (by denying the FTP PUT command).

---

[2]In some literature, unfiltered also refers to traffic that is not processed at all by a firewall.

[3]Filtered traffic may also refer to traffic that is processed by the firewall and discarded, so be careful with the terms filtered and unfiltered.

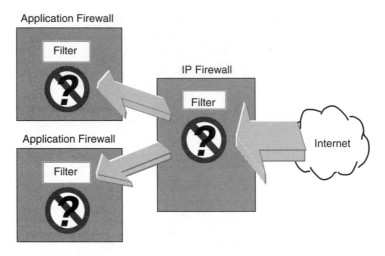

Figure 4–3   Application (proxy firewalls)

NCSA GUIDANCE

The National Computer Security Association (NCSA) provides guidance on how to handle policing protocols for certain port numbers [NCSA96]. Additional information is available in [CHAP95][4] and [GRAF92].[5]

(a) FTP, port 69, trivial FTP, used for booting diskless workstations, terminal servers and routers, can also be used to read any file on the system if set up incorrectly.

(b) X Windows, OpenWindows, ports 6000+, port 2000, can leak information from X window displays including all keystrokes (intruders can even gain control of a server through the X-server).

(c) RPC, port 111, Remote Procedure Call services including NIS and NFS, which can be used to steal system information such as passwords and read and write to files.

(d) rlogin, rsh, and rexec, ports 513, 514, and 512 service, which, if improperly configured, can permit unauthorized access to accounts and commands.

---

[4][CHAP95]. Chapman, D. Brent. *Building Internet Firewalls,* O'Reilly & Assoc. 1995.

[5][GRAF92]. Garfinkle, Simson and Spafford, Gene. *Practical UNIX Security,* O'Reilly & Assoc. 1992.

Other services according the NCSA95 are usually filtered and possibly restricted to only those systems that need them. These include:

(e) TELNET, port 23, often restricted to certain systems.

(f) FTP, ports 20 and 21, like TELNET, often restricted to certain systems.

(g) SMTP, port 25, often restricted to a central email server.

(h) RIP, port 520, routing information protocol, can be spoofed to redirect packet routing.

(i) DNS, port 53, domain names service zone transfers, contains names of hosts and information about hosts that could be helpful to attackers, could be spoofed.

(j) UUCP, port 540, UNIX-to-UNIX CoPy, if improperly configured can be used for unauthorized access.

(k) NNTP, port 119, Network News Transfer Protocol, for accessing and reading network news.

(l) gopher, http, ports 70 and 80, information servers, and client programs for gopher and WWW clients, should be restricted to an application gateway that contains proxy services.

As a general rule, providing service to TELNET or FTP should be restricted to certain systems. In most instances, not all users will need access to TELNET or FTP. Consequently, restricting these types of protocols improves security but it does not entail any additional costs to the organization. Once again, we must reemphasize the idea that the basic approach is to deny any service unless it is expressly permitted.

MANAGED FIREWALL SERVICES (MFWS)

Managed firewall services (MFWS) are a relatively new "weapon" in the Internet security wars. An organization providing this service takes on the responsibilities of setting up and managing a company's firewall, including the overall planning of a complete security association, software licensing, installation, maintenance, and even key management operations.

In evaluating a potential MFWS, one should look very carefully at the staff of the company; indeed perhaps the biggest complaint about firewall providers is the lack of depth of their security personnel. But this lament is common throughout the industry; there simply are not enough skilled people to go around. Nonetheless, the failure to have competent personnel in the MFWS that is managing your firewalls can create a lot of problems, AKA security breaches. More on this subject later.

As depicted in Figure 4–4, the firewall provider gives the customer two options on where the firewall is located: (a) on the customer's site, or (b) at the provider's site. Most of their services are being provided by ISPs and long-distance carriers, so option (b) usually entails placing the firewall at

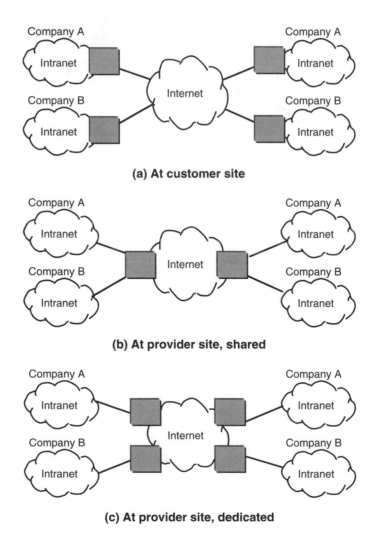

(a) At customer site

(b) At provider site, shared

(c) At provider site, dedicated

Figure 4–4   Managed firewall services (MFWS)

the provider's data center, on a server farm (at for example, an ISP's point-of-presence, or POP). There are pros and cons to each option.

For option (a), it is easier to collect the security efforts into a concentration point, and one is assured of having a dedicated firewall, with confidence of precise filters. For option (b), the company does not have to use its space for equipment, nor allocate staff for the firewall. However, option (b) may mean the security efforts are dispersed at multiple server locations. Also, option (b) may mean that the firewall is shared with other customers. But dispersion is not necessarily a bad thing. It can lead to less delay, and a reduced hop distance. For option (b), it is a good idea to know how many sites the provider has, since traffic can be shared by multiple locations (for example, in the United States, Europe, Asia, etc.). As Figure 4–4 shows, a non-dedicated arrangement actually entails two variations, shown as (b) and (c).

Evaluating a Firewall Service Provider

Several criteria are used when evaluating a provider of managed firewall services [MAKR99].[6] One consideration is the availability of the service, which pertains to how many network operations centers (NOCs) are available to support the firewall service. Typical numbers range from one to six. Another important consideration is the support of different user technologies, such as Frame Relay, X.25, and ATM.

The provider's firewall products may provide only access filtering, or proxy filtering (application filtering). As discussed earlier, the potential customer must evaluate if it is better to have the firewall on-site, or off-site, and if it is off-site, if it is better to have a dedicated or stand-alone setup.

In reference to costs, they do vary quite a bit between the offerings, with prices structured per firewall, and perhaps per user. Some providers charge extra for encryption management; others charge partially based on location of the customer. The cost per firewall can range from $500 per firewall for a few users to $20,000 for several hundred users. Practically all providers include in their fees the ongoing consulting services.

The selection of the software for the firewall is another consideration. Some providers have their own, and others buy it from vendors. It is a good idea to check the capabilities of this software.

---

[6][MAKR99]. Makris, Joanna. "More Bark than Bite," *Data Communications,* March, 1999, or jmakris@data.com.

Another aspect to examine is how many changes are allowed to the filter parameters, and how they are given to the provider. Some MFWSs allow unlimited changes and others charge for changes that exceed a certain number per week. These changes may be given by email, by phone, by fax, etc., but the procedure does vary among the providers.

Check the service level agreement (SLA) regarding up-time, and the penalties the MFWS agrees to for any SLA "infraction."

Finally, check the competency of the personnel and the depth of the staff!

FIREWALLS WITH INTERNET SECURITY PROTOCOLS (IPSec)

Figures 4–5 and 4–6 show a model that supports the implementation of IPSec with a firewall [RFC 2709]. These examples are for a tunnel mode operation, one in which the firewalls support a secure tunnel between them.

Figure 4–5 depicts the operations on an outgoing packet at the firewall. The user packet is examined for a match to an outbound security policy. Recall that the match can be made on IP addresses, the IP Protocol ID, and port numbers. Based on a match or no-match, the packet is (a) forwarded in the clear (without alteration), (b) dropped (no more processing), or (c) subjected to the operations dictated by the outbound security policy (in this example, the IPSec operations).

Figure 4–6 depicts the operations on an incoming packet at the firewall. The secure packet arrives at the firewall where it is detunneled (decapsulated). The IP packet is then compared for a match to an inbound SA policy. If a match occurs, it is subjected to the operations dictated by the inbound security policy (once again, the IPSec operations). Otherwise, it is dropped.

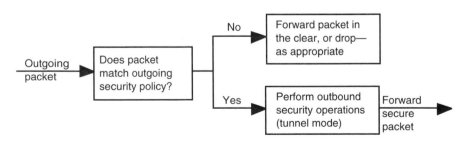

Figure 4–5 IPSec at a firewall (outbound packet)

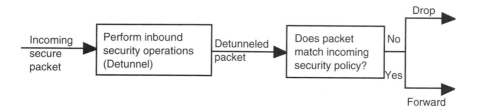

Figure 4–6   IPSec at a firewall (inbound packet)

SOCKS

SOCKS Version 4 is a procedure that provides for unsecured fire-wall traversal for TCP-based client-server applications, including TEL-NET, FTP, HTTP, and GOPHER. SOCKS Version 5 model includes UDP. It also extends the framework to include provisions for strong authentication schemes, and extends the addressing scheme to encompass domain-name and IPv6 addresses [VANH99].[7]

When a TCP-based client wishes to establish a connection to an object that is reachable only through a firewall, it must open a TCP connection to the appropriate SOCKS port on the SOCKS server system. The SOCKS service is located on TCP port 1080. If the connection request succeeds, the client enters into a negotiation for the authentication method to be used, authenticates with the chosen method, then sends a relay request. The SOCKS server evaluates the request, and either establishes the appropriate connection or denies it. The SOCKS specification defines several authentication methods. The one described in this book (in Chapter 6) is CHAP. For more information see [VANH99].

SUMMARY

Firewalls are used to implement an organization's security policies. The firewall is placed in a physical machine, such as a router or server, to filter the traffic coming from untrusted networks.

---

[7][VANH99]. *www.ietf.org,* click on working drafts, and find draft-ietf-aft-socks-pro-v5-04.

5

Prominent Internet Security Procedures

This chapter describes the more widely used procedures that are used with the Internet security protocols. Many of these procedures were developed outside of the Internet Engineering Task Force (IETF). They have been incorporated into many Internet security services, and in some cases, published as RFCs.

Our approach in this chapter is to extend the discussion of several of the subjects discussed in a general way in Chapter 3. The focus in this chapter is on how the procedures are used in the Internet.

For the past four chapters, we have laid the groundwork for a more detailed analysis of the Internet security procedures protocols. As I mentioned earlier, this book is not intended to be a treatise on all aspects of network security; I know of no book that can make that claim. Nonetheless, it will serve us well to pause here and take a look at some of the more recent and notable contributions to many of the topics covered in this and subsequent chapters. We start with public key encryption, introduced in Chapter 3, a methodology that is surely the most revolutionary occurrence to happen to security in many decades or even centuries. We will not revisit the material in Chapter 3—only make reference to it, as appropriate, and move directly into the Internet-specific aspects of the topics.

Because of the many details associated with this material, the approach is to provide a general description of the subject in this chapter, and refer you to sections in Appendix A if you wish to review code and or algorithms.

DIFFIE-HELLMAN

Whitfield Diffie and Martin Hellman are credited with establishing the foundation for public key encryption and decryption. Diffie and Hellman had been thinking and writing about public key exchanges for many years, and part of their focus in the 1970s was how to send keys in another manner than physically transporting them from one point to another. The problem was replete with inefficiencies.[1]

The key distribution problem is like a dog chasing its tail. Let's say Alice and Bob wish to have secure communications with each other. However, before they can communicate securely, they must share a secret key that is used to encrypt their traffic. But how do they transfer this key to each other in a secure manner? In the old days, young Ensigns flew around the Far East, acting as couriers for the distribution of these keys. But as introduced in Chapter 3, Diffie and Hellman (and another pioneer, Ralph Merkle) persevered in their ideas that there was another way. Going against the conventional wisdom at that time (what they were trying to do was simply counterintuitive), Hellman made a breakthrough in 1976. And in that year, their discovery was revealed in the June 1976 National Computer Conference.

Notwithstanding their astounding achievements, in retrospect their key exchange idea had some problems. But for this discussion, we will focus on their achievement, their discovery, and address some enhancements later.

We learned in Chapter 3 that Diffie concocted the idea of the asymmetric key: the encryption and decryption keys are not identical. Moreover, these researchers were focused on a one-way function (one that is easy to do, but very difficult to undo), a topic also discussed in Chapter 3.

---

[1]In the 1960s, I served as a crypto officer in the US Navy. One of my jobs was that of a courier. Periodically, I transported secret keys from various communications centers ("crypto shacks") in the Far East to my ship. The rules required me to carry a side arm when I was on my journey between my ship and the center. Another rule required the courier bag containing the keys and other security material to be handcuffed to my wrist. I sometimes wondered if my wrist was really a deterrent to someone who might really want that courier pouch. Had I known about public keys in those days, I am sure I would have been in favor of their use.

This idea is quite important, because it implies that a Mallory cannot (easily) tap a channel, and glean sufficient information from it to reverse-engineer the data to reveal the key to decrypt the traffic.

However, they did not reach the point of finding a proven method of realizing a one-way function with asymmetric ciphers. The individuals that are credited with this feat are Ronald Rivest, Adi Shamir, and Leonard Adleman, known as RSA. We will talk about RSA shortly. For now, let us examine how Diffie-Hellman is applied in the Internet security protocols.

Diffie-Hellman and RFC 2631

For the Internet implementation of the Diffie-Hellman ideas, RFC 2631 (which cites ANSI X9.42) has been published. With this specification, the Diffie-Hellman key operation requires both the sender and recipient of a message to have key pairs. As explained in Chapter 3, by combining one's private key and the other party's public key, both parties can compute the same shared secret number. This number can then be converted into cryptographic keying material. That keying material is typically used as a key-encryption key (KEK) to encrypt a content-encryption key (CEK) which is in turn used to encrypt the message data. If you are not familiar with these ideas, please refer back to Figures 3–3 and 3–7 in Chapter 3.

Key Agreement.   The first stage of the key agreement process is to compute a shared secret number, called ZZ. When the same originator and recipient public/private key pairs are used, the same ZZ value will result. The ZZ value is then converted into a shared symmetric cryptographic key. When the originator employs a static private/public key pair, the introduction of a public random value ensures that the resulting symmetric key will be different for each key agreement. Box 5–1 provides a summary of these concepts.

Generation of Keying Material.   X9.42 defines an algorithm for generating an arbitrary amount of keying material from ZZ. The RFC 2631 algorithm is derived from that algorithm by mandating some optional fields and omitting others:

$$KM = H\,(\,ZZ \mid\mid \text{OtherInfo})$$

Box 5–1   RFC 2631 Diffie-Hellman concepts

ANSI X9.42 defines that the shared secret ZZ is generated as follows:

$$ZZ = g \wedge (xb * xa) \bmod p$$

The individual parties actually perform the computations:

$$ZZ = (yb \wedge xa) \bmod p = (ya \wedge xb) \bmod p$$

Where $\wedge$ denotes exponentiation.
The following relationships exist:

1. *ya* is party *a*'s public key; $ya = g \wedge xa \bmod p$
2. *yb* is party *b*'s public key; $yb = g \wedge xb \bmod p$
3. *xa* is party *a*'s private key
4. *xb* is party *b*'s private key
5. *p* is a large prime, enormous if possible
6. *q* is a large prime, enormous if possible
7. $g = h \wedge \{(p - 1) / q\} \bmod p$,
   where: *h* is any integer with $1 < h < p - 1$ such that $h\{(p - 1) / q\} \bmod p > 1$
   (*g* has order q mod *p*; i.e. $g \wedge q \bmod p = 1$ if $g! = 1$)
8. *j is* a large integer such that $p = qj + 1$

H is the message digest function SHA-1 [FIPS-180 and discussed later]. *ZZ* is the shared secret value. Leading zeros must be preserved, so that *ZZ* occupies as many octets as *p*. For instance, if *p* is 1024 bits, *ZZ* should be 128 bytes long. OtherInfo is the encoding of the following structure:

```
OtherInfo ::= SEQUENCE {
  keyInfo KeySpecificInfo,
  partyAInfo [0] OCTET STRING OPTIONAL,
  suppPubInfo [2] OCTET STRING
}
KeySpecificInfo ::= SEQUENCE {
  algorithm OBJECT IDENTIFIER,
  counter OCTET STRING SIZE (4..4) }
```

The object counter is a 32-bit number, represented in network byte order. Its initial value is 1 for any *ZZ*, i.e., the byte sequence 00 00 00

01(hex), and it is incremented by one every time the above key generation function is run for a given KEK. The object partyAInfo is a random string provided by the sender. If provided, partyAInfo must contain 512 bits. The object suppPubInfo is the length of the generated KEK, in bits, represented as a 32-bit number in network byte order.

To generate a KEK, one generates one or more *KM* blocks (incrementing counter appropriately) until enough material has been generated. The *KM* blocks are concatenated left to right, i.e., *KM*(counter = 1) || *KM*(counter = 2)...

KEK Computation.   Each key encryption algorithm requires a specific size key (n). The KEK is generated by mapping the left n-most bytes of *KM* onto the key. For 3DES (explained in Chapter 6, see Figure 6–9), which requires 192 bits of keying material, the algorithm must be run twice, once with a counter value of 1 (to generate K1′, K2′, and the first 32 bits of K3′) and once with a counter value of 2(to generate the last 32 bits of K3). K1′, K2′ and K3′ are then parity adjusted to generate the 3 DES keys K1, K2 and K3. For RC2-128, which requires 128 bits of keying material, the algorithm is run once, with a counter value of 1, and the left-most 128 bits are directly converted to an RC2 key. Similarly, for RC2-40, which requires 40 bits of keying material, the algorithm is run once, with a counter value of 1, and the leftmost 40 bits are used as the key.

RIVEST, SHAMIR, AND ADLEMAN (RSA)

The contributions of the Diffie-Hellman-Merkle key exchange have been cited. We explained in Chapter 3, their ideas were workable, but they were not yet perfected. The final piece to the puzzle was provided by Ronald Rivest, Adi Shamir, and Leonard Adleman.

These men worked at MIT in the computer science department in the 1970s doing various kinds of research. They became interested in asymmetric ciphers after Ron Rivest brought to their attention the work of Diffie and Hellman. After a year of work and corroboration, they came up with their ideas. Once again, if you skipped Chapter 3, go back to the section titled, "The Next Step: RSA."

RSA in RFC 2437

RFC 2437 does not lend itself to a summary. The best approach is to describe how RFC 2437 treats the public and private keys.

RSA Public Key.   An RSA public key consists of two components: (a) n, the modulus, a nonnegative integer, and (b) e, the public exponent, a nonnegative integer. In a valid RSA public key, the modulus n is a product of two odd primes p and q, and the public exponent e is an integer between 3 and n − 1 satisfying gcd $(e, \lambda(n)) = 1$, where $\lambda(n) = lcm$ $(p − 1, q − 1)$.

RSA Private Key.   An RSA private key may have either of two representations. The first representation consists of the pair (n, d), where the components have the following meanings: (a) n, the modulus, a nonnegative integer, and (b) d, the private exponent, a nonnegative integer. The second representation consists of a quintuple $(p, q, dP, dQ, qInv)$, where the components have the following meanings:

- p: First factor, a nonnegative integer
- q: Second factor, a nonnegative integer
- dP: First factor's exponent, a nonnegative integer
- dQ: Second factor's exponent, a nonnegative integer
- $qInv$: CRT coefficient, a nonnegative integer

In a valid RSA private key with the first representation, the modulus n is the same as in the corresponding public key and is the product of two odd primes p and q, and the private exponent d is a positive integer less than n satisfying: $ed \equiv 1$ (mod $\lambda(n)$), where e is the corresponding public exponent and $\lambda(n)$.

In a valid RSA private key with the second representation, the two factors p and q are the prime factors of the modulus n, the exponents dP and dQ are positive integers less than p and q, respectively, satisfying:

$$e(dP) \equiv 1 (\text{mod}(p − 1))$$
$$e(dQ) \equiv 1 (\text{mod}(q − 1)),$$

The CRT coefficient $qInv$ is a positive integer less than p satisfying:

$$q(qInv) \equiv 1 \ (\text{mod } p).$$

If you wish to go beyond this general discussion of the RSA keys, RFC 2437 provides a syntax for interchanging RSA private keys between implementations, which includes components from both representations, see Section 11.1.2 of RFC 2437.

MD5

The MD5 Message Digest Algorithm, published in RFC 1321 by Ron Rivest, is a widely-used hash function. In the past few years, it has been criticized for its vulnerability to attack, and it is known that it is possible to find two different inputs that will produce the same digest. In spite of this problem, I highlight MD5 in this chapter for two reasons. The first reason is that MD5 can be protected by an operation called the Keyed Hashing for Message Authentication (HMAC), and MD5-HMAC is not susceptible to this collision attack. The second reason is that MD5 is used in many routers for protecting a variety of routing protocols, such as RIP, OSPF, and BGP. This part of the chapter provides a summary of RFC 1321, and more information is provided in Appendix A.

The MD5 algorithm is designed for 32-bit machines. It is an extension of MD4, with several enhancements, discussed shortly. It takes a message of arbitrary length, and produces a 128-bit message digest. It processes the input message in 512-bit blocks (sixteen 32-bit words). It is designed for Digital Signatures. The MD5 operation consists of 5 steps:

Step 1: Append Padding bits. As seen in Figure 5–1, the message is padded (a 1 bit followed by 0s of up to 512 bits) so that its length is always 64 bits less than an integer multiple of 512 bits.

Step 2: Append Length. Figure 5–1 also shows the result of step 2, in which the results of step 1 are appended with a 64-bit representation of the length of the message before the padding bits were added. In the event that the original message is greater than 2^{64}, then only the low-order 64 bits of the length are used. The result of step 2 is the resulting message has a length of integer multiples of 512 bits. Equivalently, this message has a length that is an exact multiple of sixteen 32-bit words. Let $M[0 \dots N-1]$ denote the words of the resulting message, where N is a multiple of 16. Therefore, $N = L \times 16$.

Step 3: Initialize MD buffer: A 128-bit buffer (represented as four 32-bit registers) is used to hold the results of the MD5 hash function. The registers, identified as A, B, C, and D, are initialized to the following 32-bit integers (shown in hex, and with low-order bytes first [little-endian format]):

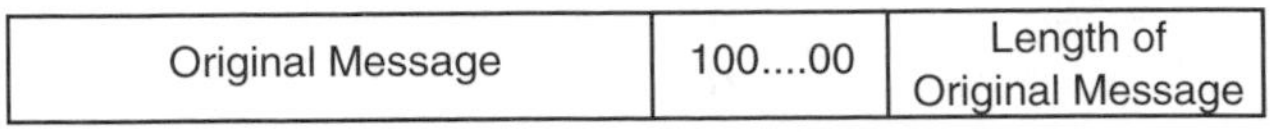

Original Message	100....00	Length of Original Message

Figure 5–1   Message padding

word A:	01	23	45	67
word B:	89	AB	CD	EF
word C:	FE	DC	BA	98
word D:	76	54	32	10

Step 4: Process message in 512-bit (16-word) blocks: The major operations of MD5 are contained in this step, which consists of four processing rounds (or passes) over each 16-byte block of the message. The process uses a different constant for each word on each round. There are four rounds, each using 16 message words, creating 64 32-bit constants. These values are stored in a 64-element table, identified as Table T and provided in Appendix A. T is based on the sine function, and for those readers that are curious: $Ti = \lfloor 2^{32} |\sin i| \rfloor$ [KAUF95].[2]

Four auxiliary functions each take as input three 32-bit words and produce as output one 32-bit word. The rounds use a different structure, as shown here (and identified as *F, G, H,* and *I*):

$$F(X,Y,Z) = XY \: v \: \text{not}(X) \: Z$$
$$G(X,Y,Z) = XZ \: v \: Y \: \text{not}(Z)$$
$$H(X,Y,Z) = X \: x \: \text{or} \: Y \: x \: \text{or} \: Z$$
$$I(X,Y,Z) = Y \: x \: \text{or} \: (X \: v \: \text{not}(Z))$$

RFC 1321 describes the operations for each round, and also provides coding examples. This code, also sourced from RFC 1321, explains the processing algorithm for step 4.

```
/* Process each 16-word block. */
   For i = 0 to N/16-1 do

     /* Copy block i into X. */
     For j = 0 to 15 do
     Set X[j] to M[i*16+j].
     end /* of loop on j */

     /* Save A as AA, B as BB, C as CC, and D as DD. */
     AA = A
     BB = B
     CC = C
     DD = D
```

[2][KAUF95]. Kaufman, Charlie, et al., *Network Security: Private Communication in a Public World,* Prentice Hall, 1995.

```
/* Round 1. */
/* Let [abcd k s i] denote the operation
    a = b + ((a + F(b,c,d) + X[k] + T[i]) <<< s). */
/* Do the following 16 operations. */
[ABCD 0 7 1] [DABC 1 12 2] [CDAB 2 17 3] [BCDA 3 22 4]
[ABCD 4 7 5] [DABC 5 12 6] [CDAB 6 17 7] [BCDA 7 22 8]
[ABCD 8 7 9] [DABC 9 12 10] [CDAB 10 17 11] [BCDA 11 22 12]
[ABCD 12 7 13] [DABC 13 12 14] [CDAB 14 17 15] [BCDA 15 22 16]


/* Round 2. */
/* Let [abcd k s i] denote the operation
    a = b + ((a + G(b,c,d) + X[k] + T[i]) <<< s). */
/* Do the following 16 operations. */
[ABCD 1 5 17] [DABC 6 9 18] [CDAB 11 14 19] [BCDA 0 20 20]
[ABCD 5 5 21] [DABC 10 9 22] [CDAB 15 14 23] [BCDA 4 20 24]
[ABCD 9 5 25] [DABC 14 9 26] [CDAB 3 14 27] [BCDA 8 20 28]
[ABCD 13 5 29] [DABC 2 9 30] [CDAB 7 14 31] [BCDA 12 20 32]


/* Round 3. */
/* Let [abcd k s t] denote the operation
    a = b + ((a + H(b,c,d) + X[k] + T[i]) <<< s). */
/* Do the following 16 operations. */
[ABCD 5 4 33] [DABC 8 11 34] [CDAB 11 16 35] [BCDA 14 23 36]
[ABCD 1 4 37] [DABC 4 11 38] [CDAB 7 16 39] [BCDA 10 23 40]
[ABCD 13 4 41] [DABC 0 11 42] [CDAB 3 16 43] [BCDA 6 23 44]
[ABCD 9 4 45] [DABC 12 11 46] [CDAB 15 16 47] [BCDA 2 23 48]


/* Round 4. */
/* Let [abcd k s t] denote the operation
    a = b + ((a + I(b,c,d) + X[k] + T[i]) <<< s). */
/* Do the following 16 operations. */
[ABCD 0 6 49] [DABC 7 10 50] [CDAB 14 15 51] [BCDA 5 21 52]
[ABCD 12 6 53] [DABC 3 10 54] [CDAB 10 15 55] [BCDA 1 21 56]
[ABCD 8 6 57] [DABC 15 10 58] [CDAB 6 15 59] [BCDA 13 21 60]
[ABCD 4 6 61] [DABC 11 10 62] [CDAB 2 15 63] [BCDA 9 21 64]


/* Then perform the following additions. (That is increment
   each of the four registers by the value it had before this
   block was started.) */
A = A + AA
B = B + BB
C = C + CC
D = D + DD


end /* of loop on i */
```

Step 5: Output, the final step, is the result of the processing of all L 512-bit blocks.

MD5 Vulnerabilities?

In the words of the author of MD5 (Ron Revist) the design intent of MD5 is as follows: "It is conjectured that it is computationally infeasible to produce two messages having the same message digest, or to produce any message having a given pre-specified target message digest."

It is indeed very unlikely that two messages chosen at random will result in the same hash code. However, several researchers have found vulnerabilities in MD5. While it remains the most prominent message digest tool in the Internet, other alternatives are available that are known to be more resistant to compromise, and are discussed next. Those of you that would like to delve into more detail about these MD5 "problems," see [DOBB96].[3]

But before proceeding further, it must be emphasized that MD5 will most likely continue to be a preferred message digest algorithm, because IPSec defines its use with HMAC, the Keyed-Hashing for Message Authentication specification, published in RFC 2104. We will also examine HMAC in this chapter.

RFC 2537: RSA, MD5, and DNS

The Domain Name System (DNS) is the global database system for Internet addressing, mail proxy, and other information. The DNS has been extended to include Digital Signatures and cryptographic keys as described in RFC 2535. Thus the DNS can now be secured and used for secure key distribution. RFC 2537 describes how to store RSA keys and RSA/MD5-based signatures in the DNS. Implementation of the RSA algorithm in DNS is recommended. Here is a summary of RFC 2537.

RSA Public KEY Resource Records

RSA public keys are stored in the DNS as KEY Resource Records (RRs) using algorithm number 1 from RFC 2535. The structure of the algorithm-specific portion of the RDATA part of the RRs is shown here.

---

[3][DOBB96]. Dobbertin, H, et al., "The Status of MD5 After a Recent Attack," *Crypto-Bytes*, Summer, 1996.

Field	Size
Exponent length	1 or 3
Exponent	as specified by length field
Modulus	remaining space

For interoperability, the exponent and modulus are each currently limited to 4096 bits in length. The public key exponent is a variable length unsigned integer. Its length in octets is represented as 1 octet if it is in the range of 1 to 255 and by a 0 octet followed by a 2-octet unsigned length if it is longer than 255 bytes. The public key modulus field is a multi-precision unsigned integer. The length of the modulus can be determined from the RDLENGTH and the preceding RDATA fields including the exponent. Leading 0 octets are prohibited in the exponent and modulus.

RSA/MD5 SIG Resource Records

The signature portion of the SIG RR RDATA area, when using the RSA/MD5 algorithm, is calculated as shown below. The data signed is determined as specified in RFC 2535.

hash = MD5 (data)
signature = (00 | 01 | FF* | 00 | prefix | hash) ** e (mod n)

Where MD5 is the message digest algorithm documented in RFC 1321, "|" is concatenation, e is the private key exponent of the signer, and n is the modulus of the signer's public key. 01, FF, and 00 are fixed octets of the corresponding hexadecimal value. "prefix" is the ASN.1 BER MD5 algorithm designator prefix, that is,

hex 3020300c06082a864886f70d020505000410

The size of n, including most and least significant bits (which will be 1) must be not less than 512 bits and not more than 4096 bits. n and e should be chosen such that the public exponent is small. Leading 0 bytes are permitted in the RSA/MD5 algorithm signature.

Performance Considerations

General signature generation speeds are roughly the same for RSA and DSA [RFC 2536]. With sufficient pre-computation, signature generation with DSA is faster than RSA. Key generation is also faster for DSA.

However, signature verification is an order of magnitude slower with DSA when the RSA public exponent is chosen to be small as is recommended for KEY RRs used in DNS data authentication.

THE SECURE HASH STANDARD (SHA-1) AND THE SECURE HASH ALGORITHM (SHA)

The secure hash algorithm (SHA), generally referred to as the secure hash standard (SHA-1), is published by the U.S. National Institute of Standards and Technology (NIST). It is based on a predecessor to MD5, called MD4. The main differences between SHA-1 and these MDs is that it produces a 160-bit message digest, instead of the 128-bit digest of the MDs. This longer digest makes SHA-1 less vulnerable to attack and compromise. SHA-1 involves more processing to produce the longer digest. However, SHA-1 is one of the more widely used hash algorithms (it and MD5), because of its resistance to collision.

While SHA-1 is a stronger message digest, if HMAC is applied to MD5, then MD5 maintains its integrity, and operates more efficiently (it is faster to compute) than SHA-1. Computational speed is important, since each packet leaving and entering a node must have security calculations performed on it. I refer you to NIST FIPS PUB 180 for more information on SHA-1.

RIPEMD-160

Because of the concern with MD4 and MD5, the European RACE Integrity Primitives Evaluation (RIPE) developed RIPEMD-160. It, too, was developed from MD4, but its digest length is 160 bits. However, like SHA-1, RIPEMD is considerably less efficient than MD5.

COMPARISONS OF MD5, SHA-1, RIPEMD-160, AND MD5-HMAC

Table 5–1 provides a comparison of the major features of MD5, SHA-1, and RIPEMD-160 [STAL99]. Table 5–2 shows speed benchmarks for some of the most popular hash algorithms [DAI99].[4] MD5-HMAC is

---

[4][DAI99]. Dai, Wei. http://www.eskimo.com/~weidai/benchmark.html.

Table 5–1　Comparison of Security Hash Functions [DAI99]

Cipher	Total Bytes	Time	Bytes/Second
MD5	2,147,483,648	37.534	57,214,356
SHA-1	536,870,912	21.12	25,420,024
RIPEMD-160	536,870,912	22.232	24,148,566
MD5-HMAC	1,073,741,824	21.491	49,962,396

discussed next in this chapter, and it is included here to make the point that placing MAC onto MD5 reduces MD5 to perform worse than SHA-1, and RIPEMD-160.

All were coded in C++ or ported to C++ from C implementations, compiled with Microsoft Visual C++ 6.0 SP2 (optimize for speed, Pentium Pro code generation), and ran on a Celeron 450MHz machine under Windows 2000 beta 3. No assembly language was used.

HMAC

References to HMAC have been made several times in this book. This part of the chapter provides the details for this operation. First, HMAC is published in RFC 2104, and its authors are Hugo Krawczyk, Mihir Bellare, and Ran Canetti, who furnish coding examples of HMAC (Appendix A of this book). HMAC is a keyed hash function. IPSec requires that all message authentication be performed using HMAC. RFC 2104 states the design objectives of HMAC (and I quote directly):

Table 5–2　Comparison of MD5, SHA-1, and RIPEMD-160 [STAL99]

	MD5	SHA-1	RIPEMD-160
Digest length	128 bits	160 bits	160 bits
Basic unit of processing	512 bits	512 bits	512 bits
Number of steps	64 (4 rounds of 16)	80 (4 rounds of 20)	160 (5 paired rounds of 16)
Maximum message size	Any	$2^{64} - 1$ bits	$2^{64} - 1$ bits
Primitive logical functions	4	4	5
Additive constants used	64	4	9
Endianness	Little-endian	Big-endian	Little-endian

1. To use, without modifications, available hash functions. In particular, hash functions that perform well in software, and for which code is freely and widely available.
2. To preserve the original performance of the hash function without incurring a significant degradation.
3. To use and handle keys in a simple way.
4. To have a well understood cryptographic analysis of the strength of the authentication mechanism based on reasonable assumptions on the underlying hash function.
5. To allow for easy replaceability of the underlying hash function in case faster or more secure hash functions are found or required.

One of HMAC's unique characteristics is the use of a nested key hash operation, one inside the other. The idea is based on the use of two pad values, one is called an inner pad (ipad), the other is called an outer pad (opad), and are used with the hash algorithm H of message H using key K:

$$\text{HMAC }(K,M) = H(K \text{ XOR opad}, H(K \text{ XOR ipad}, M))$$

Where: B = number of bits in a block
         ipad = the byte 0x36 repeated B times
         opad = the byte 0x5C repeated B times.

Which translates to:

1. Append zeros to the end of K to create a B-byte string (e.g., if K is of length 20 bytes and $B = 64$, then K will be appended with 44 zero bytes 0x00)
2. XOR the B-byte string computed in step (1) with ipad
3. Append the stream of data "text" to the B-byte string resulting from step (2)
4. Apply H to the stream generated in step (3)
5. XOR the B-byte string computed in step (1) with opad
6. Append the H result from step (4) to the B-byte string resulting from step (5)
7. Apply H to the stream generated in step (6) and output the result

PERFORMANCE AND SECURITY OF HMAC

Stallings has a fine explanation of the security and performance aspects of HMAC. I quote directly [STAL99]:[5]

The security of any MAC function based on an embedded hash function depends in some way on the cryptographic strength of the underlying hash function. The appeal of HMAC is that its designers have been able to prove an exact relationship between the strength of the embedded hash function and the strength of HMAC.

The security of a MAC function is generally expressed in terms of the probability of successful forgery with a given amount of time spent by the forger and a given number of message-MAC pairs created with the same key. In essence, it is proved in [BELL96a] that for a given level of effort (time, message-MAC pairs), by a legitimate user and seen by an attacker, the probability of successful attack on HMAC is equivalent to one of the following attacks on the embedded hash function:

1. The attacker is able to compute an output of the compression function even with an IV that is random, secret, and unknown to the attacker.
2. The attacker finds collisions in the hash function even when the IV is random and secret.

In the first attack, we can view the compression function as equivalent to the hash function applied to a message consisting of a single b-bit block. For this attack, the IV of the hash function is replaced by a secret random value of n bits. An attack on this hash funciton requires either a brute-force attack on the key, which is a level of effort on the order of 2^n, or a birthday attack, which is a special case of the second attack, discussed next.

In the second attack, the attacker is looking for two messages M and M' that produce the same hash: H(M) = H(M'). This is the birthday attack.... We have shown that this requires a level of effort $2^{n/2}$ for a hash length of n. On this basis, the security of MD5 is called into question, because a level effort of 2^{64} looks feasible with today's technology. Does this mean that a 128-bit hash function such as MD5 is unsuitable for HMAC? The answer is no, because of the following argument: To attack MD5, the attacker can choose any set of messages and work on these off line on a dedicated computing facility to find a collision. Because the attacker knows the hash algorithm and the default IV, the attacker can generate the hash code for each of the messages that the at-

---

[5][STAL99]. Stallings, William. *Cryptography and Network Security*. Prentice Hall, Upper Saddle River, NJ 1999. This is another excellent book on security. Of the references cited in this book, Stallings provides the best overall treatise on the theory and mathematical foundations of the subject. For a more general and leisurely read, the Singh book (cited in Chapter 3) is first-rate.

tacker generates. However, when attacking HMAC, the attacker cannot generate message/code pairs off line because the attacker does not know K. Therefore, the attacker must observe a sequence of messages generated by HMAC under the same key and perform the attack on these known messages. For a hash code length of 128 bits, this requires 2^{64} observed blocks (2^{73} bits) generated using the same key. On a 1-Gbps link, one would need to observe a continuous stream of messages with no change in key for about 2,250,000 years in order to succeed. Thus, if speed is a concern, it is fully acceptable to use MD5 rather than SHA-1 or RIPEMD-160 as embedded hash functions for HMAC.

HMAC WITH IPSec

In the Internet standards, HMAC is designed to operate with the two IPSec protocols: (a) Authentication Header (AH), and (b) Encapsulating Security Payload (ESP). These operations are described in Chapter 9, in the section titled, "HMAC Applied to AH and ESP."

THE OAKLEY KEY DETERMINATION PROTOCOL

RFC 2412 [ORMA98][6] describes the protocol, OAKLEY. This protocol defines how two authenticated parties agree on secure keying material. The basic mechanism for OAKLEY is the Diffie-Hellman key exchange algorithm. The OAKLEY protocol supports secrecy, compatibility with the ISAKMP protocol for managing security associations, user-defined abstract group structures for use with the Diffie-Hellman algorithm and key updates.

OAKLEY is a feature-rich protocol and gives its users considerable flexibility in configuring their security operations pertaining to keying material. Our approach is to provide a summary of RFC 2412, and to set the stage for how it is used with the Internet Security Association and Key Management Protocol (ISAKMP) and the Internet Key Exchange Protocol (IKE), which are covered in later chapters. First, a few words about two protocols on which OAKLEY relies.

The Diffie-Hellman key exchange algorithm allows two parties to agree on a shared value without requiring encryption. The shared value is immediately available for use in encrypting subsequent traffic, either

---

[6][ORMA98]. Orman, H. "The Oakley Key Determination Protocol," RFC 2412, November, 1998.

for privacy or authentication services. The STS protocol defines how to embed the algorithm in a secure protocol. STS provides the security of a shared secret, and the identities of the communicating parties.

OAKLEY is a generic key exchange protocol, and the keys that it generates can be used for encrypting data that must be secure for a long time; as stated in RFC 2412, 20 years or more. The protocol has two options for adding to the difficulties faced by an attacker who has a large amount of recorded key exchange traffic at his disposal (a passive attacker). These options are useful for deriving keys which will be used for encryption.

ISAKMP is discussed in Chapter 10, and provides fields for specifying the security association (SA) parameters for use with the IPSec AH and ESP protocols. These security association payload types are specified in the ISAKMP specifications; the payload types can be protected with OAKLEY keying material and algorithms.

As you read this next material, be aware that I will mention ISAKMP in the discussion of OAKLEY. We will fill in the gaps of the OAKLEY and ISAKMP relationship in Chapter 10.

Beyond Diffie-Hellman and STS

The OAKLEY protocol is related to STS. It also shares the similarity of authenticating the Diffie-Hellman exponentials and using them for determining a shared key, and also of achieving perfect forward secrecy for the shared key, but it differs from the STS protocol in several ways, which RFC 2412 calls "extensions."

The first extension is the addition of a weak address validation mechanism to help avoid denial of service. The second extension is to allow the two parties to select mutually agreeable supporting algorithms for the encryption method, the key derivation method, and the authentication method. The third extension is that the authentication does not depend on encryption using the Diffie-Hellman exponentials; instead, the authentication validates the binding of the exponentials to the identities of the parties.

Fourth, OAKLEY adds additional security to the derivation of keys meant for use with encryption (as opposed to authentication) by including a dependence on an additional algorithm. The derivation of keys for encryption is made to depend not only on the Diffie-Hellman algorithm, but also on the cryptographic method used to authenticate the communicating parties to each other.

The fifth extension is that OAKLEY defines how the two parties can select the mathematical structures (group representation and operation) for performing the Diffie-Hellman algorithm; they can use standard groups or define their own. User-defined groups provide an additional degree of long-term security.

OAKLEY has several options for distributing keys. In addition to the Diffie-Hellman exchange, it can be used to derive a new key from an existing key and to distribute an externally derived key by encrypting it. OAKLEY also allows the parties to use anti-clogging and perfect forward secrecy operations. To give its users flexibility in their selection of security services, it permits the use of authentication based on symmetric encryption or non-encryption algorithms.

OAKLEY Key Exchange Processing

In its simplest terms, OAKLEY provides a means to exchange secure common keying information between two parties. OAKLEY calls this information "state information." This state information consists of a key name, secret keying material, the IDs of the two parties, and three algorithms for use during authentication: (1) encryption, for privacy (2) hashing, for protecting the integrity of the messages, and (3) authentication, or verifying the two parties.

OAKLEY message processing between the two parties involves a negotiation in which the initiator sends a message that contains how much information he/she wishes the first message to contain. The responder replies, supplying as much information as the responder wishes. The two sides can exchange additional messages, supplying more information each time, until their requirements are satisfied with regard to their specific security association.

The choice of how much information to include in each message depends on which options are desirable. Additional features may increase the number of message exchanges needed for the keying material determination.

The Essential Key Exchange Message Fields

There are 12 fields in an OAKLEY key exchange message, and we will see how they are used with ISAKMP in Chapter 10. For this discussion, the approach is to explain their functions with regards to the key exchange operation. Not all the fields are used in every message exchange; if a field is not relevant it can have a null value or not be present. The fields perform the following functions (the information in Box 5–1 will be useful while reading this section):

- *CKY-I:* Originator cookie; a 64-bit pseudo-random number. The number generated must ensure that its use with the destination IP address is unique over some time, such as one hour.
- *CKY-R:* Responder cookie, with the same stipulations as CKY-I.
- *MSGTYPE:* Message type in the ISAKMP header.
- *GRP:* The SA payload, and the name of the Diffie-Hellman group used for the exchange.
- *g^x (or g^y):* Variable length integer representing a power of a group generator.
- *EHAO or EHAS:* Encryption, hash, authentication functions, selected during the negotiation operations.
- *IDP:* Indicator as to whether or not encryption with g^{xy} follows (perfect forward secrecy for IDs).
- *ID(I):* Identity for the initiator.
- *ID(R):* Identity for the responder.
- *Ni*: Nonce supplied by the initiator.
- *Nr:* Nonce supplied by the responder.

The construction of the cookies is implementation-dependent. RFC 2412 recommends making them the result of a one-way function applied to a secret value (changed periodically), the local and remote IP address, and the local and remote UDP port. In this way, the cookies remain stateless and expire periodically. In addition, in order to support pre-distributed keys, RFC 2412 recommends that implementations reserve some portion of their cookie space to permanent keys. The encoding of these depends on the local implementation.

SUMMARY

Scores of security procedures are available to the network administrator to enhance security services to the user community. The Diffie-Hellman and the RSA mechanisms are two of the most prevalent. MD5 is the prevalent message digest algorithm and is now made more secure with the MD5-HMAC specification.

6

PPP, ECP, TLS, EAP, DESE-bis, and 3DESE

T he focus of this chapter is on the Point-to-Point Protocol (PPP) and several PPP extensions: PPP Encryption Control Protocol (ECP), Transport Level Security (TLS), PPP Extensible Authentication Protocol (EAP), PPP DES Encryption Protocol, Version 2 (DESE-bis), and PPP Triple-DES Encryption Protocol (3DESE) protocols. A separate book in this series is dedicated to PPP.

PPP AND HDLC

PPP operates over the High Level Data Link Control (HDLC) protocol, and consists of two major protocols; see Figure 6–1.

The Link Control Protocol (LCP) is the first procedure that is executed when a PPP link is set up. It defines the operations for configuring and testing the link. As part of LCP, or as a separate "phase," the authentication option (AUTH) can be invoked.

PPP then uses a Network Control Protocol (NCP) to negotiate certain options and parameters that will be used by an L_3 protocol. The IPCP (The IP Control Protocol), which is an example of a specific NCP, is used to negotiate various IP parameters, such as IP addresses, compression, etc.

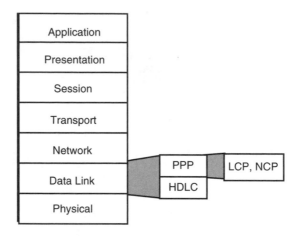

Where:
   LCP   Link Control Protocol
   NCP   Network Control Protocol

Figure 6–1   The PPP entities

The PPP PDU uses the HDLC frame as stipulated in ISO 3309-1979 (and amended by ISO 3309-1984/PDAD1). HDLC is beyond the scope of this book, so this material is restricted to showing the HDLC frame format and its relationship to PPP. Figure 6–2 shows this format. The flag sequence is the standard HDLC flag of 01111110 (hex 7E), the address field is set to all 1s (hex FF), which signifies an all stations address. PPP does not use individual station addresses because it is a Point-to-Point Protocol. The control field is set to identify an HDLC unnumbered information (UI) command. Its value is 00000011 (hex 03).

The protocol field is used to identify the PDU that is encapsulated into the I field of the frame. The field values are assigned by the Internet, and the values beginning with a 0 identify the network protocol that resides in the I field. Values beginning with 8 identify a control protocol that is used to negotiate the protocols that will actually be used. Up-to-date values of the Protocol field are specified in the most recent "Assigned Numbers" RFC.

The protocol number for LCP is xC021, and the contents of the remainder of the information field are a function of the code field. For LCP, the code field value identifies a Configure-Request message, and Configure-Ack message, etc. The ID field is used to match and coordinate

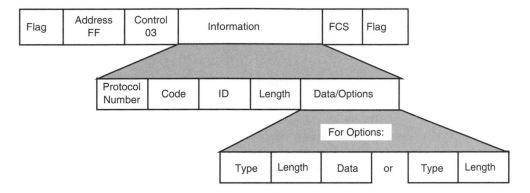

Figure 6–2   PPP packet contents

request messages to their associated response messages. The length field defines the length (in octets) of the contents of the information field, with the exception of the protocol number.

Thereafter, the remainder of the information field is propagated with options. This field is coded with two or three values: (a) Type-Length-Data, or (b) Type-Length. The options field is used between the PPP nodes to inform each other about their desires and capabilities. It is explained in more detail later.

LCP

The purpose of LCP is to support the establishment of the PPP connection and to allow for certain configuration options to be negotiated. The protocol also maintains the connection and provides procedures for terminating the connection.

PPP requires that LCP be executed to open the connection between two stations before any network layer traffic is exchanged. This requires a series of packet exchanges which are called configure packets. After these packets have been exchanged and a configure acknowledge packet has been sent and received between the stations, the connection is considered to be in an open state and the exchange of traffic can begin. LCP confines itself only to link operations. It does not understand how to negotiate the implementation of Network Layer Protocols. Indeed, it does not care about the upper layer negotiations relating to the network protocols.

Link quality determination is optional and allows LCP to check if the link is of sufficient quality to actually bring up the network layer. Although the link quality determination phase is defined in the standard, the actual implementation procedures are not specified. This tool exists to provide an LCP echo request and an LCP echo-type packet. These packets are defined within the protocol and exist within the state transition tables of the protocol.

After the link establishment (and if the link quality determination phase is implemented), the protocol configuration allows the two stations to negotiate/configure the protocols that will be used at the network layer. This is performed by the appropriate Network Control Protocol (NCP). The particular protocol that is used here depends on which family of NCPs is implemented.

LCP is also responsible for terminating the link connection. It is allowed to perform the termination at its discretion. Unless problems have occurred which create this event, the link termination is usually provided by a upper layer protocol or a user-operated network control center.

GENERAL EXAMPLE OF PPP OPERATIONS

Figure 6–3 shows an example of how PPP can be used to support network configuration operations. Routers, hosts, etc. exchange the PPP frames to determine which Network Layer Protocols are supported. In this example, two machines negotiate the use of the Internet Protocol (IP) and its OSI counterpart, ISO 8473, the Connectionless Network Protocol (CLNP). The LCP operations are invoked first to set up and test the link. Next NCP operations are invoked to negotiate which network protocols (and associated procedures) are to be used between the machines. After this negotiation is complete, datagrams are exchanged. At any point, either node can terminate the session.

PPP PHASE DIAGRAM

In the process of configuring, maintaining and terminating the PPP link, the PPP link goes through several distinct phases, shown in Figure 6–4. This phase diagram is generalized for this explanation. Also, PPP (RFC 1661, Section 4) describes in considerable detail a state machine that explains the PPP events between PPP layers inside the machine. This chapter does not cover this aspect of PPP.

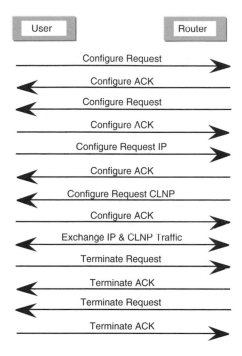

Figure 6–3   Example of a PPP link operation

Link Dead (Physical Layer Not Ready)

The link begins and ends with this phase. When an external event (such as carrier detection or network administrator configuration) indicates that the physical-layer is ready to be used, PPP will proceed to the Link Establishment phase.

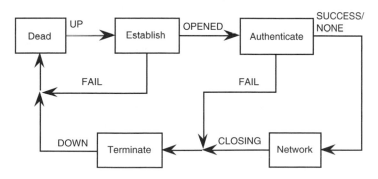

Figure 6–4   The PPP phase diagram

Typically, a link will return to this phase automatically after the disconnection of a modem. In the case of a hard-wired link, this phase may be extremely short—merely long enough to detect the presence of the device.

Link Establishment Phase

The Link Control Protocol (LCP) is used to establish the connection through an exchange of Configure packets. This exchange is complete, and the LCP Opened state is entered, once a Configure-Ack packet has been both sent and received. The receipt of the LCP Configure-Request causes a return to the Link Establishment phase from the Network Layer Protocol phase or Authentication phase.

Authentication Phase

Authentication is not required. If an implementation desires that the peer authenticate with some specific authentication protocol, then it requests the use of that authentication protocol during Link Establishment phase. The method of authentication is implementation-specific. Later sections in this chapter explain this phase.

Network Layer Protocol Phase

Next, each Network Layer Protocol (such as IP, IPX, or AppleTalk) is separately configured by the appropriate Network Control Protocol (NCP).

After an NCP has reached the Opened state, PPP will carry the corresponding Network Layer Protocol packets. Any supported Network Layer Protocol packets received when the corresponding NCP is not in the Opened state must be silently discarded. During this phase, link traffic consists of any possible combination of LCP, NCP, and Network Layer Protocol packets.

Link Termination Phase

LCP is used to close the link through an exchange of Terminate packets. When the link is closing, PPP informs the Network Layer Protocols so that they may take appropriate action. After the exchange of Terminate packets, the physical layer is usually notified to disconnect.

LCP PACKETS

This section describes the LCP packets.

- *Link Configuration* packets are used to establish and configure a link (Configure-Request, Configure-Ack, Configure-Nak and Configure-Reject).
- *Link Termination* packets are used to terminate a link (Terminate-Request and Terminate-Ack).
- *Link Maintenance* packets are used to manage and debug a link (Code-Reject, Protocol-Reject, Echo-Request, Echo-Reply, and Discard-Request).

Each Configuration Option specifies a default value. This ensures that such LCP packets are always recognizable, even when one end of the link mistakenly believes the link to be open. Exactly one LCP packet is encapsulated in the PPP Information field, where the PPP Protocol field indicates type hex C021 (Link Control Protocol).

The Link Control Protocol packet format is shown Figure 6–5. The fields are transmitted from left to right.

The fields in the LCP packet are as follows:

- *Code field*: Identifies the kind of LCP packet, currently defined in PPP for these codes:
  - 1 Configure-Request
  - 2 Configure-Ack
  - 3 Configure-Nak
  - 4 Configure-Reject
  - 5 Terminate-Request
  - 6 Terminate-Ack
  - 7 Code-Reject

0	1-6	7	8	9-14	15	16-30	31
	Code			Identifier		Length	
Data							

Figure 6–5   Format of Link Control Packet (LCP)

8   Protocol-Reject
9   Echo-Request
10 Echo-Reply
11 Discard-Request

- *Identifier:* Used in matching requests and replies.
- *Length:* Indicates the length of the LCP packet, including the Code, Identifier, Length, and Data fields.
- *Data:* Format of the Data field is determined by the Code field.

The following section provides a brief explanation of the functions of each LCP packet.

Configure-Request

An implementation wishing to open a connection transmits a Configure-Request. The Options field is filled with any desired changes to the link defaults. Upon reception of a Configure-Request, an appropriate reply is transmitted.

Configure-Ack

If every Configuration Option received in a Configure-Request is recognizable, and all values are acceptable, then the receiver implementation transmits a Configure-Ack.

Configure-Nak

If every instance of the received Configuration Options is recognizable, but some values are not acceptable, then the receiver transmits a Configure-Nak. The Options field is filled with the unacceptable Configuration Options from the Configure-Request. All acceptable Configuration Options are filtered out of the Configure-Nak.

Each Configuration Option is modified to a value acceptable to the Configure-Nak sender. The default value can be used, when this differs from the requested value.

When a particular type of Configuration Option can be listed more than once with different values, the Configure-Nak includes a list of all values for that option which are acceptable to the Configure-Nak sender. This includes acceptable values that were present in the Configure-Request.

Configure-Reject

If some Configuration Options received in a Configure-Request are not recognizable or are not acceptable for negotiation, the receiver transmits a Configure-Reject. The Options field is filled with the unacceptable Configuration Options from the Configure-Request.

Terminate-Request and Terminate-Ack

PPP closes a connection by sending a Terminate-Request. Terminate-Request packets continue to be sent until Terminate-Ack is received, the lower layer indicates that it has gone down, or a sufficiently large number of these packets have been transmitted such that the peer is down with reasonable certainty. Upon reception of a Terminate-Request, a Terminate-Ack is transmitted.

Code-Reject

Reception of a LCP packet with an unknown Code indicates that the peer is operating with a different version. This information is conveyed in the unknown Code by transmitting a Code-Reject packet.

Protocol-Reject

Reception of a PPP packet with an unknown Protocol field indicates that the peer is attempting to use a protocol which is unsupported. This usually occurs when the peer attempts to configure a new protocol. Upon reception of a Protocol-Reject, the implementation stops sending packets of the indicated protocol at the earliest opportunity.

Echo-Request and Echo-Reply

LCP includes Echo-Request and Echo-Reply Codes in order to provide a data link layer loopback mechanism for use in exercising both directions of the link. This is useful as an aid in debugging, link quality determination, performance testing, and for numerous other functions.

Discard-Request

LCP includes a Discard-Request Code in order to provide a data link layer sink mechanism for use in exercising the local to remote direction of the link.

OTHER SUPPORTING CAST MEMBERS
FOR PPP SECURITY SERVICES

In addition to the protocols discussed in Chapter 7, several other PPP-related protocols have emerged over the past several years. They extend PPP's security services. The remainder of this chapter provides a summary of their major features and operations. To help you track these discussions (and go to *www.ietf.org* for more information), the subjects are covered in this order:

RFC 2276   Transport Layer Security Protocol (TLS)
RFC 1968   PPP Encryption Control Protocol (ECP)
RFC 2287   PPP Extensible Authentication Protocol (EAP)
RFC 2419   PPP DES Encryption Protocol, Version 2 (DESE-bis)
RFC 2420   PPP Triple-DES Encryption Protocol (3DESE)

TRANSPORT LAYER SECURITY PROTOCOL (TLS)

You might be wondering at this point in the book why yet another security protocol has been published by the IETF. TLS is based on Netscape's SSL 3.0. The idea is to publish the protocol as a formal RFC, and lend it some non-proprietary status. The approach taken in this section is to describe TLS in a general way and refer you to RFC 2276 and the SSL specification [FRIE96],[1] for details.

Goals of TLS

The TLS Protocol is composed of two layers: the TLS Record Protocol and the TLS Handshake Protocol. The TLS Record Protocol operates over TCP or UDP and provides the following security services:

- *Symmetric cryptography* is used for data encryption. The keys for the symmetric encryption are generated uniquely for each connection and are based on a secret negotiated by another protocol (such as the TLS Handshake Protocol). The Record Protocol can also be used without encryption.

---

[1][FRIE96]. Frier A., Karlton P., and Kocher P., "The SSL 3.0 Protocol," *Netscape Communications Corp.*, Nov 18, 1996.

- *Message transport* includes a message integrity check using a keyed MAC. Secure hash functions (e.g., SHA, MD5, etc.) are used for MAC computations.

The TLS Record Protocol is used for encapsulation of various higher layer protocols. One such encapsulated protocol, the TLS Handshake Protocol, allows the server and client to authenticate each other and to negotiate an encryption algorithm and cryptographic keys before the application protocol transmits or receives data. The TLS Handshake Protocol provides connection security that has these three properties:

- The peer's identity can be authenticated using public key cryptography (e.g., RSA, DSS, etc.). This authentication may be optional, but is generally required for at least one of the peers.
- The negotiated secret is unavailable to eavesdroppers, and for any authenticated connection the secret cannot be obtained, even by an attacker who can place himself in the middle of the connection.
- No attacker can modify the negotiation communication without being detected by the parties to the communication.

PPP ENCRYPTION CONTROL PROTOCOL (ECP)

The Encryption Control Protocol (ECP) is responsible for configuring and enabling data encryption algorithms on both ends of the point-to-point link. The specification is published in RFC 1968. It uses most of the same mechanisms as LCP. However, ECP packets are not exchanged until PPP has reached the network layer phases. A few differences exist between ECP and LCP:

- One ECP packet is encapsulated in the PPP Information field, where the PPP Protocol field indicates type x8053 (Encryption Control Protocol).
- When individual link data encryption is used in a multiple link connection to a single destination, the PPP protocol field indicates type x8055 (Individual link Encryption Control Protocol).
- ECP uses (decimal) codes 1 through 7 (Configure-Request, Configure-Ack, Configure-Nak, Configure-Reject, Terminate-Request, Terminate-Ack and Code-Reject); it may also use code 14 (Reset-Request) and code 15 (Reset-Ack).

- An implementation cannot transmit data until ECP negotiation has completed successfully. If ECP negotiation is not successful, the link should be brought down.

Only one encryption algorithm in each direction can be in use at a time. The PPP protocol field of the encrypted datagram indicates that the frame is encrypted, but not the algorithm with which it was encrypted. ECP includes Reset-Request and Reset-Ack codes in order to provide a mechanism for indicating a decryption failure in one direction of a decrypted link without affecting traffic in the other direction.

The ECP Option Type field values are specified in the *www.ietf.org* page. Currently, the codes are 0 for organization unique ID (a vendor-specific implementation), and 1 for DESE, discussed shortly. DESE is supposed to be implemented on all ECP products.

PPP EXTENSIBLE AUTHENTICATION PROTOCOL (EAP)

The PPP Extensible Authentication Protocol (EAP) is a general PPP protocol supporting multiple authentication mechanisms and published in RFC 2284. EAP does not select a specific authentication mechanism during the LCP operations, but defers this operation to the authentication phase. During this phase, the authenticator can request more information from the challenged party before determining the specific authentication mechanism. The idea allows the PPP authenticator to pass the authentication exchange to a server to execute the specific authentication operation.

Figure 6–6 shows how EAP is executed (a) in relation to the PPP phase diagram (top part of the figure), and (b) in relation to the protocol flow.

The EAP is identified by PPP protocol number xC227. The code field values are conventional (a) Request, (b) Response, (c) Success, and (d) Failure. The format of the PPP data field is determined by the code field. The type field identifies the structure of the EAP Request or Response packet. Thus far, these types have been defined in RFC 2284:

- *Identity:* A displayable message in the Request packet.
- *Notification:* A displayable message (from authenticator to challenged), used to inform the end user about situations such as a password that is about to expire.

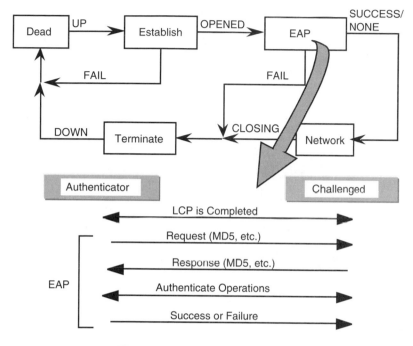

Figure 6–6   EAP Operations

- *NAK:* Used only in Response packets. Indicates the authentication type in the Request packet is not acceptable.
- *MD5 challenge:* Identical to CHAP, and contains a challenge message to the challenged party.
- *One-Time Password:* Defined in RFC 1938 for a one-time password system.
- *Generic Token Card:* A type to support user input into the operation.

PPP DES ENCRYPTION PROTOCOL, VERSION 2 (DESE-bis)

The DES Encryption Protocol (DESE-bis) describes how a user specifies the necessary details of a specific protocol given the context of the generic PPP Encryption Control Protocol, and also to provide at least one commonly understood means of secure data transmission between PPP implementations. As suggested by the title of the RFC, the emphasis is on DES.

While the US Data Encryption Standard (DES) algorithm provides multiple modes of use, this specification selects the use of only one mode in conjunction with the PPP Encryption Control Protocol (ECP): the Cipher Block Chaining (CBC) mode.

The initialization vector for this mode is deduced from an explicit 64-bit nonce, which is exchanged in the clear during the negotiation phase. The 56-bit key required by all DES modes is established as a shared secret between the implementations.

Appendix A provides the details for the generation and retrieval of the ciphertext for the DESE [see Appendix A, section titled: "Generation of and Retrieval of Ciphertext in RFC 1969: PPP DES Encryption Protocol (DESE-bis)"].

Configuration Option for ECP

The ECP DESE Configuration Option indicates that the issuing node wishes to use ECP DESE for decrypting communications on the link. The option has the fields shown in Figure 6–7. The fields perform the following functions.

- *Type:* Set to 3 to indicate the DESE-bis protocols
- *Length:* Set to 10
- *Initial Nonce:* Used by the peer to encrypt the first packet transmitted after the sender reaches the opened state. To guard against replay attacks, RFC 2419 recommends a different value is used during each ECP negotiation. An example might be to use the number of seconds since January 1, 1970 (GMT/UT) in the upper 32 bits, and the current number of nanoseconds relative to the last second mark in the lower 32 bits.

Packet Format for DESE

The format for the DESE packets are shown in Figure 6–8. The fields in the packets perform the following functions.

0	1-6	7	8	9-14	1 5	16-30	3 1
	Type			Length		Initial nonce	

Figure 6–7　ECP DESE configuration option

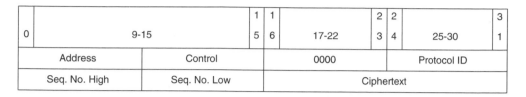

0	9-15		1 5	1 6	17-22	2 3	2 4	25-30	3 1
Address		Control			0000			Protocol ID	
Seq. No. High		Seq. No. Low			Ciphertext				

Figure 6–8   DES Encryption Protocol Packet Format

- *Address and Control:* These fields are present unless the PPP Address and Control Field Compression option (ACFC) has been negotiated.
- *Protocol ID:* The value of this field is x53 or x55; the latter indicates that ciphertext includes headers for the Multilink Protocol, and requires that the Individual Link Encryption Control Protocol has reached the opened state. The leading zero may be absent if the PPP Protocol Field Compression option (PFC) has been negotiated.
- *Sequence Numbers:* These 16-bit numbers are assigned by the encryptor sequentially starting with 0 (for the first packet transmitted once ECP has reached the opened state).
- *Ciphertext:* The generation of this data is described Appendix A.

PPP TRIPLE-DES ENCRYPTION PROTOCOL (3DESE)

The DES algorithm is a well-studied, understood and widely implemented encryption algorithm. Triple-DES means that this algorithm is applied three times on the data to be encrypted before it is sent over the link. The variant used is the DES-EDE3-CBC. Because of the use of the CBC mode, a sequence number is provided to ensure the right order of transmitted packets so lost packets can be detected.

The Algorithm

The DES-EDE3-CBC algorithm is a simple variant of the DES-CBC algorithm, see Figure 6–9. In DES-EDE3-CBC, an Initialization Vector (IV) is XOR'd with the first 64-bit (8 octet) plaintext block (P1). The keyed DES function is iterated three times, an encryption (E) followed by a decryption (D) followed by an encryption (E), and generates the ciphertext (C1) for the block. Each iteration uses an independent key: k1, k2, and k3. For successive blocks, the previous ciphertext block is XOR'd

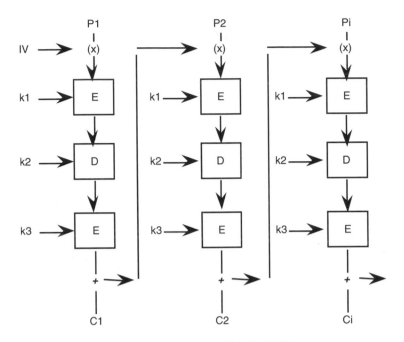

Figure 6–9   The Triple DES

with the current 8-octet plaintext block (Pi). The keyed DES-EDE3 en-cryption function generates the ciphertext (Ci) for that block.

To decrypt, the order of the functions is reversed: decrypt with k3, encrypt with k2, decrypt with k1, and XOR with the previous cipher-text block. When all three keys (k1, k2 and k3) are the same, DES-EDE3-CBC is equivalent to DES-CBC.

Keys

The secret DES-EDE3 key shared between the communicating par-ties is 168 bits long. This key consists of three independent 56-bit quanti-ties used by the DES algorithm. Each of the three 56-bit subkeys is stored as a 64-bit (8 octet) quantity, with the least significant bit of each octet used as a parity bit.

3DESE Configuration Option for ECP

The ECP 3DESE Configuration Option indicates that the issuing implementation is offering to employ this specification for decrypting communications on the link, and may be thought of as a request for its

0	1-6	7	8	9-14	1 5	16-30	3 1
	Type			Length		Initial Nonce	

Figure 6–10   ECP 3DESE Configuration Option

peer to encrypt packets in this manner. The ECP 3DESE Configuration
Option format is shown in Figure 6–10. The fields perform the following
functions.

- *Type:* Set to 2, to indicate the 3DESE protocol.
- *Length:* Set to 10.
- *Initial Nonce:* Used by the peer implementation to encrypt the first
  packet transmitted after the sender reaches the opened state. To
  guard against replay attacks, the implementation should offer a
  different value during each ECP negotiation.

Packet Format for 3DESE

The 3DESE packets that contain the encrypted payload are shown
in Figure 6–11. The fields in the packet perform the following functions.

Address and Control: These fields must be present unless the PPP
Address and Control Field Compression option has been negotiated.

Protocol ID: The value of this field is x53 or x55; the latter indicates
the use of the Individual Link Encryption Control Protocol and that the
ciphertext contains a Multilink fragment. Protocol Field Compression
may be applied to the leading zero if negotiated.

Sequence Number: These numbers are assigned by the encryptor sequentially starting with 0 (for the first packet transmitted once ECP has
reached the opened state).

Ciphertext: The encrypted data.

0	9-15	1 5	1 6	17-22	2 3	2 4	25-30	3 1
	Address		Control		0000		Protocol ID	
	Seq. No. High		Seq. No. Low		Ciphertext			

Figure 6–11   DESE Encryption Protocol Packet Format

SUMMARY

PPP is enhanced considerably with the addition of several security protocols. These protocols are extensions to PPP, and use the overall message syntax rules defined in the PPP specification, such as protocol numbers and option codes. In addition, VPN gateways often incorporate the DES-based protocols into their security services.

7

Dial-in Operations with PAP, CHAP, RADIUS and DIAMETER

T his chapter explains several Internet dial-in security protocols. The survey begins with the Password Authentication Protocol (PAP), followed by the Challenge-Handshake Authentication Protocol (CHAP). Protocols based on a client/server operation are then examined, with a look at the Remote Authentication Dial-in User Service (RADIUS). The successor to RADIUS, called DIAMETER, is then examined in considerable detail. The chapter concludes with examples of the internetworking of the Internet security protocols (DIAMETER extensions) with telephony networks.

PAP AND CHAP

An older specification, RFC 1334, defines PPP authentication procedures for two authentication protocols: (a) the Password Authentication Protocol (PAP), and (b) the Challenge-Handshake Authentication Protocol (CHAP). CHAP is now published in a more recent specification, RFC 1994 (this RFC does not include PAP).

PAP

PAP is a simple procedure for a peer (usually a host, or router) to establish its identity using a two-way handshake. This operation is performed upon initial link establishment. Once the link establishment phase is complete, an ID/Password pair is repeatedly sent by the peer to the authenticator (the node that is responsible for verifying the operation) until authentication is acknowledged or the connection is terminated.

PAP is not intended to be a strong authentication procedure, and all passwords and IDs are sent across the link in the clear. The nodes have no protection against monitoring, or security attacks. Then why use it? It is most appropriately used where a plaintext password must be available to simulate a login at a remote host. In such use, this method provides a similar level of security to the conventional user login at the remote host.

Figure 7–1 shows the format of the PPP protocol data unit for PAP. The PPP Protocol field is set to xC023 for PAP. The code field identifies one of three PPP packets: (a) the Authenticate-Request, (b) the Authenticate-Ack, and (c) the Authenticate-Nak. The ID and Length fields are coded in accordance with conventional rules discussed earlier. The Data field is coded with a Peer-ID and Password in the Authenticate-Request packet, and a message in the ack or nak packets.

Key Aspects of PAP

Here is a summary of the key aspects of PAP. First, the Authenticate-Request packet is used to begin the PAP operations. The link peer must use the Authenticate-Request packet during the Authentication phase. The Authenticate-Request packet is repeated until a valid reply packet is received, or an optional retry counter expires.

The authenticator expects the peer to send an Authenticate-Request packet. Upon reception of an Authenticate-Request packet, some type of Authenticate reply is returned.

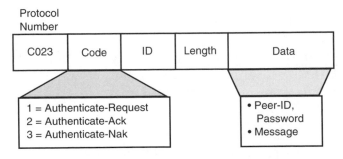

Figure 7–1   PAP in the PPP packet

If the Peer-ID/Password pair received in an Authenticate-Request is both recognizable and acceptable, then the authenticator sends an Authenticate-Ack. Otherwise, it sends an Authenticate-Nak. In this case, this party is not authenticated, and L_3 packets cannot be exchanged, because the recipient of the nak must clear the link.

CHAP

The Challenge-Handshake Authentication Protocol (RFC 1994) is a strong authentication protocol. Like PAP, it is designed to operate over PPP dial-up links between a host and another node, such as a router. In this part of our analysis, we take a look at the major attributes of CHAP.

CHAP periodically verifies the identity of the peer using a three-way handshake during the initial link establishment. Thereafter, CHAP can be invoked at any time.

After the completion of the PPP link establishment phase, the authenticator sends a challenge message to its peer. This peer must then calculate a one-way hash function and send this information to the authenticator. The authenticator verifies the hash value with its complementary calculation and responds with an ack if the values match. Otherwise, the connection is terminated.

CHAP uses an incrementally changing identifier and a variable challenge value. The use of repeated challenges is intended to limit the time of exposure to any single attack. The authenticator is in control of the frequency and timing of the challenges. The authentication method depends upon a secret known only to the authenticator and that peer. The secret is not sent over the link.

Authentication is one-way, but PPP's two-way behavior allows CHAP to actually operate in a two-way fashion.

CHAP can be used to authenticate different systems, so name fields are used as an index to locate the proper secret in a table of secrets. This concept also makes it possible to support more than one name/secret pair per system, and to change the secret in use at any time during the session. Figure 7–2 shows an example of a CHAP exchange.

CHAP Messages

The CHAP messages are (a) Challenge, (b) Response, (c) Success, and (d) Failure. They are coded in two formats, shown in Figure 7–3. The overall structure of the PPP packet is described earlier, and CHAP is as-

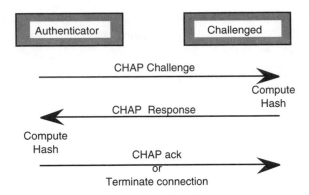

Figure 7–2   Example of a CHAP authentication

signed protocol number xC223. For CHAP, the identifier is changed each time a Challenge is sent, and this field is copied into the associated Response.

The Value-Size field indicates the size of the Value field. The Value field in the Challenge message is the Challenge value. Each Challenge

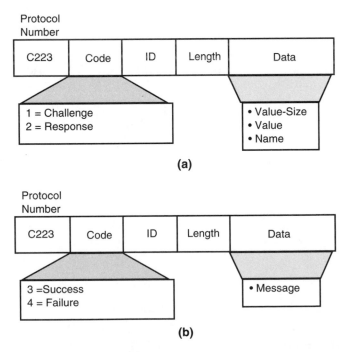

Figure 7–3   CHAP messages in PPP packets

value should be unique, since repetition of a Challenge value in conjunction with the same secret would permit an attacker to reply with a previously intercepted response. Furthermore, each value should be as random and unpredictable as possible, and must be changed with each Challenge.

The Response Value is the result of the hash calculation. It is calculated over a stream of concatenated octets consisting of the Identifier, followed by the secret, followed by the Challenge Value. The length of the Response Value depends of the hash algorithm (for example, it is 128 bits for MD5, which is the prevalent algorithm used in dial-up authentication). As expected, the one-way hash algorithm is chosen such that it is computationally infeasible to determine the secret from the known challenge and response values.

The Name field is used to identify the system that transmits the CHAP message. No limitation is placed on how this field is coded.

A Success is sent back to the peer if the Value received is the same as the expected value. Otherwise, a Failure is returned. In the latter case, the link should be terminated. For the Success and Failure messages, the Message field is implementation-specific.

RADIUS

In a large organization, security operations are a significant task. One of the concerns is the possible compromise of the organization's resources due to the dispersal of security measures throughout the system, resulting in a fragmented approach. To compound matters, employees, contractors, and customers need access to information, and these individuals dial-in to the organization's computers from practically anywhere. Considerable administrative support is needed to manage the many serial dial-in links and supporting modem pools.

Authentication of these diverse sources must be accomplished in accordance with the organization's security policy. But how? Should there be an authentication system (a server) at each of the organization's sites? If so, how are these servers managed, how are their activities coordinated? Alternatively, should the organization deploy one centralized server to reduce the coordination efforts?

To aid an organization in establishing an integrated approach to security management, the Internet Network Working Group has published RFC 2138, the Remote Authentication Dial-In User Service (RADIUS). This specification defines the procedures to implement an authentication server, containing a central database that identifies the dial-in users, and the associated information to authenticate the users.

RADIUS also permits the server to consult with other servers; some may be RADIUS-based, and some may not. With this approach, the RADIUS server acts as proxy to the other server. The specification also details how the user's specific operations can be supported, such as PPP, rlogin, TELNET, etc.

RADIUS CONFIGURATION

Figure 7–4 shows the configuration for RADIUS, which is built on a client/server mode. The end user communicates with the Network Access Server (NAS) through a dial-up link. In turn, the NAS is the client to the RADIUS server. The NAS and RADIUS server communicate with each other through a network, or a point-to-point link. As mentioned earlier, the RADIUS server may communicate with other servers, some may operate the RADIUS protocol, and some may not. Also, the idea is to have a

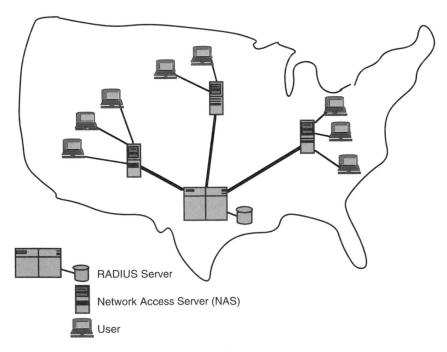

RADIUS Server

Network Access Server (NAS)

User

Figure 7–4   RADIUS setup

central repository for the authentication information, shown in Figure 7–4 as the database icon.

The user is required to present authentication information to the NAS (called client hereafter), such as a user name and a password, or a PPP authentication packet. The client may then access RADIUS. If so, the client creates an Access Request message, and sends to the RADIUS node (called server hereafter). This message contains information about the user that are called Attributes. The Attributes are defined by the RADIUS system manager, and therefore can vary. Examples of Attributes are the user's password, ID, destination port, client ID, etc.

If sensitive information is contained in the Attributes field, it must be protected by MD5. All transactions between the client and the RADIUS server must be authenticated with the use of a shared secret, and all user passwords sent between these devices must be encrypted.

Example of a RADIUS Message Exchange

The RADIUS-based request from the client must be a shared secret with the server, see Figure 7–5. Otherwise, the request is silently discarded (nothing happens . . . no further processing). If the initial check is

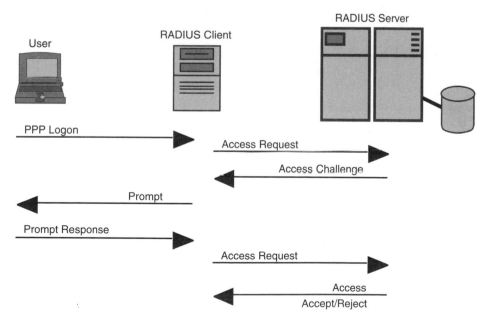

Figure 7–5   Example of RADIUS message exchange

satisfactory, the server consults a database to authenticate the user. The database contains the information needed to validate the user.

If the authentication conditions are met, the server issues a challenge to the user in the form of an Access Challenge message. The client may relay this information to the user in the form of a prompt. Whatever the scenario may be between the user and the client, the client must resubmit the Access Request message. This message contains some different fields; the salient one for this example is an encrypted response to the challenge. The user is "challenged" by being presented with a random number, and tasked with encrypting it, and sending back the result of the encryption.

The server receives and examines this message. If all conditions are satisfied, the server returns an Access Accept message to the client. However, the RADIUS protocol goes much further that the support of authentication operations. The Access Accept message contains configuration information, such as PPP, Login User, etc. The idea is to use the RADIUS node to give the user all the information that is needed to support the user session with the network. For example, the configuration information can be an IP address for the session, compression services, maximum transmission unit size (MTU), etc.

The NAS client may support PAP and CHAP. If so, the NAS client sends the PAP ID and password in the Access Request message (in the User-Name and User-Password fields of the message). If CHAP is used, the NAS client generates a challenge and sends it to the user. In accordance with CHAP conventions, the user responds with the CHAP ID and CHAP user name. The NAS client then sends to the RADIUS sever the Access Request message, containing the CHAP user name in the Access Request message User Name, and the CHAP ID.

Use of UDP

RADIUS operates over UDP for the following reasons: If the request to a primary authentication server fails, a secondary server must be queried. TCP is not designed for forking these kinds of transactions. Therefore, timers and retransmission operations are maintained by RADIUS, and UDP is employed for the following reasons (the RADIUS port assignment is 1812):

- The timing requirements are different than the support offered by TCP; the full features of lost data detection, and round trip time (RTT)-based retransmissions are not needed. After all, a user may not want to wait very long to be authenticated, and the user of an alternate server (instead of waiting for TCP to resolve matters) may be more efficient.

- The stateless nature of RADIUS simplifies the use of UDP. As clients and servers are taken-down, brought-up, rebooted, etc., TCP connections become more difficult to manage.
- Use of UDP simplifies the use of multi-threading (wherein, a user request has several processes spawned to reduce the delay in getting the authentication completed).

RADIUS Message Format

Figure 7–6 shows the format of the RADIUS packet. One RADIUS packet is encapsulated into UDP, with the packet containing the following fields:

- *Code*: Identifies the type of RADIUS packet as follows:
  - 1 = Access-Request
  - 2 = Access-Accept
  - 3 = Access-Reject
  - 4 = Accounting-Request
  - 5 = Accounting-Response
  - 11 = Access-Challenge
  - 12 = Status-Server (experimental)
  - 13 = Status-Client (experimental)
  - 255 = Reserved
- *Identifier:* Matches requests and replies.
- *Length:* Indicates length of packet, including all fields.

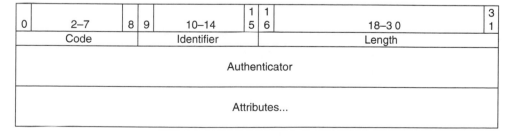

Figure 7–6   The RADIUS packet

- *Authenticator:* Used to authenticate the reply from the RADIUS server. In the Access-Request packet, this value is a 16-octet random number, called the request authenticator. This value along with a shared secret is processed with MD5 to create 16-octet digest value which is XORed with the password entered by the user. The XORed result is placed in the user-password attribute in the Access-Request packet. In the Access-Accept, Access-Reject, or Access-Challenge packets, this value is called the response authenticator, and is an MD5 function computed over these fields of the Access-Request packet: code, identifier, length, and authenticator.
- *Attributes:* Described in the next section of this chapter.

RADIUS Attributes

Attributes convey the information needed between the RADIUS nodes for authentication, authorization, and configuration operations. RFC 2138 defines several of these attributes, and the attribute identifiers are contained in the "Assigned Numbers," RFC 1700.[1] This section highlights several of the more prominent attributes. Others, such as address, name, port numbers, etc., are not covered here since they are either self-evident, and/or self-descriptive (the user-password attribute was just explained).

Service-type Attribute.   This attribute identifies the type of service the user has requested. The following services are defined:

- *Login:* The user should be connected to a host.
- *Framed:* A framed protocol should be started for the user, such as PPP async frames.
- *Callback login:* The user should be disconnected and called back, then connected to a host.
- *Callback framed:* The user should be disconnected and called back, then a framed protocol should be started for user.
- *Outbound:* The user should be granted access to outgoing devices.
- *Administrative:* The user should be granted access to the administrative interface to the NAS from which privileged commands can be executed.

---

[1]RFC 1700 no longer contains all the Internet assigned numbers. Go to *www.ietf.org* and click on IANA.

- *NAS prompt:* The user should be provided a command prompt on the NAS from which non-privileged commands can be executed.
- *Authenticate only:* Only authentication is requested, and no authorization information needs to be returned in the Access-Accept (typically used by proxy servers rather than the NAS itself).
- *Callback NAS prompt:* The user should be disconnected and called back, then provided a command prompt on the NAS from which non-privileged commands can be executed.

Framed-MTU. Defines the maximum transmission unit (MTU) to be configured for the user. This may not be needed if PPP is used to negotiate the MTU.

Login-IP-Host. Used to indicate to the server the system that is preferred for a host connection. It is a hint which the server does not have to honor.

Login-Service. Identifies which service should be used to connect the user to the login host. Examples are TELNET, Rlogin, and LAT.

Callback-Number. Identifies a dialing string to be used for a callback. It can serve as a hint to the sever about a callback, but the server is not obligated to honor the callback request.

Framed-Route. Provides routing information pertaining to the user on the NAS. It should contain a destination address, and a gateway address.

Session-Timeout. Sets the maximum number of seconds of service to be provided before the termination of a session or the issuance of a prompt.

Idle-Timeout. Sets the maximum number of consecutive seconds of idle connection allowed before the termination of a session or the issuance of a prompt.

Termination-Action. Indicates what action the NAS is to take when a service is completed.

Calling-Station-ID. Identifies the calling party number.

Proxy-State.   Sent by a proxy server to another server when the proxy server is forwarding an Access-Request message.

NAS-Port-Type.   Identifies the type of physical port at the NAS that is authenticating the user. Examples are asynchronous, synchronous, ISDN synchronous, ISDN asynchronous V.120, and ISDN asynchronous V.110.

Examples of RADIUS Operations

This part of the chapter shows some examples of packet flows between the NAS (RADIUS client) and the RADIUS server. In the first example shown in Figure 7–7, The NAS at 192.168.1.16 sends an Access-Request packet to the RADIUS Server for a user named "uyless" logging in on port 3. The request authenticator (RA) is set to a 16-octet random number (RN). The user-password is a 16-octet of password (padded at end with nulls) XORed with MD5 (shared secret | request authenticator). The RADIUS server authenticates the message, and sends an Access-Accept packet to the NAS telling it to TELNET "uyless" to host 192.168.1.3. The RA is the 16-octet MD5 checksum of the code, ID,

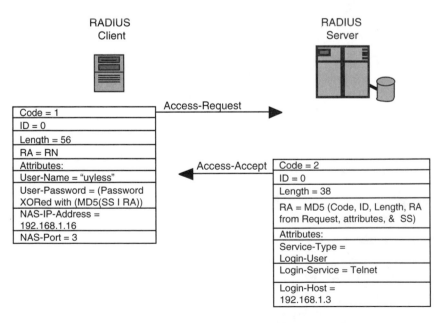

Figure 7–7   User TELNETS to a specified host [RFC2138]

length, RA from the Access-Request, the attributes in this reply and the shared secret.

The second example is shown in Figure 7–8, which depicts a user who executes a framed protocol (PPP), and is authenticated with CHAP (Figure 7–5 shows the user side of this exchange). The NAS at 192.168.1.16 sends an Access-Request UDP packet to the RADIUS Server for a user named "uyless" logging in on port 20 with PPP, and authenticating using CHAP. The NAS sends the Service-Type and Framed-Protocol attributes as hints to the RADIUS server that the user is executing PPP. The RADIUS server authenticates "uyless," and sends an Access-Accept packet to the NAS telling it to start the PPP service and assign an IP address for the user. Notice that the server also returns additional attributes pertaining to framing operations.

Problems with RADIUS

RADIUS is somewhat limited because of its command and attribute address space structure, and the resulting restriction on introducing new services. RADIUS operates over UDP, and UDP has no timing and re-

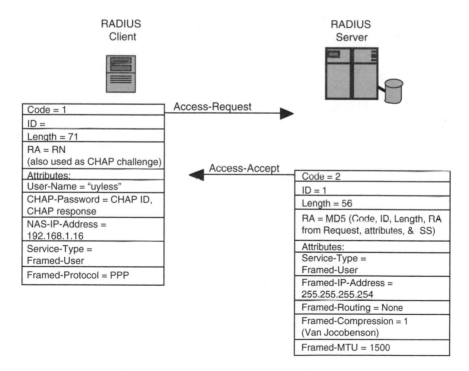

Figure 7–8   PPP and CHAP Support

sending mechanisms. Therefore, vendors have implemented their own implementations for these procedures. In addition, RADIUS assumes that there are no unsolicited messages from a server to a client, which further restricts its flexibility. Its successor, DIAMETER, solves these problems.

DIAMETER

DIAMETER is a relatively new protocol to emerge in Internet security standards inventory. It came about because as the number of new internet services has increased, routers and network access servers (NAS) have had to be changed to support them. In addition, vendors and working groups have been defining their own protocol for these operations.

DIAMETER provides a standard for the definition of headers, and security extensions, commands, and Attribute Value Pairs (AVPs). The idea is for a new service to use DIAMETER instead of the varying procedures developed earlier. DIAMETER is considered a successor to RADIUS, and is intended to provide a framework for any services that need authentication, accounting, and authorization (AAA) policy support. The DIAMETER architecture is defined in [CALH98],[2] and the following is a summary of this working paper.

DIAMETER MESSAGE FORMATS

This section describes the DIAMETER message formats, including headers and AVPs.

Message Header

Figure 7–9 shows the format for the DIAMETER message header. The fields in the message perform the following functions:

- *RADIUS PCC (Packet Compatibility Code):* Used to achieve backward compatibility with RADIUS. Its value is set to 254 to identify a DIAMETER packet, thus allowing a server to support both protocols
- *Flags:* Used to identify DIAMETER options.

---

[2][CALH98]. Calhoun, Pat R., draft-calhoun-diameter-07.txt.NOVEMBER 1998.

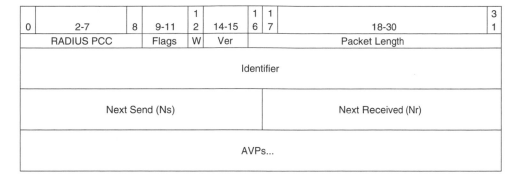

0	2-7	8	9-11	1 2	14-15	1 6	1 7	18-30	3 1
RADIUS PCC			Flags	W	Ver			Packet Length	

Identifier

Next Send (Ns)	Next Received (Nr)

AVPs...

Figure 7–9   DIAMETER header

- *"W" bit option:* This bit is set when the Next Send (Ns) and Next Received (Nr) fields are present in the header. This bit is set unless TCP is providing traffic integrity support.
- *Version:* This field is set to 1.
- *Packet length:* Indicates the length of the packet, including the header.
- *Identifier:* Used to match requests to their replies.
- *Next Send:* The send sequence number of the message.
- *Next Received:* The receive sequence number, used to acknowledge previously sent messages.
- *AVPs:* Attribute value pairs, described next.

Message Body for the AVP

DIAMETER message attributes carry authentication, accounting, and authorization (AAA) information. They also contain configuration details for the session. The message body of an AVP format is depicted in Figure 7–10. The fields in this message body perform the following functions:

- *AVP Code:* Identifies the specific AVP code. The first 256 values are reserved for RADIUS compatibility. These values are available at *www.ietf.org* (click on IANA). Any numbers above 256 are reserved for DIAMETER, and are allocated through the IANA.
- *AVP length:* Indicates the length of the attribute.
- *Reserved:* Reserved for future use.

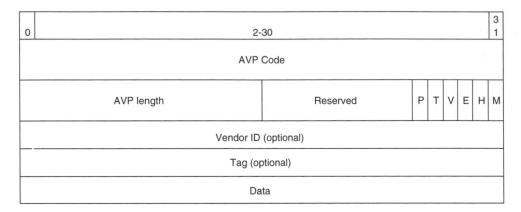

Figure 7–10   Message body of AVP

- *AVP flags:* Six flags are defined for this field, and they inform the DIAMETER host how each attribute is to be handled. The M (mandatory) bit indicates whether support of this AVP is required. If the receiver does not support this AVP, the request is rejected. The H bit indicates that the AVP data is encrypted on a hop-by-hop basis, whereas the E bit indicates that the AVP data is encrypted end-to-end. The V bit (the vendor-specific bit) indicates if the vendor ID field is in the AVP header. The T bit (the tag bit) groups sets of AVPs together if multiple AVPs are needed to express a condition. The P bit (the protected AVP bit) indicates whether the AVP is protected by a Digital Signature.
- *Vendor ID:* Used by a vendor to implement extensions to the DIAMETER attribute values.
- *Tag:* Used to group attributes in the same packet which refer to the same tunnel.
- *Data:* Contains the information specific to the attribute.

DIAMETER-Command AVP

This AVP follows the DIAMETER header, and its format is shown in Figure 7–11. It identifies the command associated with the message. The fields in this message body perform the following functions:

- *AVP code:* Set to 256 to identify a DIAMETER-Command.
- *AVP length:* Length of AVP.

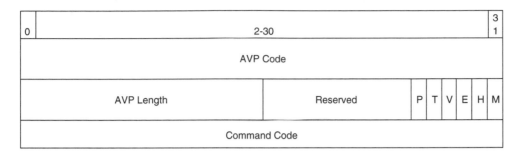

Figure 7–11   DIAMETER-command AVP

- *AVP flags:* These bits were explained earlier. For this AVP, the *M* bit is set. The *H* and *E* are set depending upon the security model used. The *V* may be set if the Command Code is vendor specific. The *T* and the *P* bits must not be set.
- *Command code:* Contains the command number, with these commands mandatory:

       Message-Reject-Ind = 256

       Device-Reboot-Ind = 257

       Device-Watchdog-Ind = 258

Message-Reject-Ind Command

This command is used to provide diagnostics about (and indicate errors in) received messages. Its format is shown in Figure 7–12. This message contains the same identification and session-ID as the message to which it is responding. The fields in this message perform the following functions:

- *AVP code:* Set to 256
- *AVP length:* Length of message
- *AVP flags:* The *M* bit is set. The *H* and *E* may be set depending upon the security model used. The *V, T,* and the *P* bits must not be set.
- *Command code:* Set to 256.

Approach to the Remainder of Message Descriptions

The DIAMETER messages follow the same format as those described so far. For purposes of brevity, the remaining explanations pro-

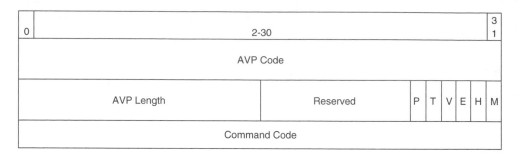

Figure 7–12   The message-reject-ind command

vide a description of the functions of the message without repeating the figures showing the message syntax.

Device-Reboot-Ind (DRI).   A DIAMETER device sends the Device-Reboot-Ind message to inform all of its peers either of an upcoming reboot or that it has just rebooted. This message is also used to exchange the supported protocol version number as well as all supported extensions.

Device-Watchdog-Ind (WDI).   This message is a keepalive procedure employed between two DIAMETER peers.

Host-IP-Address and Host-Name.   These attributes are simply the IP address and host-name of the sender; they are used to inform the peer of the sender's identity.

State.   When a server sends messages that span multiple round-trip messages, this AVP is used to maintain server-state information. DIAMETER uses a reliable transport mechanism (with timing) to support its operations.

Class.   This AVP is defined by the specific implementation, and it is used during authentication. It may contain accounting information to be used by an accounting server.

Session-Timeout.   This Attribute sets the maximum number of seconds of service to be provided to the user before terminating the session or prompt. This attribute is available to be sent by the server.

Extension-ID.   The Extension-ID AVP is used in order to identify a specific DIAMETER extension. This AVP may be used in the Device-

Reboot-Ind and the Device-Feature-Reply command in order to inform the peer what extensions are locally supported.

Integrity-Check-Vector (ICV). The Integrity-Check-Vector AVP is used for hop-by-hop authentication and integrity; it is not recommended for use with untrusted proxy servers. The DIAMETER header as well as all AVPs (including padding) up to this AVP is protected by the Integrity-Check-Vector. The Timestamp AVP is present to provide replay protection and the Initialization-Vector AVP is present to add randomness to the packet.

The use of the ICV AVP requires a preconfigured shared secret. Although this mechanism does not scale as well as the Digital Signature, it may be desirable to use this mechanism in the case where asymmetric technology is not required or available.

The HMAC operation is performed as follows:

```
hmac_md5(DIAMETERMessage, MessageLength, Secret, Secretlength, Output)
```

Transform ID. The Transform ID field contains a value that identifies the transform that was used to compute the ICV. MD5-HMAC-96 is stipulated for DIAMETER operations.

Initialization-Vector. The Initialization-Vector AVP must be present prior to the Integrity-Check-Vector AVPs within a message and is used to ensure randomness within a message. The content of this AVP must be a random value of at least 128 bits.

Timestamp. The Timestamp AVP is used to add replay protection to the DIAMETER protocol. This AVP must appear prior to the Integrity-Check-Vector AVP or any other Integrity AVP defined in separate extensions. The value of time is the most significant 4 octets returned from a Network Time Protocol (NTP) server that indicates the number of seconds expired since January 1, 1970.

Session-ID. The Session-ID AVP is used to identify a specific session. Note that in some applications there is no concept of a session (i.e., data flow) and this field may be used to identify objects other than a session. The session ID is created by the DIAMETER device initiating the session, which in most cases is done by the client. A Session-ID can be used by more than one extension.

Vendor-Name. The Vendor-Name attribute is used in order to inform a DIAMETER peer of the Vendor Name of the DIAMETER device. This may be used in order to know which vendor specific attributes may be sent to the peer.

Firmware-Revision. This AVP is used to inform a peer of the revision number of the device that sent the message.

Result-Code. The Result-Code AVP is used to indicate whether a particular command was completed successfully or whether an error occurred. The Result-Code AVP must be present in all DIAMETER messages of type Request or Answer. AVP Format. The Integer 32 field contains the result code that is associated with the DIAMETER command. The list below are these codes:

- DIAMETER_SUCCESS = 0: The Request was successfully completed.
- DIAMETER_FAILURE = 1: The Request was not successfully completed, and the reject message containing this code should also contain the AVPs that created the problem.
- DIAMETER_POOR_REQUEST = 2: The Request was poorly constructed, and the reject message containing this code should also contain the AVPs that created the problem.
- DIAMETER_INVALID_MAC = 3: The request did not contain a valid integrity-check-vector or Digital Signature.
- DIAMETER_UNKNOWN_SESSION_ID = 4: The request contained an unknown session-ID.
- DIAMETER_SEE_ERROR_CODE = 5: This diagnostic contains specific information about the problem; once again, the AVPs that led to the failure.
- DIAMETER_COMMAND_UNSUPPORTED = 6: The DIAMETER request message contained a command code that is not recognized or supported.
- DIAMETER_ATTRIBUTE_UNSUPPORTED = 8: The DIAMETER request message contained an AVP that is not supported.

Error-Code. The Error-Code AVP contains the message-specific error code, if any. This AVP only needs to be present if the Result-Code AVP is present with the DIAMETER_SEE_ERROR_CODE.

Unrecognized-Command-Code. The Unrecognized-Command-Code AVP contains the offending Command Code that resulted in sending the Message-Reject-Ind message.

Reboot-Type. If a reboot of a DIAMETER node occurs, the AVP indicates the type of reboot that is performed, such as peer has just been rebooted and is ready to accept traffic, peer is in the process of rebooting, etc.

Reboot-Time. The Reboot-Time AVP indicates the number of seconds before the issuer expects to be ready to receive new DIAMETER messages. The value indicated by this AVP should be used as an estimate and is not a hard rule.

Failed-AVP-Code. The Failed-AVP-Code AVP provides debugging information in cases where a request is rejected or not fully processed due to erroneous information in a specific AVP.

User-Name. This attribute contains the User-Name in a format consistent with the NAI specification.

BASIC OPERATIONS

The AVP Encryption with shared secrets method is the simplest to use and is supposed to be supported by all DIAMETER implementations. This section provides a summary of DIAMETER operations, taken from the IETF working drafts.

The "H" bit is only set if a shared secret exists between both DIAMETER peers. If the "II" bit is set in any DIAMETER AVP, the Initialization-Vector AVP must be present prior to the first encrypted AVP.

The ClearText data field contains the data of AVP that is to be obscured.

An MD5 hash is performed on the concatenation of:

- the 2-octet Command Code of the AVP
- the shared authentication secret
- an arbitrary length random vector

The value of the random vector used in this hash is passed in the data field of an Initialization-Vector AVP. This Initialization-Vector AVP must appear in the message before any hidden AVPs. The same Initialization-Vector may be used for more than one hidden AVP in the same message. If a different Initialization-Vector is used for the hiding of subsequent AVPs then a new Initialization-Vector AVP must be placed before the first AVP to which it applies.

The MD5 hash value is then XORed with the first 16-octet or less segment of the AVP Subformat and placed in the data field of the AVP. If the AVP Subformat is less than 16 octets, the Subformat is transformed as if the Value field had been padded to 16 octets before the XOR, but only the actual octets present in the Subformat are modified, and the length of the AVP is not altered. If the Subformat is longer than 16 octets, a second one-way MD5 hash is calculated over a stream of octets consisting of the shared secret followed by the result of the first XOR. That hash is XORed with the second 16-octet or less segment of the Subformat and placed in the corresponding octets of the Data field of the AVP. If necessary, this operation is repeated, with each XOR result being used along with the shared secret to generate the next hash to XOR the next segment of the value with. This technique results in the content of the AVP being obscured, although the length of the AVP is still known.

On receipt, the Initialization-Vector is taken from the last Initialization-Vector AVP encountered in the message prior to the AVP to be decrypted. The above process is then reversed to yield the original value. For more details on this hiding method, consult RFC 2138.

Note that in the case where the DIAMETER message needs to be processed by an intermediate non-trusted DIAMETER server (also known as a proxy server, depicted as DIA2 in Figure 7–13) the AVP needs to be decrypted using Shared-Secret-1 and re-encrypted by DIA2 using Shared-Secret-2.

Figure 7–13   Non-trusted DIAMETER server

DIAMETER SUPPORT OF DIAL-INS TO/FROM SS7

One of the biggest challenges facing Internet telephony is interfacing with the current world-wide telephone network. There are different views on how this interface should occur. Some believe that it should be minimal, and the telephone network should be avoided as much as possible. Others believe that Internet dial-in services should be designed to interwork with the telephone system to take advantage of the many service features and intelligent network services available through the telephone system's SS7 and advanced intelligent network capabilities.

Whatever one's view is on this matter, this section of the chapter explains the operations of a gateway that sits between the telephone network and an internet network access server (NAS) and summarizes the key points of [GREE98].[3]

[GREE98] describes an architectural framework for standardization for telephony interworking with the internet. Interworking deals with both signaling and bearer connections (i.e., media streams, such as a VoIP flow), which can either be carried together (e.g., in-band, BRI, PRI) or separately (e.g., SS7).

When signaling is carried together with the bearer connections, it arrives directly at the NAS. When signaling is carried separately, it passes through a Signaling Gateway and/or a NAS Controller before arriving at a Network Access Server (NAS). [GREE98] describes extensions to DIAMETER to allow session setup to occur from the NAS to the Signaling Gateway/NAS Controller and from the Signaling Gateway/NAS Controller to a NAS. This part of the chapter is a summary of the main points of [GREE98].

Session Setup Messages Signaling Gateway/ NAS Controller Interaction

Session-Setup-Request. A Session-Setup-Request message is issued from a NAS to an SGNC, or from an SGNC to a NAS. This command may be used from the NAS to the SGNC when the signaling for the call is co-located with the NAS. This situation is the case with PRI sig-

---

[3][GREE98] *www.ietf.org.*, greene-diameter-ss7-session-00.txt, July, 1998.

naling. If authentication of the user is required, then the authentication procedures defined in [CALH98a][4] should be used instead.

This command is issued from an SGNC to a NAS, when the signaling for the call is co-located with the SGNC. This situation is the case with SS7 signaling. For incoming calls that require end-user authentication see [CALH98a]. In this case, the AA-Request/Response message exchange initiated from the NAS to the SGNC would be bracketed with a Session-Setup-Request/Response exchange initiated from the SGNC. Note that the Session-ID used for all messages would be the same.

For the incoming part of a VoIP call, the Session-Setup-Request message goes from the SGNC to the NAS or VoIP gateway, or vice versa depending on the signaling termination location. For the outgoing part, the message always flows from the SGNC to the VoIP gateway, if there is PRI signaling then the Session-Setup-Response message is issued as the call is completed. If it is SS7 signaling, the Session-Setup-Request message is issued after the outgoing leg has been set through the SS7 signaling).

The Resource-Token AVP contains all resources currently assigned to the user for this session. For example, it may include information describing the trunk that a particular SS7 call is assigned to. Actual resources for particular signaling and VoIP gateways are described as AVPs in another DIAMETER extension.

The Extension-ID indicates to which DIAMETER extension this message (and the AVPs it uses) belongs. If it belongs to more than one, then more than one will be listed.

Session-Setup-Response. A Session-Setup-Response message contains the same Session-ID as that in the Session-Setup-Request. The Result-Code must be present. This indicates whether the session was set up successfully or not.

Resource-Add-Request. A Resource-Add-Request message is issued from an SGNC to a NAS, or from a NAS to an SGNC. When it is issued from the SGNC to a NAS, it is assumed that authorization to use the resources required has already been granted. If Resource-Add-Request contains a Session-ID already in use, then the requested re-

---

[4][CALH98a]. Calhoun, P. R., Billy, W., "DIAMETER User Authentication Extensions," draft-calhoun-diameter-authent-03.ttxt, April 1998

source(s) is (are) added to that session. If the resource is engaged in a session the Resource-Add-Request message is interpreted as "Resource Modify." For example, for a tunnel resource, an application may request that the tunnel parameters be changed so that all future data sent over the tunnel is encrypted. It is possible for a resource to belong to more than one session. For example, a tunnel could support more than one session simultaneously.

The Resource-Add-Request message may contain the Session-ID for the maintenance session. Resource messages sent using the maintenance session apply to resources outside any session, or to resources shared by more than one session.

Resource-Add-Response. The Resource-Add-Response message is sent in response to a Resource-Add-Request message. The Resource-Token AVP is only present if the session has resources to be managed.

Message Exchanges Examples

This section provides several examples of message exchanges between the PSTN, the SGNC, and the NAS. The first two examples are message exchanges for SS7 session setup. Figure 7–14 is an example of a SS7 session setup originating from SGNC. Figure 7–15 is an example of the SS7 session setup originating from NAS.

Figure 7–16 shows a session setup from SGNC to NAS, with a successful continuity test. It depicts how the Session and Resource messages can be used when a continuity test should be performed on the channel prior to the call establishment.

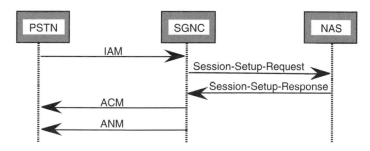

Figure 7–14   SS7 session setup originating from SGNC

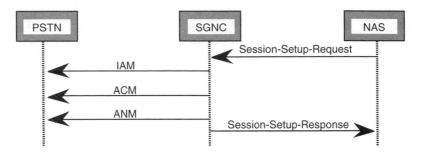

Figure 7–15   SS7 session setup originating from NAS

The Resource-Add-Request message from the SGNC to the NAS is used to initiate the continuity test loopback. If the remote end-point indicates to the SGNC that the continuity test succeeded, the SGNC proceeds with Session Setup-Request.

Figure 7–17 shows an SS7 session setup from SGNC to NAS, with failed continuity test. If the remote end indicates failure, the SGNC will send a Resource-Add-Request message to the NAS requesting that the channel be placed into the in maintenance state. Session setup is initiated by the SGNC.

Figure 7–18 shows an SS7 session setup from NAS to SGNC, with a successful continuity test and how the session and resource messages can be used when a continuity test should be performed on the channel prior to the call establishment. The session setup is initiated by the NAS.

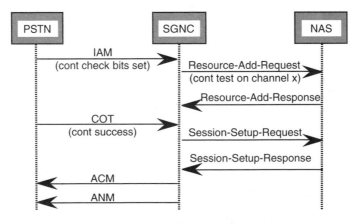

Figure 7–16   Session setup with continuity test

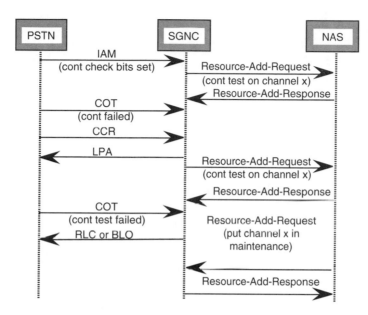

Figure 7–17   Session setup to initiate a loopback test

The Session-Setup-Request message from the NAS to the SGNC is used to initiate the session. The Resource-Add-Request initiates continuity test loopback. The NAS decides whether the continuity test has succeeded, and tells the SGNC in the Resource-Add-Response. If successful, the SGNC proceeds with Session-Setup-Response.

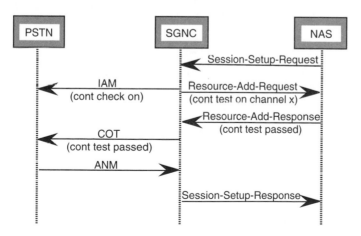

Figure 7–18   SS7 session setup from NAS to SGNC with successful continuity test

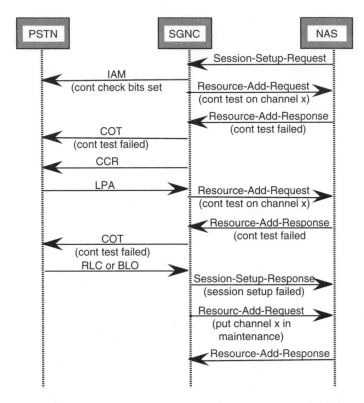

Figure 7–19   SS7 session setup from NAS to SGNC with failed continuity test

Figure 7–19 shows an SS7 session setup from NAS to SGNC, with failed continuity test. If the NAS indicates failure, the SGNC will send a Resource-Add-Request message to the NAS requesting that the channel be placed into the in maintenance state.

SUMMARY

PAP and CHAP have been the mainstays of Internet dial-in operations. PAP is not used (or should not be used) across untrusted links since it is a weak authentication protocol. CHAP typically used MD5 for its authentication. RADIUS and DIAMETER are significant enhancements to these dial-in operations and support the deployment of remote network access servers (NAS).

8

IPSec Architecture

T his chapter describes the IPSec architecture, the primary Internet protocol for transporting secure traffic across an untrusted link or untrusted network. The security association (SA), introduced in Chapter 1, is explained in relation to how it is implemented with two IPSec databases, the security policy database (SPD), and the security association database (SAD). IPSec transport and tunnel modes are explained, and the IPSec rules for combining tunnels and SAs are discussed.

Note: The terms IP Protocol ID, Protocol, and Next Protocol refer to a field in the IPv4 or IPv6 header. The value in this field identifies the type of traffic residing in the data portion of the IP datagram, such as TCP, UDP, OSPF, or ICMP traffic.

BASICS OF IPSec

IPSec is being developed by the Internet Engineering Task Force (IETF) IPSec Working Group. The full set of specifications for IPSec are not finished as of this writing, but they are nearing completion, and the basic RFCs are complete. I will give you the latest information on the specifications, and I will provide references, as well as additional bibliography. In addition, this explanation of IPSec includes a specific approach from IBM on implementing the emerging RFCs. I refer you to [CHEN98][1] for an example of an organization's implementation of IPSec and related specifications.

IPSec Services

IPSec is designed to provide the following services (described in Chapter 1) for IP traffic (IPv4 or IPv6): (a) access control, (b) connection-less integrity, (c) origin authentication, (d) replay protection, which includes partial sequence integrity, and (e) privacy/confidentiality (traffic encryption).

Of course, the quality of these services depends on the decisions of the security administrator. IPSec is a tool, and a powerful tool, but its effectiveness depends on how it is implemented.

IPSec places no requirements on where it operates. Nonetheless, the services should operate in a user host or a security gateway. The security gateway is a separate machine from the host, such as a router or a server.

IPSec Traffic Security Protocols

The IPSec services are provided by two traffic security protocols, the Authentication Header (AH), and the Encapsulating Security Payload (ESP). Additionally, other protocols are employed, such as key management protocols, which are not defined in the IPSec specifications. AH and ESP are part of IPSec. They are introduced in this chapter and described in more detail in Chapter 9.

Security Association (SA) Databases

IPSec needs considerable information to perform the security services for the users. In simplest terms, it must know about the user's security association (SA). Recall that an SA defines the security services that are provided to a user.

The requirements for these SA services are stored in two security databases. They are known collectively as Security Association Databases. They are the information repositories for the IPSec operations, and their contents (how they are configured by the security administrator) govern the "behavior" of IPSec. I introduce them in our initial discus-

---

[1][CHEN98]. Cheng, P. C., Garay, J. A., Herzberg, A., Krawczyk, H. "A Security Architecture for the Internet Protocol," *IBM System Journal,* Vol. 37, No. 1, 1998.

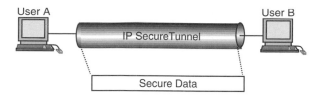

Figure 8–1   The IP secure tunnel

sions of IPSec. Later discussions will focus on these databases in more detail.

The IPSec Tunnel

To explain IPSec further, we first need to clarify the concept of an IP secure tunnel in the context of how it is used in IPSec. See Figure 8–1. Broadly speaking, a tunnel conveys the idea of the secure transport of traffic between two systems across a nonsecure network (an untrusted network). The Internet is an untrusted network and so is a dial-up line.

The passing of traffic is an instantiation of the security policies existing between the sending and receiving systems. The security policies (also referred to as meta-characteristics) include the addresses of the endpoints, an encapsulation method (by which the traffic is encapsulated inside other protocol data units), the cryptographic algorithms, the parameters for the algorithms (which include the size of the key and the lifetime of the key).

An IP secure tunnel refers to *all* the procedures, including protocols, encryption methods, etc., that ensures the safe passage of the traffic between two systems. Once again, this set of capabilities is called a security association (SA). Be aware that a security association is not the tunnel itself, but an instantiation of the tunnel during a particular time, based on the SA.

THE SECURITY ASSOCIATION (SA)

We learned that a security association defines a set of items (and procedures) that are shared between two communicating entities. Its purpose is to protect the communications process between the parties. An IPSec SA defines the following information as part of the security associations. See Figure 8–2 for a graphical depiction of the ideas.

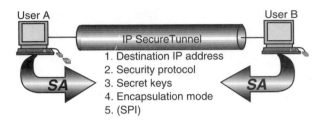

Figure 8–2   Security association (SA) for IP secure tunnels

- *Destination IP address*
- *Security protocol* that is to be used. This part of the SA defines if the traffic is to be provided with integrity as well as secrecy support. It also defines the key size, key lifetime, and cryptographic algorithms (the algorithms are called transforms in IPSec).
- *Secret keys* to be used by the cryptographic transforms.
- *Encapsulation mode* which defines how the encapsulation headers are created and which parts of the headers and user traffic are protected during the communicating process.
- *Security parameter index (SPI)* is one of the identifiers of the SA. It provides information to the receiving device on how to process the incoming traffic.

Taken as a whole, the operations that are to be performed on the user traffic are defined by the security protocol, the cryptographic operations, and the encapsulation mode.

An SA must be identified by: (a) an SPI, (b) a destination IP address, and (c) an identifier of the security protocol (AH or ESP).

The specific SA is unidirectional, in that it defines the operations that occur in the transmission in one direction only. Notwithstanding, a secure tunnel can also be bi-directional. This means that a pair of SAs are used for the transport of traffic in both directions. The idea of a bi-directional process is to have the two SAs use the same meta-characteristics but employ different keys. This concept is known as a bi-directional SA.

SAs may also be grouped together (an SA bundle) to provide a required security feature for the traffic. For example, one SA could be used to guarantee the secrecy of the traffic and another SA could be used to guarantee the integrity of the traffic. The rule with regard to the use of SA bundles is that the destination addresses of SAs must always be the same.

CASES OF SECURITY ASSOCIATIONS: A GENERAL VIEW

The Network Working Group of the IETF has described several security associations that are common in internets. These associations are called "cases," and the four that are explained in this part of the chapter are required for IPSec-compliant hosts and security gateways. These cases are explained in a general way here. Later, we re-visit the cases and show the conventions for creating various combinations of secure tunnels.

Figures 8–3 through 8–6 show the four cases. I have changed terminology slightly from previous explanations. My descriptions of [KENT98][2] will use the terms defined in this document. Thus, the term host is used to describe an IPSec-compliant user machine, and the term security gateway is used to describe an IPSec-compliant router, or some machine that services the host (perhaps a terminal server, etc.).

Case 1: Figure 8–3 shows the security association and its associated tunnel running between two hosts, thus providing an end-to-end security service. For this case, the Internet or an intranet is not aware of, and does not participate in, the security association.

Case 2: Figure 8–4 places the security association and its associated tunnel between two security gateways. The hosts are relieved of implementing the security association, and their communications with the security gateways are assumed to be through trusted intranets. This case could use a single SA for all traffic between (say) a contiguous group of subnetworks.

Case 3, shown in Figure 8–5 is a combination of Cases 1 and 2. It relies on a tunnel between security gateways, as well as an end-to-end tunnel.

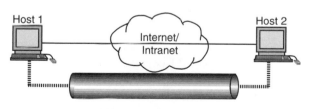

Figure 8–3   Case 1

---

[2][KENT98]. Kent, Stephen, "Security Architecture for the Internet Protocol," draft-ietf-ipsec-sec-07-txt., obsoletes RFC 1825, July 1998.

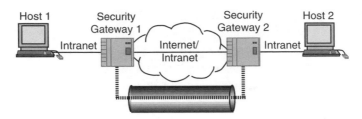

Figure 8–4   Case 2

In Figure 8–6, Case 4 covers a common situation in which a remote host (Host 1) dials-in through the Internet to its organization, or a server located behind the security gateway. The connection occurs through the Internet. Examples of this case are mobile phone users, travelers staying at hotels, etc.

This situation requires more elaborate procedures than those implemented in Cases 1–3. For example, how does the host locate the security gateway? How does the host know its dial-in is to the proper gateway, and vice versa? IPSec provides information on how to resolve these questions.

Not shown in these figures are the various components in the Internet to effect this connection, such as ISPs. They are not important to this discussion, since the idea is to establish a security association and its associated tunnel between the host and the organization's security gateway (a firewall, explained in Chapter 4).

Types of SAs: Transport Mode and Tunnel Mode

IPSec defines two types of IPSec mode SAs. Section 4.1 of IPSec describes these modes, and I summarize them here [KENT98c].[3] Also, see Table 8–1 for a general description of the transport and tunnel modes. Figure 8–7(a) shows the packet structure for an original IP packet, Figure 8–7(b) shows a transport mode packet, and Figure 8–7(c) shows a tunnel mode packet. It should be noted that if ESP is used, there will be two other fields in these packets. They are an ES trailer and a MAC value, and both are placed behind the L_7 field. The L_7 field represents the Internet layer 7 traffic, such as FTP, HTTP, Rlogin, etc.

---

[3][KENT98c]. Kent, Stephen, "Security Architecture for the Internet Protocol," draft-ietf-ipsec-sec-07-txt., obsoletes RFC 1825, July 1998.

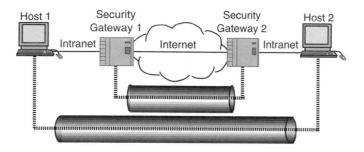

Figure 8–5   Case 3

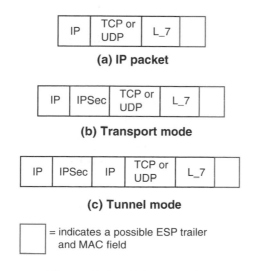

Figure 8–6   Case 4

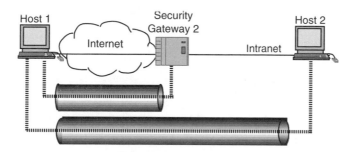

Figure 8–7   IPSec modes

Table 8–1   Modes of Security Associations

- Transport Mode:
  - Between hosts
  - Uses one IP header
  - Protects upper layer protocols (ULPs)
  ...and maybe parts of IP header
- Tunnel Mode:
  - Between hosts or gateways
  - Uses two IP headers
  - Protects ULPs *and* inner IP header
  ...and parts of an outer IP header
- Host must support both transport and tunnel modes
- Security gateway must support tunnel mode

Where Security Services Are Provided.   A transport mode SA is a security association between two hosts.[4] For ESP, a transport mode SA provides security services only for the higher layer protocols (layers 4 and above), not for the IP header or any extension headers preceding the ESP header. For AH, the protection is extended to selected portions of the IP header, selected portions of extension headers, and selected options (contained in the IPv4 header, IPv6 Hop-by-Hop extension header, or IPv6 Destination extension headers).

A tunnel mode SA is an SA applied to an IP tunnel. Whenever either end of a security association is a security gateway, the SA must be tunnel mode. An SA between two security gateways is always a tunnel mode SA, as is an SA between a host and a security gateway. Two hosts may establish a tunnel mode SA between themselves.

The term "selected portions" refers to the fields in the header that do not change (immutable) during the transmission of the header through the system.

The tunnel mode SA defines an "outer" IP header that specifies the IPSec processing destination, plus an "inner" IP header that specifies the

---

[4]In IPv4, a transport mode security protocol header appears immediately after the IP header and any options, and before any higher layer protocols (e.g., TCP or UDP). In IPv6, the security protocol header appears after the base IP header and extensions, but may appear before or after destination options, and before higher-layer protocols.

ultimate destination for the packet. The security protocol header appears after the outer IP header, and before the inner IP header. If AH is employed in tunnel mode, portions of the outer IP header are afforded protection, as well as all of the tunneled IP packet (i.e., all of the inner IP header is protected, as well as the higher-layer protocols). If ESP is employed, the protection is afforded only to the tunneled packet, not to the outer header.

COMBINING SECURITY ASSOCIATIONS: A MORE DETAILED VIEW

IP datagrams are not given protection by both AH and ISP. An individual SA is given protection by one or the other, but not both. However, it is possible to use multiple SAs to implement a security policy, and IPSec defines two ways for SAs to be combined into bundles, described by the term an "SA bundle."

The first is called transport adjacency. This method applies more than one security protocol to the same IP datagram, without any tunneling involved. It combines the AH and ESP, and does no further nesting; that is, only one level of combination. The idea is that strong algorithms are used in both AH and ESP so further nesting would yield no more benefits. Receiver processing is performed only once—at the final destination.

The second method is called iterated tunneling, and refers to the use of multiple (layered) security protocols through IP tunneling. This method allows for multiple layers of nesting. Each tunnel can originate or terminate at different IPSec sites along the path from the source to the destination.

There is one case of transport adjacency and three cases of iterated tunneling, shown in Figure 8–8. Figure 8–8(a) shows the transport adjacency case with the one level of SA combination. Figure 8–8(b) shows one case of iterated tunneling in which both endpoints for the SAs are the same. The inner and outer tunnels can be either AH or ESP, and both tunnels could be the same (but that is unlikely). Figure 8–8(c) shows another case of iterated tunneling in which one endpoint of the SAs is the same. The inner or outer tunnels can be either AH or ESP. Figure 8–8(d) shows the last case of iterated tunneling in which neither endpoint for the SAs is the same. The inner and outer tunnels can be either AH or ESP.

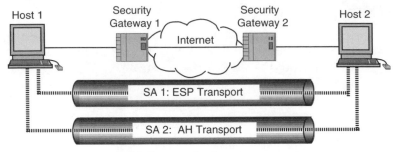

(a) Transport adjacency

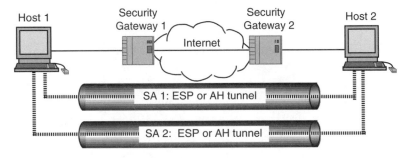

(b) Iterated Tunneling, both endpoints of the SAs are the same

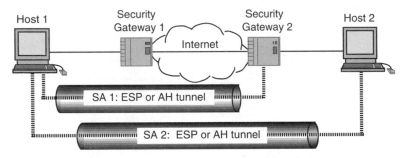

(c) Iterated Tunneling, one endpoint of the SAs is the same

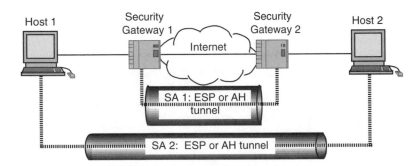

(d) Iterated Tunneling, neither endpoint of the SAs is the same

Figure 8–8   Combining Security Associations

PLACEMENTS OF IPSec

As you might expect, the specific placement of IPSec in hardware or software is not defined as requirements in the Internet specifications, only as suggestions. There are three likely scenarios, shown in Figure 8–9. The first is to place the IPSec software directly into the IP source code, which could be applicable to the host or the security gateway software. This approach is called "bump-in-the-code" (BITC).

The second scenario is to place IPSec under the IP protocol stack, which means it would operate over the line driver. This approach would typically be applicable to hosts, with IPSec running on top of the Media Access Control (MAC) local area network layer. This approach is called "bump-in-the-stack" (BITS).

The third scenario is to use a separate piece of equipment, and attach it to a host or a gateway. For example, the equipment could be a

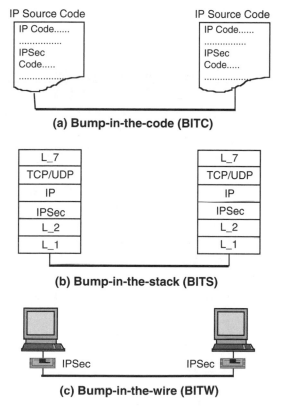

Figure 8–9   Possible Placements of IPSec

crypto processor (for example, used by the military). This approach is called "bump-in-the-wire" (BITW). The BITW device is usually accessed with IP addressing, and if supporting a host, it appears as BITS to the host. When operating with a router or a firewall, it appears to be a security gateway, and must be configured to complement the security functions of the firewall.

THE IPSec DATABASES

IPSec defines the use of two databases called the Security Policy Database (SPD) and the Security Association Database (SAD). An associated concept, called a selector, is also defined. The functions of these three IPSec tools are as follows:

- *Security Policy Database (SPD):* The SPD stores the IPSec policies that define *which* traffic is to be treated (that is, a traffic match) and *how* this traffic is treated (discard, bypass IPSec, or apply IPSec). It defines how to treat both inbound and outbound traffic, and is therefore consulted for each inbound and outbound packet. Three treatments are defined: (1) Discard means the traffic cannot go anywhere, and applies to inbound and outbound traffic. (2) Bypass IPSec means that outbound traffic is not subject to IPSec protection, and it is assumed that inbound traffic has not been given any protection. (3) Apply IPSec means inbound traffic must have had IPSec applied, and outbound traffic will have IPSec applied.
- *Security Association Database (SAD):* The SAD stores information about each active security association. Since SAs are unidirectional, the SAD stores pairs of SAs, one of each direction of the SA.
- *Selector:* A set of IP and ULP fields, and used by the SPD to map traffic to a security policy (an SA). The selectors are (a) IP source address, (b) IP destination address, (c) a DNS or X.500 name, (d) the IP protocol ID field, (e) source port number, and (f) destination port number.

SELECTORS AND SAD/SPD OPERATIONS

All traffic between two hosts may be carried via a single SA, and provided one set of security services. Alternatively, traffic between a pair of hosts might be spread over multiple SAs, depending on the applications being used (as defined by the Next Protocol and Port fields), with different security services offered by different SAs.

The following selector parameters must be supported in an IPSec implementation. Note that both source and destination addresses can be IPv4 or IPv6 addresses.

Destination IP Address

This address may be a single IP address [unicast, anycast, broadcast (IPv4 only), or multicast group], a range of addresses [high and low values (inclusive)], address + mask, or a wildcard address. The last three addresses are used to support more than one destination system sharing the same SA (e.g., behind a security gateway).

This selector is conceptually different from the Destination IP Address field in the <Destination IP Address, IPSec Protocol, SPI> tuple used to uniquely identify an SA.

When a tunneled packet arrives at the tunnel endpoint, its SPI/Destination Address/Protocol values are used to look up the SA for this packet in the SAD. This Destination Address comes from the encapsulating IP header.

Once the packet has been processed according to the tunnel SA and has come out of the tunnel, its selectors are "looked up" in the Inbound SPD. The Inbound SPD has a selector called Destination Address. This IP destination address is the one in the inner (encapsulated) IP header.

Source IP Address

This address may be a single IP address [unicast, anycast, broadcast (IPv4 only), or multicast group], range of addresses (high and low values inclusive), address + mask, or a wildcard address. The last three are used to support more than one source system sharing the same SA (e.g., behind a security gateway or in a multihomed host).

Name

A name may take the form of a fully qualified DNS name, an X.500 distinguished name, or an X.500 general name.

Transport Layer Protocol

This ID is obtained from the IPv4 Protocol or the IPv6 Next Header fields. This value may be an individual protocol number.

Source and Destination Ports

These values may be individual UDP or TCP port values or a wild-card port.

Selectors and SAD/SPD Entries

The specific IPSec implementation determines how selectors are used. For example, a host implementation integrated into the stack may make use of a socket interface. When a new connection is established, the SPD can be consulted and an SA (or SA bundle) bound to the socket. Thus, traffic sent via that socket need not result in additional lookups to the SPD/SAD.

Table 8–2 lists several types of entries in the SPD and SAD. The table shows how they relate to the fields in data traffic being subjected to IPSec screening. (Note: the "wild" or "wildcard" entry for src and dst addresses includes a mask, range, etc.)

Looking Up the SA in the SAD

The following packet fields are used to look up the SA in the SAD:

- Outer header's destination IP address.
- IPSec protocol, AH, or ESP.
- The SPI value used to distinguish among different SAs terminating at the same destination and using the same IPSec protocol.

For each of the selectors, the SA entry in the SAD must contain the value or values which were negotiated at the time the SA was created.

Table 8–2   Typical Entries in the SAD and SPD

Field	Traffic Value	SAD Entry	SPD Entry
src addr	single IP addr	single, range, wild	single, range, wildcard
dst addr	single IP addr	single, range, wild	single, range, wildcard
xpt protocol*	xpt protocol	single, wildcard	single, wildcard
src port*	single src port	single, wildcard	single, wildcard
dst port*	single dst port	single, wildcard	single, wildcard
user id*	single user id	single, wildcard	single, wildcard
sec. labels	single value	single, wildcard	single, wildcard

*The SAD and SPD entries for these fields could be "OPAQUE" because the traffic value is encrypted.

For the sender, these values are used to decide whether a given SA is appropriate for use with an outbound packet. For the receiver, these values are used to check that the selector values in an inbound packet match those for the SA and thus indirectly those for the matching policy.

The following SAD fields are used doing IPSec processing:

- *Sequence number counter:* a 32-bit value used to generate the sequence number field in AH or ESP headers.
- *Sequence counter overflow:* a flag indicating whether overflow of the sequence number counter should generate an auditable event and prevent transmission of additional packets on the SA.
- *Anti-replay window:* a 32-bit counter and a bit-map (or equivalent) used to determine whether an inbound AH or ESP packet is a replay.
- AH authentication algorithm, keys, etc.
- ESP encryption algorithm, keys, IV mode, IV, etc.
- ESP authentication algorithm, keys, etc. If the authentication service is not selected, this field will be null.
- Lifetime of this security association: a time interval after which an SA must be replaced with a new SA (and new SPI) or terminated, plus an indication of which of these actions should occur.
- *IPSec protocol mode:* tunnel, transport or wildcard. Indicates which mode of AH or ESP is applied to traffic on this SA. Note that if this field is "wildcard" at the sending end of the SA, then the application has to specify the mode to the IPSec implementation. This use of wildcard allows the same SA to be used for either tunnel or transport mode traffic on a per packet basis, e.g., by different sockets. The receiver does not need to know the mode in order to properly process the packet's IPSec headers.
- *Path MTU:* any observed path MTU and aging variables.

EXAMPLES OF IPSec SENDING AND RECEIVING OPERATIONS

This section examines the procedures at the sending and receiving IPSec nodes. The exact procedures vary, depending upon the vendor's implementation. We will use IBM's model that was introduced earlier [CHEN98].

Figure 8–10 shows the major operations that occur at the IPSec sending node. The user data is extracted from a buffer queue (usually

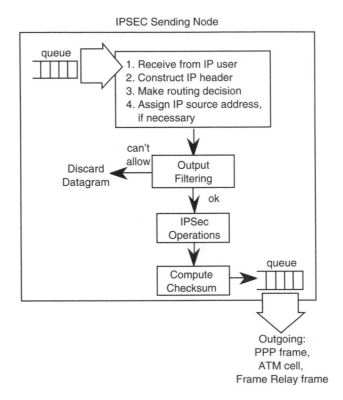

Figure 8–10   IPSec processing at the sending node

from TCP/UDP, OSPF, ICMP, etc.) and processed with the conventional IP-based logic. The IP header is constructed, and routing decisions are made. The routing decisions determine if IPSec operations are to be invoked for this datagram, based on (a) the outgoing link, and (b) the next node that is to receive that traffic. If the user application has not furnished an address with its protocol data unit, one is assigned.

Output filtering may or may not be performed. It is an implementation-specific decision. In some companies, output filtering is applied to prevent unmitigated use of a resource, or of course to institute security screening functions. Output filtering results in the denial of service, with the discard of the datagram, or the passing of the datagram to the IPSec module for IPSec operations and encapsulation.

The completed protocol data unit has its checksum computed. It is then placed in an output queue for the outgoing interface. Here, layer 2 takes over, encapsulates the IPSec PDU into an L_2 frame and sends the frame to the physical layer and the physical link. After IPSec processing, the complete IPSec packet may undergo fragmentation operations, which are not shown in this example.

IPSec also defines the sending node processing as follows. In a security gateway or BITW implementation (and in many BITS implementations), each outbound packet is compared against the SPD to determine what processing is required for the packet. If the packet is to be discarded, this is an auditable event. If the traffic is allowed to bypass IPSec processing, the packet continues through "normal" processing for the environment in which the IPSec processing is taking place. If IPSec processing is required, the packet is either mapped to an existing SA (or SA bundle), or a new SA (or SA bundle) is created for the packet. Since a packet's selectors might match multiple policies or multiple extant SAs and since the SPD is ordered, but the SAD is not, IPSec must:

- Match the packet's selector fields against the outbound policies in the SPD to locate the first appropriate policy, which will point to zero or more SA bundles in the SAD.
- Match the packet's selector fields against those in the SA bundles found in (1) to locate the first SA bundle that matches. If no SAs were found or none match, create an appropriate SA bundle and link the SPD entry to the SAD entry. If no key management entity is found, drop the packet.
- Use the SA bundle found/created in (2) to do the required IPSec processing, e.g., authenticate and encrypt.

In a host IPSec implementation based on sockets, the SPD will be consulted whenever a new socket is created, to determine what, if any, IPSec processing will be applied to the traffic that will flow on that socket.

Figure 8–11 shows the major operations for the processing of an IPSec packet at an incoming node. The incoming packet is error-checked (the external IP header's checksum) and edited for a well-formed protocol data unit. If these checks pass, the packet goes through input filtering, which is part of the overall IPSec operations at this machine, and part of the security policy.

If the filter permits the packet to pass past into the firewall, it is processed by conventional IP procedures ("IP processing" in the figure). Prior to performing AH or ESP processing, any IP fragments are reassembled. During this process, the IP Protocol Number is examined to determine if the IPSec mode is ESP or AH and passed to "IPSec decapsulate" operational. Also, during these operations, the ID of the secure tun-

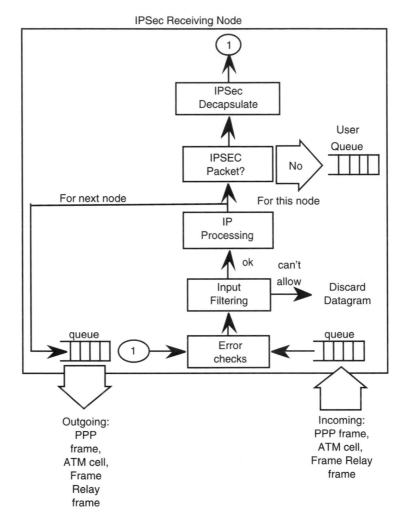

Figure 8–11   IPSec processing at the receiving node

nel is made known, which reveals the way in which the packet is protected. The packet is passed back to error-checking, input filtering, etc., but with additional information furnished to these modules. Therefore, it may be discarded, as a result of this operation. On this second go-around, the ID of the secure tunnel through which the packet came is known, and indicates the manner in which the packet has been protected.

SELECTING AND USING AN SA OR SA BUNDLE

During the processing of the inbound packet, just described, the mapping of the IP datagram to the appropriate SA is simplified because of the presence of the SPI in the AH or ESP header. Note that the selector checks are made on the inner headers not the outer (tunnel) headers. The steps defined by IPSec are:

1. Use the packet's destination address (outer IP header), IPSec protocol, and SPI to look up the SA in the SAD. If the SA lookup fails, drop the packet and log/report the error.

2. Use the SA found in step 1 to do the IPSec processing, e.g., authenticate and decrypt. This step includes matching the packet's (Inner Header if tunneled) selectors to the selectors in the SA. Local policy determines the specificity of the SA selectors (single value, list, range, wildcard). In general, a packet's source address must match the SA selector value. However, an ICMP packet received on a tunnel mode SA may have a source address other than that bound to the SA and thus such packets should be permitted as exceptions to this check. For an ICMP packet, the selectors from the enclosed problem packet (the source and destination addresses and ports should be swapped) should be checked against the selectors for the SA. Note that some or all of these selectors may be inaccessible because of limitations on how many bits of the problem packet the ICMP packet is allowed to carry.

Do steps 1 and 2 for every IPSec header until a transport protocol header or an IP header that is not for this system is encountered. Keep track of what SAs have been used and their order of application.

3. Find an incoming policy in the SPD that matches the packet. This could be done, for example, by use of backpointers from the SAs to the SPD or by matching the packet's selectors (Inner Header if tunneled) against those of the policy entries in the SPD.

4. Check whether the required IPSec processing has been applied, i.e., verify that the SAs found in steps 1 and 2 match the kind and order of SAs required by the policy found in step 3. After

going through this process again (with different decisions made on different headers), all IPSec information is removed. The protocol data unit is no longer a security-based packet, the original IP header reveals the IP datagram is destined for this node, and it is delivered to a queue to pass to the user application.

SUMMARY

IPSec is the primary Internet protocol for transporting secure traffic across an untrusted link or untrusted network. The security association (SA) is implemented with two IPSec databases, the security policy database (SPD), and the security association database (SAD). IPSec transport and tunnel modes can be set up in several ways to provide for transport adjacency and iterated tunneling.

9

The IPSec AH and ESP Protocols

The IPSec AH and ESP protocols are introduced in Chapter 8. This chapter picks up on this introduction and goes into more details about the specific operations of AH and ESP. The authoritative source for AH is RFC 2402, and for ESP, RFC 2406. This chapter provides a tutorial on these RFCs, plus the author's comments on their operations.

SERVICES OF THE IPSec PROTOCOLS

We learned in Chapter 8 that IPSec defines two protocols to support user security operations, and Table 9–1 provides a summary of their operations (services). The IP Authentication Header (AH) provides (a) integrity (called connectionless integrity in the specifications), (b) data origin authentication, and (c) anti-replay services. The latter service is optional, and is established by the receiver when a security association is established. AH may be used alone or in conjunction with ESP.

The IP Encapsulating Security Payload (ESP) may provide: (a) confidentiality (encryption), (b) limited traffic flow confidentiality, (c) connectionless integrity, (d) data origin authentication, and (e) anti-replay services. For ESP, one of these options must be implemented. The set of services offered by ESP depends on the options selected when the secu-

Table 9–1   IPSec Protocols: AH and ESP

- Two protocols
    - Define types of:
    - (a) security services
    - (b) methods of encapsulation
- IP Authentication Header (AH) may provide:
    - Integrity
    - Authentication
    - Anti-replay
- IP Encapsulating Security Payload (ESP) may provide:
    - Confidentiality/privacy/security
    - Integrity
    - Authentication
    - Anti-replay
- Does not define mechanisms for implementing keys
    - Assumes they are available

rity association is established. ESP allows confidentiality services to be provided independently of all other services, but the exclusion of integrity/authentication services may result in active attacks on the traffic that could compromise the confidentiality services.

ESP data origin authentication and connectionless integrity are joint services and are called authentication. They are offered as an option in conjunction with confidentiality. The anti-replay service may be selected only if data origin authentication is selected, and at the discretion of the receiver. Traffic flow confidentiality requires selection of the tunnel mode.

Both protocols are tools for access control, and may be used alone or applied in combination with each other. They support IPv4 or IPv6.

IPSec itself does not define the mechanisms for implementing cryptographic keys (shared secret values), but relies on another set of specifications that deal with public-key based operations, and automatic key management. They are discussed in Chapters 10 and 11.

INTEGRITY CHECK VALUE (ICV)

IPSec uses the term integrity check value (ICV) to define a message authentication code (MAC). IPSec requires that the following procedures be implemented:

- MD5-HMAC-96
- HMAC-SHA-1-96

Relationships of AH, ESP, and the Transport and Tunnel Modes

Table 9–2 shows the relationships of the IPSec transport and tunnel modes to the AH and ESP operations and headers. The table is self-explanatory, but a couple of points can be made about AH and ESP. The reason that ESP has some (optional) features that are also found in AH is to give the network security administrator more flexibility. In addition, the application of both AH and ESP provides the administrator with more options in supporting security associations. I will embellish on these general points later in this chapter.

Handling Mutable Fields

If a field may be modified during transit, the value of the field is set to zero for purposes of the ICV computation. If a field is mutable, but its value at the (IPSec) receiver is predictable, then that value is inserted into the field for purposes of the ICV calculation. The authentication data field is also set to zero in preparation for this computation.

The IPv4 base header fields are classified as follows:

- Immutable
    Version
    Internet header length
    Total length
    Identification
    Protocol (this is the value for AH)
    Source address
    Destination address (without loose or strict source routing)

Table 9–2   Relationships of IPSec Modes and the IPSec Protocols

	Transport	Tunnel
AH	Authenticates IP payload and selected portions of IP header	Authenticates entire inner IP header and payload, and selected portions of outer IP header
ESP	Encrypts and optionally authenticates IP payload, but not IP header	Encrypts and optionally authenticates inner IP header and payload

- Mutable but predictable
    Destination address (with loose or strict source routing)
- Mutable (zeroed prior to ICV calculation)
    Type of service (TOS)
    Flags
    Fragment offset
    Time to live (TTL)
    Header checksum
- TOS: This field is excluded because some routers are known to change the value of this field, even though the IP specification does not consider TOS to be a mutable header field.
- Flags: This field is excluded since an intermediate router might set the DF bit, even if the source did not select it.
- Fragment offset: Since AH is applied only to non-fragmented IP packets, the Offset Field must always be zero, and thus it is excluded (even though it is predictable).
- TTL: This field is changed en route as a normal course of processing by routers, and thus its value at the receiver is not predictable by the sender.
- Header checksum: This field will change if any of these other fields changes, and thus its value upon reception cannot be predicted by the sender.
- Options: This field has many rules associated with it, depending on the specific option. I refer you to Appendix A of RFC 2402 for the details.

The IPv6 base header fields are classified as follows:

- Immutable
    Version
    Payload length
    Next header (this is the value for AH)
    Source address
    Destination address (without routing extension header)
        Mutable but predictable
        Destination address (with routing extension header)

- Mutable (zeroed prior to ICV calculation)
    Class
    Flow label
    Hop limit

PROTECTION COVERAGE OF THE AH AND ESP PACKETS

Figures 9–1 through 9–6 show the protection coverage given to the AH and ESP packets. These figures are used throughout the chapter to aid in explaining AH and ESP operations. Note that in all these figures the arrows show where authentication and encrypted (privacy) services are provided (in all but the mutable fields).

AH Protection

Figure 9–1 shows the IPv4 protection coverage by AH in transport mode. In this mode, AH is inserted after the IP header and before an upper layer protocol, e.g., TCP, UDP, ICMP, etc. or before any other IPSec headers that have already been inserted. In the context of IPv4, this calls for placing AH after the IP header (and any options that it contains), but before the upper layer protocol (ULP). The term "transport" mode should not be misconstrued as restricting its use to TCP and UDP. For example, ICMP, OSPF, IGMP, etc., messages may be sent using either transport mode or tunnel mode. In addition, the term upper-layer protocols refers to the content of any other protocols carried in the IP datagram. Once again, these protocols can be TCP, UDP, OSPF, ICMP, etc.

For IPv6 protection, AH is viewed as an end-to-end payload, and thus should appear after hop-by-hop, routing, and fragmentation exten-

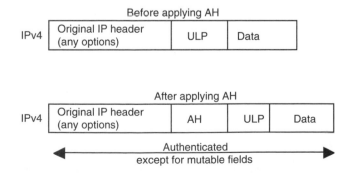

Figure 9–1   AH protection for IPv4 in transport mode

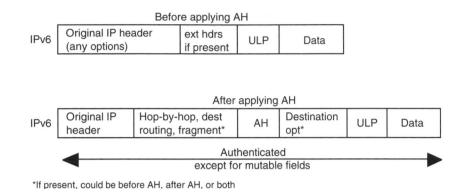

*If present, could be before AH, after AH, or both

Figure 9–2   AH protection for IPv6 in transport mode

sion headers. The destination options extension header(s) could appear either before or after the AH header depending on the semantics desired. Figure 9–2 illustrates AH transport mode positioning for a typical IPv6 packet.

Figure 9–3 shows the AH Protection for IPv4 and IPv6 in tunnel mode. Tunnel mode AH may be employed in either hosts or security gateways (or in so-called "bump-in-the-stack" or "bump-in-the-wire" implementations). When AH is implemented in a security gateway (to protect transit traffic), tunnel mode must be used. In tunnel mode, the "inner" IP header carries the ultimate source and destination addresses, while an "outer" IP header may contain distinct IP addresses, e.g., addresses of security gateways. In tunnel mode, AH protects the entire inner IP packet, including the entire inner IP header. The position of AH in tunnel mode, relative to the outer IP header, is the same as for AH in transport mode.

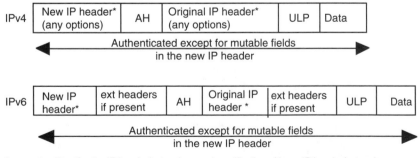

* = construction of outer IP header/extensions and modification of inner IP header/extensions
   is discussed in text

Figure 9–3   AH protection for IPv4 and IPv6 in tunnel mode

SERVICES AND OPERATIONS OF AH

AH has been published in two "versions." The first is defined in RFC 1826, and this part of the chapter will deal briefly with this earlier specification, since there are implementations in existence using this RFC.

RFC 1826

Figure 9–4 shows the format of the AH header. The next header field identifies the next payload after the authentication payload. The payload length is the length of the authentication data field in 32-bit words. The reserved field is reserved for future use.

The security parameters index (SPI) field is used to identify the security association (SA) for the datagram. If set to 0, it indicates that no security association exists. The SPI values of 1–255 are reserved for use by the Internet Assigned Numbers Authority (IANA).

The authentication data field is defined by the security association of this datagram. The destination IP address and the SPI can be used to locate the SA for the datagram, and this field's use and size. This field is calculated using a message digest (MD) algorithm, which must be a strong one-way function.

RFC 2402

RFC 2402 is the latest release for AH, and the emphasis in this chapter is on this AH version. Figure 9–5 shows the format for the AH header. AH is identified with an IP protocol ID value of 51. The fields in this header are all required, and are included in the integrity check value (explained shortly). They perform the following functions.

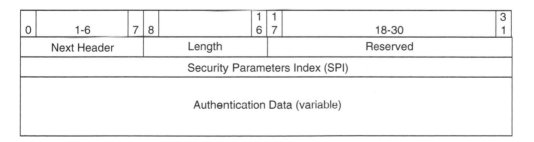

Note: Numbers at the top of the figure are the bit positions of the fields

Figure 9–4   Authentication header (AH) in RFC 1826

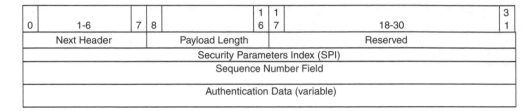

Figure 9–5   Authentication header (AH) format in RFC 2402

- *Next Header:* Identifies the type of the next payload after the authentication header. The value is chosen from the set of IP protocol numbers defined in *www.ietf.org,* (click on IANA).
- *Payload Length:* Specifies the length of AH.
- *Reserved:* Reserved for future use.
- *Security Parameters Index (SPI):* A value that, in combination with the destination IP address and security protocol (AH), uniquely identifies the security association for this datagram. The SPI is usually selected by the destination node during the establishment of an SA.
- *Sequence Number:* This field is always present even if the receiver does not elect to enable the anti-replay service for a specific SA. If anti-replay is used (the default), the transmitted sequence number is not allowed to cycle. Consequently, the sender's counter and the receiver's counter is reset (by establishing a new SA and thus a new key) prior to the transmission of the 2^{32}nd packet on an SA.
- *Authentication Data:* Contains the integrity check value (ICV), described next.

Integrity Check Value (ICV) for Outbound Packets

The AH ICV is computed on (a) the IP header fields that are immutable or are predictable at the receiver node, (b) the AH header (and padding bytes, if any), and (c) all upper-layer headers and data.

If fragmentation is in effect, it occurs after AH processing. Thus, transport mode AH is applied only to complete IP datagrams, and not to IP fragments. An IP packet to which AH has been applied may itself be fragmented by routers en route, and such fragments must be reassembled prior to AH processing at a receiver. In tunnel mode, AH is applied to an IP packet, the payload of which may be a fragmented IP packet. For example, a security gateway or a "bump-in-the-stack" or "bump-in-the-wire" IPSec may apply tunnel mode AH to such fragments.

Integrity Check Value (ICV) for Inbound Packets

If fragmentation is in effect, reassembly of the fragments is performed prior to AH processing. The SA is determined by an examination of the destination IP address, the AH, and the SPI. If there is no valid SA, the packet must be discarded. The use of the sequence number to guard against anti-replay is required for AH. However, if the receiver does not execute anti-replay, then of course the sequence number is ignored.

The receiving node then computes ICV over the appropriate field of the packet and compares its results to the ICV in the authentication data field of the packet. If they match, the datagram is valid. The algorithm for the operations can vary, but recall that a compliant AH implementation must support the: (a) HMAC with MD5, and (b) HMAC with SHA-1.

SERVICES AND OPERATIONS OF ESP

As introduced earlier, the Encapsulating Security Payload (ESP) is a mechanism for providing integrity and confidentiality to IP datagrams. It may also provide data origin authentication, depending upon the algorithms used. Non-repudiation and traffic analysis protection are not provided by ESP. Like AH, data origin authentication and connectionless integrity are joint services, and are referred to as "authentication." Traffic flow confidentiality requires the selection of tunnel mode.

The ESP payload appears after the IP header and before the transport layer protocol. It has been assigned Protocol Number 50 by the IANA. ESP contains an unencrypted header followed by encrypted data. The encrypted data includes protected ESP header fields, and user data, which may be an entire IP datagram, including the headers of upper layers, and end-user data.

ESP Protection

Like AH, ESP may be employed in two ways: transport mode or tunnel mode. The former mode is applicable only to host implementations and provides protection for upper-layer protocols, but not the IP header. (In this mode, for "bump-in-the-stack" or "bump-in-the-wire" implementations, inbound and outbound IP fragments may require an IPSec implementation to perform extra IP reassembly/fragmentation in order to both conform to this specification and provide transparent IPSec support.)

Figure 9–6 shows the transport mode ESP coverage. ESP is inserted after the IP header and before an upper layer protocol, e.g., TCP, UDP, ICMP, etc., or before any other IPSec headers that have already been inserted. In the context of IPv4, this translates to placing ESP after the IP header (and any options that it contains), but before the upper layer protocols. The "ESP trailer" encompasses any padding, plus the pad length, and next header fields.

Figure 9–7 shows the transport ESP coverage for IPv6. ESP is viewed as an end-to-end payload, and thus should appear after hop-by-hop, routing, and fragmentation extension headers. The destination options extension header(s) could appear either before or after the ESP header depending on the semantics. However, since ESP protects only fields after the ESP header, it generally may be desirable to place the destination options header(s) after the ESP header.

Tunnel mode ESP coverage is depicted in Figure 9–8. Tunnel mode ESP may be employed in either hosts or security gateways. When ESP is implemented in a security gateway (to protect subscriber transit traffic), tunnel mode must be used. In tunnel mode, the "inner" IP header carries the ultimate source and destination addresses, while an "outer" IP header may contain distinct IP addresses, e.g., addresses of security gateways. In tunnel mode, ESP protects the entire inner IP packet, including the entire inner IP header. The position of ESP in tunnel mode, relative to the outer IP header, is the same as for ESP in transport mode.

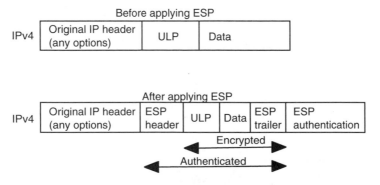

Figure 9–6   ESP protection for IPv4 in transport mode

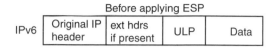

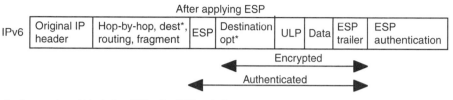

Figure 9–7   ESP protection for IPv6 in transport mode

ESP has been published in two "versions." The first is defined in RFC 1827, and this part of the chapter will deal with this earlier specification.

RFC 1827

Figure 9–9 shows the format of the RFC 1827 ESP header. It consists of an SPI field and the opaque transform data field. The SPI field identifies the security association for the datagram, and is set to zero if no security association is used.

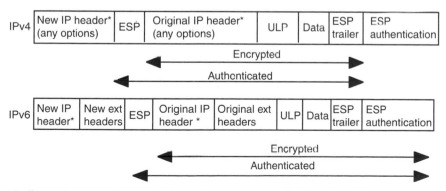

Figure 9–8   ESP protection for IPv4 and IPv6 in tunnel mode

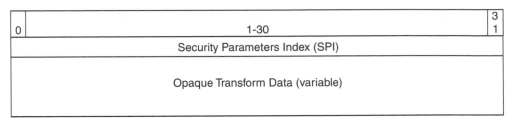

Note: Numbers at the top of the figure are the bit positions of the fields

Figure 9–9   The RFC 1827 ESP header

The opaque transform data field and the specific encryption and authentication algorithms are known as "transforms." ESP does not define the transforms; they are defined in other specifications. One that the reader might wish to examine is [KARN95].[1]

RFC 2406

RFC 2406 is the latest release for ESP, and the emphasis in this chapter is on this ESP version. Figure 9–10 shows the format for the ESP header. ESP is identified with an IP protocol ID value of 50. The fields in this header are all required, and are included in the integrity check value (explained shortly). They perform the following functions.

- *Security parameters index (SPI):* A value that, in combination with the destination IP address and security protocol (ESP), uniquely identifies the Security Association for this datagram. The SPI is usually selected by the destination node during the establishment of an SA.
- *Sequence number:* This field is always present even if the receiver does not elect to enable the anti-replay service for a specific SA. If anti-replay is used (the default), the transmitted sequence number is not allowed to cycle. Consequently, the sender's counter and the receiver's counter is reset (by establishing a new SA and thus a new key) prior to the transmission of the 2^{32}nd packet on an SA.
- *Payload data:* Contains the data as protected by encryption.

---

[1][KARN95]. Karn, P., Metzger, P., and Simpson, W., "The ESP DES-CBC Transform," RFC 1829.

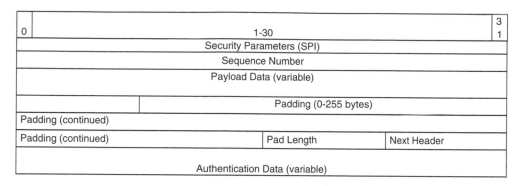

Figure 9–10   The RFC 2406 ESP Header

- *Padding:* Used to fulfil a pad requirement for the length of the plaintext. The number of PAD bytes depends on the specific implementation.
- *Pad length:* Specifies number of PAD bytes.
- *Next header:* Identifies the type of data contained in the payload data field.
- *Authentication data:* Contains the integrity check value (ICV) computed over the ESP packet. DES in CBC mode is required by IPSec.

Outbound Packet Processing

For packet encryption, the sender:

- *Encapsulates (into the ESP Payload field):* (a) for transport mode, the original upper layer protocol information, (b) for tunnel mode, the entire original IP datagram.
- Adds any necessary padding.
- Encrypts the result (payload data, padding, pad length, and next header) using the key, encryption algorithm, and algorithm mode indicated by the SA.

If authentication is selected, encryption is performed first, before the authentication, and the encryption does not encompass the authentication data field.

If authentication is selected for the SA, the sender computes the ICV over the ESP packet minus the authentication data. Thus the SPI, sequence number, payload data, padding (if present), pad length, and next header are all encompassed by the ICV computation. The last four fields will be in ciphertext form, since encryption is performed prior to authentication.

Inbound Packet Processing

If required, reassembly is performed prior to ESP processing. If a packet offered to ESP for processing appears to be an IP fragment, i.e., the offset field is non-zero or the more fragments flag is set, the receiver must discard the packet; this is an auditable event. The audit log entry for this event should include the SPI value, date/time received, source address, destination address, sequence number, and (in IPv6) the flow ID.

Security Association Lookup.   Upon receipt of a (reassembled) packet containing an ESP Header, the receiver determines the appropriate (unidirectional) SA, based on the destination IP address, security protocol (ESP), and the SPI. The SA indicates whether the sequence number field will be checked, whether the authentication data field should be present, and it will specify the algorithms and keys to be employed for decryption and ICV computations (if applicable).

Sequence Number Verification.   All ESP implementations must support the anti-replay service, though its use may be enabled or disabled by the receiver on a per-SA basis.

Integrity Check Value Verification.   If authentication has been selected, the receiver computes the ICV over the ESP packet minus the authentication data using the specified authentication algorithm and verifies that it is the same as the ICV included in the authentication data field of the packet. Details of the computation are provided below.

If the computed and received ICVs match, then the datagram is valid, and it is accepted. If the test fails, then the receiver must discard the received IP datagram as invalid; this is an auditable event.

Packet Decryption.   The receiving IPSec node:

- Decrypts the ESP payload data, padding, pad length, and next header using the key, encryption algorithm, algorithm mode, and cryptographic synchronization data (if any), indicated by the SA.
- Processes any padding as specified in the encryption algorithm specification.

- Reconstructs the original IP datagram from:

 for transport mode: original IP header plus the original upper-layer protocol information in the ESP Payload field

 for tunnel mode: tunnel IP header plus the entire IP datagram in the ESP Payload field.

AH AND ESP AND THE "CASES"

In Chapter 8, the four IPSec cases were explained. We now return to those cases and expand the explanations by describing the types of encapsulation operations supported in each. Recall that the four combinations of security associations and their associated tunnels, and encapsulations must be supported in an IPSec compliant machine.

For Figures 9–11 through 9–14, the icon for the tunnel represents one or more security associations, and the dashed line shows the IPSec nodes involved, and the logical flow of IPSec traffic. The solid line across the figure represents the physical flow of traffic. For simplicity, the ESP trailer and MAC fields (behind ULP) are not shown in these examples.

Case 1 is shown in Figure 9–11. It permits either the tunnel or transport mode to be used between hosts. Five combinations of encapsulations can be used, as depicted in the box at the bottom of the figure.

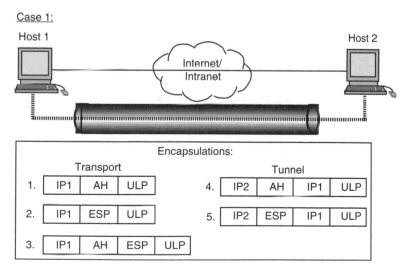

Figure 9–11   Case 1 and the encapsulations

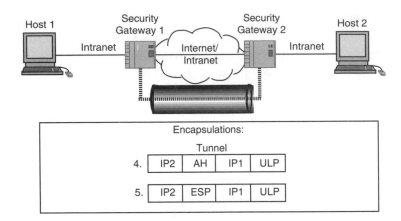

Figure 9–12   Case 2 and the encapsulations

Note also that for option 3, both AH and ESP can be applied to the data. If so, the ESP must be applied first, followed by the AH.

Case 2, shown in Figure 9–12, uses only the tunnel mode, and the encapsulation options are shown in the box at the bottom of the figure. The IPSec calls this support a virtual private network support. Note that only the tunnel mode is permitted for case 2.

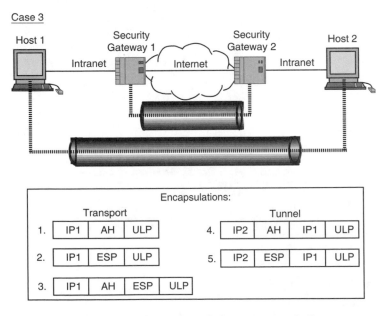

Figure 9–13   Case 3 and the encapsulations

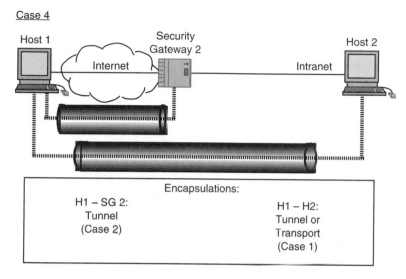

Figure 9–14   Case 4 and the encapsulations

Case 3 combines cases 1 and 2, and is shown in Figure 9–13. It adds end-to-end security operations on a host-to-host basis. The case entails no new requirements on either a host or a gateway, so we need not dwell on it further.

As discussed earlier, case 4 covers a situation in which a remote host dials-in through the Internet to its organization, see Figure 9–14. We cited examples of this case, such as mobile phone users, travelers staying at hotels, etc. As summarized in the box at the bottom of the figure, only tunnel mode is used between the host and the security gateway, in accordance with the case 2 rules. The tunnels between the two hosts can be with AH or ESP, in accordance with case 1 rules.

IP ADDRESSING IN THE HEADERS

Let's take a look at the IPSec packets in regards to addressing. The IPSec packets are coded in more than one way, and we now know that the coding depends on the security protocol employed, which in turn depends on the SA.

Tunnel mode is used when the tunnel exists between two firewalls (as shown in Figure 9–15), or between a firewall and a remote system such as a server.

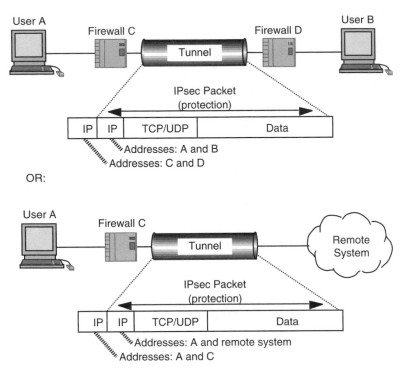

Figure 9–15   Addressing in the tunnel mode

The source and destination IP addresses in the IP header may or may not be the same as in the original IP datagram. For example, the IP addresses for users A and B may be contained in the protected IP header, whereas the IP addresses for firewalls C and D may be in the other IP header. The use of the addresses depends on where the tunnel begins and ends.

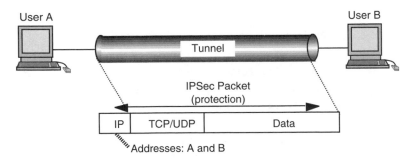

Figure 9–16   Addressing in the transport mode

The transport mode addressing is shown in Figure 9–16. The transport mode is used when the endpoints of the secure tunnel are the two end-user communicating parties.

CONSTRUCTION OF THE ESP PACKET

Figure 9–17 provides another view of the ESP packet. It is created in the following manner at the transmitter. First, the ESP header is created. The user traffic (payload) is appended to the ESP header. Next, the ESP trailer is created and appended to the payload. The trailer provides the protocol number of the encapsulated packet (such as a TCP or UDP Internet protocol number) or, if tunnel mode is used, this value will contain the IP-in-IP number (4). The ESP trailer also contains the block cipher that is used for encryption (such as DES) and padding bytes (if necessary) to pad this unit out to accommodate to the block size of the cipher. Next, the payload and ESP trailer is encrypted, which becomes the ciphertext for the packet. If traffic integrity is to be used, the MAC calculation is performed on the ESP header and ciphertext and appended at the back of the protocol data unit. Finally, the entire ESP packet is appended to the IP header to be used for tunnel operations.

The procedure for creating the AH packet is similar to the operation just discussed, see Figure 9–18. However, remember that AH is used to provide authentication operations, so there are no encryption operations involved in this mode of operation. First, the transmitting site creates the AH protocol header which (like the ESP header) contains a sequence number, the IPSec SA, the SPI, as well as a protocol number to identify

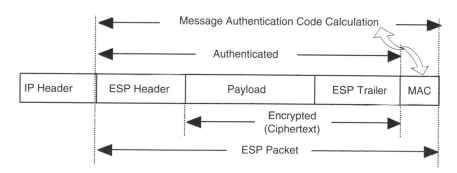

Figure 9–17   The ESP packet in more detail

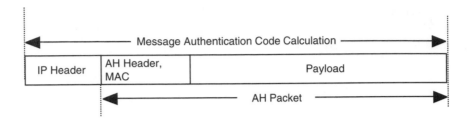

Figure 9–18   Construction of the AH Packet

the encapsulated traffic. It will also contain the MAC value (calculated later). The next operation simply appends the to-be-encapsulated packet to the AH header. The IP header is placed in front of the AH header. The final operation is the computation of the message authentication code (MAC) over the entire packet (which includes the IP header, the AH header, and the payload).

Finally, Figure 9–19 shows yet another encapsulation mode. I quote directly from [CHEN98], p. 51:

> Although ESP can provide both secrecy and integrity protection, AH is still needed for the following reasons:
>
> - If secrecy protection is not needed or prohibited by law, AH can provide integrity protection without the cost of encryption.
> - The integrity protection of AH covers part of the IP header, whereas that of ESP does not. Whether this difference in coverage is needed depends on the specific operational security requirements. (For example, a military

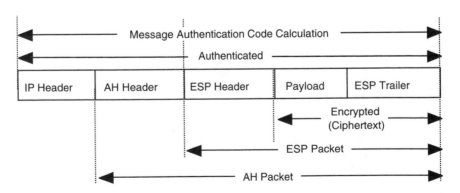

Figure 9–19   AH and ESP packet construction

application may want to protect the sensitivity labels included in the option fields of the IP header.) If both the difference in coverage and secrecy protection are needed, an IPSec SA bundle ... can be used, and the result is shown in Figure 9–19. In this figure an ISP packet is encapsulated inside an AH packet, and the AH packet is encapsulated inside an IP packet. This layout implies that the ESP packet is constructed first. The sequence number field in the AH header enables the receiver to detect a replay attack early, therefore saving the decryption operation.

HEADER CONSTRUCTION FOR TUNNEL MODE

IPSec describes the handling of the inner and outer IP headers, extension headers, and options for AH and ESP tunnels. This includes how to construct the encapsulating (outer) IP header, how to handle fields in the inner IP header, and what other actions should be taken. The general idea is modeled after the one used in RFC 2003, "IP Encapsulation with IP":

- The outer IP header Source Address and Destination Address identify the "endpoints" of the tunnel (the encapsulator and decapsulator). The inner IP header Source Address and Destination Addresses identify the original sender and recipient of the datagram, (from the perspective of this tunnel), respectively.
- The inner IP header is not changed except to decrement the TTL as noted below, and remains unchanged during its delivery to the tunnel exit point.
- No change to IP options or extension headers in the inner header occurs during delivery of the encapsulated datagram through the tunnel.
- If need be, other protocol headers such as the IP Authentication header may be inserted between the outer IP header and the inner IP header.

The tables in the next part of the chapter show the handling for the different header/option fields. The term constructed means the value in the outer field is constructed independently of the value in the inner).

Table 9–3 shows the IPv4 Header construction for tunnel mode. The notes in the table are explained in Box 9–1.

Table 9–4 shows the IPv6 header construction for tunnel mode. The notes in the tables are explained in Box 9–1.

Table 9–3   IPv4 Header Construction for Tunnel Mode

IPv4	<— How Outer Hdr Relates to Inner Hdr —>	
	Outer Hdr at	Inner Hdr at
	Encapsulator	Decapsulator
Header fields:	————————	————
version	4 (1)	no change
header length	constructed	no change
TOS	copied from inner hdr (5)	no change
total length	constructed	no change
ID	constructed	no change
flags (DF, MF)	constructed, DF (4)	no change
fragmt offset	constructed	no change
TTL	constructed (2)	decrement (2)
protocol	AH, ESP, routing hdr	no change
checksum	constructed	constructed (2)
src address	constructed (3)	no change
dest address	constructed (3)	no change
Options	never copied	no change

Table 9–4   IPv6 Header Construction for Tunnel Mode

IPv6	<— How Outer Hdr Relates Inner Hdr —>	
	Outer Hdr at	Inner Hdr at
	Encapsulator	Decapsulator
Header fields:	————————	————
version	6 (1)	no change
class	copied or configured (6)	no change
flow id	copied or configured	no change
len	constructed	no change
next header	AH, ESP, routing hdr	no change
hop limit	constructed (2)	decrement (2)
src address	constructed (3)	no change
dest address	constructed (3)	no change
Extension headers	never copied	no change

Box 9–1   Explanation of Notes in Tables 9–3 and 9–4

1. The IP version in the encapsulating header can be different from the value in the inner header.

2. The TTL in the inner header is decremented by the encapsulator prior to forwarding and by the decapsulator if it forwards the packet. (The checksum changes when the TTL.)

3. src and dest addresses depend on the SA, which is used to determine the dest address which in turn determines which src address (net interface) is used to forward the packet. In principle, the encapsulating IP source address can be any of the encapsulator's interface addresses or even an address different from any of the encapsulator's IP addresses, (e.g., if it's acting as a NAT box) so long as the address is reachable through the encapsulator from the environment into which the packet is sent. This does not cause a problem because IPSec does not currently have any IN-BOUND processing requirement that involves the Source Address of the encapsulating IP header. So while the receiving tunnel endpoint looks at the Destination Address in the encapsulating IP header, it only looks at the Source Address in the inner (encapsulated) IP header.

4. configuration determines whether to copy from the inner header (IPv4 only), clear or set the DF.

5. If Inner Hdr is IPv4 (Protocol = 4), copy the TOS. If Inner Hdr is IPv6 (Protocol = 41), map the class to TOS.

6. If Inner Hdr is IPv6 (Next Header = 41), copy the class. If inner Hdr is IPv4 (Next Header = 4), copy the TOS to class.

HMAC APPLIED TO AH AND ESP

Because of the effectiveness of HMAC (see Chapter 5, "HMAC"; you should read this section before delving into our topic here), it has been defined to operate within both AH and ESP. HMAC is defined for two hashing functions, MD5 and SHA-1. The focus of this part of the chapter is on how HMAC is deployed in the following contexts: (a) HMAC MD5 within ESP and AH (RFC 2403), and (b) HMAC SHA-1 within ESP and AH (RFC 2402). This section summarizes the key aspects of these RFCs.

To iterate a key point: These two operations are designed to ensure that the transmitted packet is (a) authentic, and (b) cannot be modified in transit.

For the MD5 and SHA-1 operations, the following holds: HMAC is a secret key authentication algorithm. Data integrity and data origin authentication as provided by HMAC are dependent upon the scope of the distribution of the secret key. If only the source and destination know the HMAC key, this operation provides both data origin authentication and data integrity for packets sent between the two parties. If the HMAC is correct, this proves that it must have been added by the source.

MD5-HMAC-96 Within ESP and AH

MD5-HMAC-96 operates on 64-byte blocks of data. Padding requirements are specified in RFC 1321 and are part of the MD5 algorithm. MD5-HMAC-96 produces a 128-bit authenticator value. For use with either ESP or AH, a truncated value using the first 96 bits must be supported. Upon sending, the truncated value is stored within the authenticator field. Upon receipt, the entire 128-bit value is computed and the first 96 bits are compared to the value stored in the authenticator field. No other authenticator value lengths are supported by MD5-HMAC-96.

No fixed key length is specified in RFC 2403. Nonetheless, for MD5-HMAC-96 use with either ESP or AH a fixed key length of 128 bits must be supported. Key lengths other than 128 bits are not allowed. A key length of 128 bits was chosen based on RFC 2104 (i.e., key lengths less than the authenticator length decrease security strength and keys longer than the authenticator length do not significantly increase security strength).

MHAC-SHA-1-96 Within ESP and AH

HMAC-SHA-1-96 operates on 64-byte blocks of data. Padding requirements are specified in FIPS-180-1 and are part of the SHA-1 algorithm. HMAC-SHA-1-96 produces a 160-bit authenticator value. This 160-bit value can be truncated as described in RFC 2104. For use with either ESP or AH, a truncated value using the first 96 bits must be supported. Upon sending, the truncated value is stored within the authenticator field. Upon receipt, the entire 160-bit value is computed and the first 96 bits are compared to the value stored in the authenticator field. No other authenticator value lengths are supported by HMAC-SHA-1-96.

As mentioned above, no fixed key length is specified in RFC 2104, but use with either ESP or AH a fixed key length of 160 bits must be supported. Key lengths other than 160 bits are not allowed (i.e., only 160-bit keys are to be used by HMAC-SHA-1-96). A key length of 160 bits was chosen based on the recommendations in RFC 2104.

IPSec AND NAT

The Network Address Translation (NAT) Protocol is a widely-used Internet operation that allows enterprises to use their own IP addresses (the reserved IP addresses for the private IP address space), yet communicate with networks that use public IP address, those that are assigned by the Internet. RFC 2709 [SRIS99][2] describes the procedures to obtain IPSec tunnel mode security for IPSec users. Before this operation is described, a couple definitions should prove helpful.

- *Normal-NAT:* The conventional NAT processing defined in RFC 2663 (a brief tutorial on NAT is provided in Appendix B, at the back of this book).
- *IPSec policy controlled NAT (IPC-NAT):* An extension of NAT transformation to IPSec transformation to packets in an IP-IP tunnel. The NAT node is a tunnel end point.

Figure 9–20 shows the operations on an outgoing packet at an IPSec node (for example, a tunnel firewall that also supports NAT). Figure 9–21 shows the operations for an incoming packet.

In accordance with RFC 2709, the major aspects of IPSec-NAT operations are:

- The NAT device administers security policies based on private realm addressing.

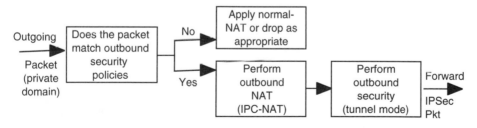

Figure 9–20 IPSec and NAT operations on an outgoing packet in tunnel mode

---

[2][SRIS99]. Srisuresh, P., RFC 2709. "Security Model with Tunnel Mode IPSec for NAT Domains," October, 1999.

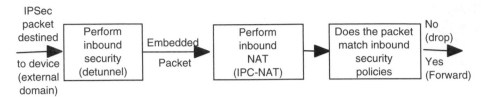

Figure 9–21   IPSec and NAT operations on an incoming packet in the tunnel mode

- The security policies determine the IPSec tunnel end-point peer. A packet may be required to undergo a different type of NAT translation depending upon the tunnel end-point.
- IPC-NAT needs a unique set of NAT maps for each security policy configured. IPC-NAT performs address translation in conjunction with IPSec processing differently with each peer, based on security policies.

Operation of an IPC-NAT device is distinguished from an IPSec gateway that does not support NAT as follows (I quote directly from RFC 2709):

(1) The IPC-NAT device has security policies administered using private realm addressing. A traditional IPSec gateway will have its security policies administered using a single realm (say, external realm) addressing.

(2) Elements fundamental to the security model of an IPC-NAT device include IPC-NAT address mapping (and other NAT parameter definitions) in conjunction with Security policies and SA attributes. Fundamental elements of a traditional IPSec gateway are limited only to security policies and SA attributes.

SUMMARY

The IP Authentication Header (AH) provides (a) integrity (called connectionless integrity in the specifications), (b) data origin authentication, and (c) anti-replay services. The latter service is optional, and is established by the receiver when a security association is established. AH may be used alone or in conjunction with ESP.

The IP Encapsulating Security Payload (ESP) may provide: (a) confidentiality (encryption), (b) limited traffic flow confidentiality, (c) connectionless integrity, (d) data origin authentication, and (e) anti-replay services. For ESP, one of these options must be implemented.

10

The Internet Key Distribution, Certification, and Management

T his chapter describes Internet operations pertaining to public key distribution, the certification of the public key, and its overall management. We begin this chapter with an overview of the issues surrounding the subject, followed by tutorials on the key Internet RFCs and working drafts.

Because of the evolution of the Internet security standards, the Internet key exchange procedures are published in RFCs that contain some overlapping procedures. A section of the chapter provides descriptions of the most important RFCs used for key exchanges, and explains the relationships of these RFCs. The sections in Chapter 3 titled "Man-in-the-Middle-Attack," and "Certification" are important prerequisites to this chapter and Chapter 11.

WHAT IS PUBLIC KEY INFRASTRUCTURE (PKI)?

A system to provide public-key encryption and Digital Signature services is known as a public-key infrastructure (PKI) [CURR97].[1] The

---

[1][CURR97]. Curry, Ian. "Trusted Public-Key Infrastructures," A White Paper, available on *www.entrust.com*. This section of the chapter is a summary of this paper. Be aware that the summary does not include many details cited in the paper, and you should visit the Entrust Web site for more information. I have also added more information on Internet-specific activities.

purpose of a PKI is to manage keys and certificates. The idea of PKI is to authenticate a user, based on the user's presentation of a certificate. A PKI user must implement the following items in a PKI to provide the required key and certificate management services:

- Public key certificates and certification authorities (CAs)
- Key backup and recovery
- Support for non-repudiation of Digital Signatures
- Automatic update of key pairs and certificates
- Management of key histories
- Support for cross-certification

Certificates and Certification Authorities (CAs)

For public-key cryptography to be effective, users must be assured that the other parties with whom they communicate are valid and trustworthy. To obtain this assurance, all PKI users have a registered identity, stored as a public key certificate.

A Certification Authoritiy (CA) represents the user in the creation of digital certificates. These certificates bind the names of users to their public keys. CAs act as agents of trust in a PKI. As long as users trust a CA for issuing and managing certificates, they can trust certificates issued by the CA. This is known as a third-party trust.

CAs create certificates for users by digitally signing a set of data that includes the following information (and additional items):

- The user's name in the format of a distinguished name (DN). The DN (an employee number, a password, etc.) specifies the user's name and any additional attributes required to uniquely identify the user.
- A public key of the user.
- The lifetime of the certificate.
- The specific operations for which the public key is to be used (authentication or privacy, or both).

The CA's signature on a certificate ensures that any tampering with the contents of the certificate can be detected. As long as the CA's signature on a certificate can be verified, the certificate has integrity, and can be trusted. The integrity of the certificate is determined by verifying the CA's signature.

Internet Certificate Authorities Activities. The Internet Policy Registration Authority (IPRA) [RFC 1422] has been established to direct the CA infrastructure for the IETF. The IPRA certifies Policy Certification Authorities (PCA). In turn, PCAs control CAs which certify users and subordinate entities. Current certificate-related work includes the Domain Name System (DNS) Security Extensions (DNSSEC), which provides signed entity keys in the DNS. The Public Key Infrastucture working group is specifying an Internet profile for X.509 certificates. There is also work going on in the industry to develop X.500 Directory Services which will provide X.509 certificates to users.

Other CA Activities. The US Post Office is developing a CA hierarchy. The NIST Public Key Infrastructure Working Group has also been doing work in this area. The DOD Multi Level Information System Security Initiative (MISSI) program has begun deploying a certificate infrastructure for the US government. Alternatively, if no infrastructure exists, the PGP Web of Trust certificates can be used to provide user authentication and privacy in a community of users who know and trust each other.

Support for Non-repudiation

Non-repudiation means that an individual cannot successfully deny the involvement in a transaction. The signature prevents repudiation of a transaction. In the electronic world, the replacement for the pen-based signature is a Digital Signature, and PKI supports the non-repudiation of a Digital Signature.

The most basic requirement for non-repudiation is that the key used to create Digital Signatures (the signing key) be generated and securely stored in a manner under the control of only the user. Unlike encryption key pairs, there is no technical or security requirement to back up or restore previous signing key pairs when users forget their passwords or lose, break, or corrupt their signing keys. In such cases, it is acceptable for users to generate new signing key pairs and continue using them from that time forward.

Key Backup and Recovery

An enterprise must be able to retrieve encrypted data even when users lose their decryption keys. The enterprise to which the user belongs requires a system for backing up and recovering the decryption keys.

Key backup and key escrow are not the same operations. Key escrow means that a third party (such as a federal agent) can obtain the decryption keys required to access encrypted information. Key backup and recovery operations have nothing to do with key escrow.

The CA supports two kinds of key pairs, introduced in Chapter 3. One key pair is used for encrypting and decrypting data (encryption key pair). Another key pair is used for digitally signing data and verifying signatures for authentication (signing key pair).

The only keys requiring backup are users' decryption keys. As long as the CA securely backs up users' decryption keys, security is not compromised and the user's data can always be recovered.

Using Two Key Pairs

To support key backup and recovery, the decryption keys must be backed up in a secure manner. To support non-repudiation, the keys used for the Digital Signature cannot be backed up and must be under the sole control of the user at all times.

To meet these requirements, a PKI must support two key pairs for each user. At any time, a user must have one current key pair for encryption and decryption, and a second key pair for Digital Signature and signature verification. Over time, users will have numerous key pairs that must be managed appropriately, as discussed in the following section.

Key Update and Management of Key Histories

In Chapters 3 and 5, we learned that cryptographic key pairs should not be used indefinitely. Consequently, PKI supports the updating of users' key pairs and the maintaining of a history of previous key pairs. The PKI process of updating key pairs is transparent to users. When encryption key pairs are updated, the history of previous decryption keys is maintained. This history of key usage ensures that users can access any of their prior decryption keys to decrypt data. The key history must also be managed by the PKI key backup and recovery system. This ensures that encrypted data can be recovered securely, regardless of what encryption public key was used to originally encrypt the data (and, by extension regardless of when the data was encrypted). When a signing key pair is updated, the previous signing key is destroyed. This destruction prevents any other person from gaining access to the signing key and is acceptable because there is no need to retain previous signing keys.

Certificate Repositories and Certificate Distribution

As mentioned earlier, the CA acts as a trusted third party issuing certificates to users. Certificate repositories store certificates so that applications can retrieve them on behalf of users. The term repository refers to a network service that allows for distribution of certificates. The repository is supported by a directory service such as LDAP (Lightweight Directory Access Protocol), or the ITU-T X.509 Directory.

Cross-certification

Cross-certification extends third-party trust relationships between Certification Authority domains. For example, two trading partners, each with their own CA, may want to validate certificates issued by the other partner's CA. Alternatively, a large, distributed organization may require multiple CAs in various geographic regions. Cross-certification allows different CA domains to establish and maintain trustworthy electronic relationships.

Once again, our discussions are a brief summary of Curry's paper, and *www.entrust.com* has the full document. This site also has several other documents on the subject.

ISAKMP, ISAKMP DOI, AND IKE

IPSec is concerned with using established security associations (SAs) to exchange secure traffic through tunnels. IPSec assumes the SAs have been established before IPSec packets are exchanged. Obviously, there must be some means of setting up SAs between the communicating parties (called nodes or peers). This latter operation is the responsibility of the Internet Security Association and Key Management Protocol (ISAKMP) and the Internet Key Exchange Protocol (IKE).

These protocols define the mechanisms (procedures and packets) to establish, delete, modify and negotiate SAs, and key establishment within a Domain of Interpretation (DOI). The basic idea is to define the IPSec DOI to define what to negotiate, which instantiates ISAKMP for use between two security peers, and then use IKE to define the actual key exchange.

Of course, the messages that are exchanged across a communications system must be protected. So these RFCs define procedures to protect the ISAKMP and IKE messages as well. Strong authentication is required for message exchanges; Digital Signatures must be part of the authentication functions, but a certificate authority is not mandated.

ISAKMP

ISAKMP was developed at the National Security Agency (NSA). It defines the procedures to establish, negotiate, modify, and delete SAs. It does not define the procedures for how the key exchange itself occurs. This latter operation is defined in IKE, discussed in the next chapter. In essence, ISAKMP is a security association management protocol, and provides a framework for SA management, independent of the key generation, encryption, and authentication mechanisms. It is also independent of (and supportive of) the various protocols in the Internet layered model protocol stack.

THE "PROTECTION SUITE"

Figure 10–1 shows the relationships of ISAKMP and the conventional Internet protocol layers. ISAKMP runs on top of the Internet L_4 (TCP/UDP). An important idea behind this protocol suite is the notion that the end user is provided with a coherent implementation set of security services, based on the "protection suite" shown in the figure.

The "Socket Layer" is not a layer per se, but the software that allows the applications and ISAKMP to interact with L_4. The security protocol consists of an entity at a point in the network stack, performing a security service for network communication. IPSec ESP and IPSec AH are security protocols. TLS is another example.

The DOI describes a broad set of security services that are specific to an organizational entity, such as a company, a government agency, etc. The Internet defines an Internet DOI, but an organization may define its own. The DOI includes all security policies, keys, and cryptographic algorithms. The ISAKMP DOI is described later in this chapter.

The Key Exchange Definition defines the method(s) of exchanging keys, such as RSA, Diffie-Hellman, etc., and defined by the IKE in RFC 1409.

The API (applications programming interface) defines the interface between the Security Protocol and ISAKMP. The API is not part of ISAKMP or the security protocols, but is published in separate Internet specifications.

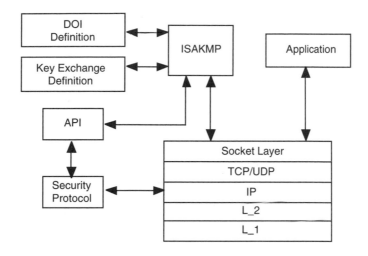

Where:
DOI   Domain of Interpretation
API   Applications Programming Interface

Figure 10–1   The protection suite

Other Thoughts on Key Exchange

A few more thoughts are pertinent to the public key discussion in relation to Internet security, as stipulated in RFC 2408. Key exchanges may be authenticated during or after the protocol exchange completion. Authentication of the key exchange during the protocol exchange is provided when each party provides proof it has the secret session key before the end of the protocol exchange. Proof can be provided by encrypting known data in the secret session key during the protocol exchange. Authentication after the protocol must occur in subsequent communications. Authentication during the protocol is preferred so subsequent communications are not initiated if the secret session key is not established with the desired party.

A key exchange provides symmetry if either party can initiate the exchange and exchanged messages can cross in transit without affecting the key that is generated. This approach is desirable so that computation of the keys does not require either party to know who initiated the exchange. While key exchange symmetry is desirable, symmetry in the entire key management protocol may provide a vulnerablity to reflection attacks.

ISAKMP NEGOTIATION PHASES

ISAKMP handshakes (a negotiation) between two ISAKMP nodes take place in two phases.

- *Phase One:* ISAKMP nodes agree on how to protect further negotiation traffic between themselves, by establishing an ISAKMP SA. The SA is used to protect the subsequent negotiations of the requested SA. The ISAKMP SAs are separate from other SAs
- *Phase Two:* ISAKMP establishes SAs for other security protocols, such as IPSec. The result of phase two is the ability of the IPSec to protect the traffic that is associated with its SA.

The ISAKMP SA is identified by two cookie fields in the header of the negotiation message, and the user-specific SA is identified by two other fields: the message ID and the SPI. The cookie fields and the message ID are used to identify the state of the negotiation process. ISAKMP operations begin with the exchange of cookies, which are 8-byte pseudo-random numbers. Each cookie is unique to the remote ISAKMP peer and a specific exchange.

Cookies in ISAKMP are used to guarantee uniqueness and prevent packet replay. Typically, the cookie is calculated by a hash function on the peer's IP address, a port and protocol number, a secret of the generator and a timestamp.

It is a good idea to complete the exchange of cookies before other exchanges occur, such as Diffie-Hellman in order to protect against a clogging attack. For example, Mallory might generate a spate of bogus ISAKMP messages with false return addresses. It would have little effect because the second message that contains the bogus cookie (bogus address) would not be accepted.

Table 10–1 shows six entries that describe which of these four fields are used during the negotiation. Entries 1 and 2 of this table are associated with phase one and entries 3–6 are associated with phase two. An "X" entry means the field is required, the "NA" means not applicable, and "O" means optional.

The events are associated with these fields in the following manner:

- *Event 1:* ISAKMP initiator places the initiator cookie (I-cookie) in the header of the transmitted message (other fields are optional [O]).

Table 10–1 Basic Negotiation Fields in the ISAKMP Messages

Event	Operation	I-Cookie	R-Cookie	Message ID	SPI
1	Start ISAKMP SA negotiation	X	0	0	0
2	Respond to SA negotiation	X	X	0	0
3	Initiate other SA negotiation	X	X	X	X
4	Respond to other SA negotiation	X	X	X	X
5	Other (KE, ID, etc.)	X	X	X/0	NA
6	Security Protocol (ESP, AH)	NA	NA	NA	X

- *Event 2:* Responder places the four fields in the response message (two are optional).
- *Event 3:* Initiator places the message ID and the SPI in the header of the transmitted message to identify each security protocol and SA for the session.
- *Event 4:* The responder sends back this information to the initiator.
- *Event 5:* The message ID field is used to keep track of the ongoing negotiation. The SPI field is not applicable during this event, because the Proposal Payload (a set of fields in the message, discussed shortly) is used only in events 3 and 4.
- *Event 6:* This event completes the negotiation. The SPI is used to identify the security services for this session.

Messages

This section explains the ISAKMP messages, and should help fill-in the gaps in the understanding of this protocol. An ISAKMP message consists of the chaining together of payload fields to the header. The chaining operation permits the construction of modular messages with different payload types. The specifc types are identified by the exchange type field in the ISAKMP header. Figure 10–2 shows the format for the header. The fields in the header perform the following functions:

- *Initiator Cookie:* Cookie of entity that initiated SA establishment, SA notification, or SA deletion.
- *Responder Cookie:* Cookie of entity that is responding to an SA establishment request, SA notification, or SA deletion.

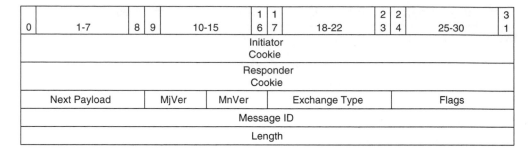

0	1-7	8	9	10-15	16	17	18-22	23	24	25-30	31
Initiator Cookie											
Responder Cookie											
Next Payload		MjVer		MnVer		Exchange Type			Flags		
Message ID											
Length											

Figure 10–2   The ISAKMP Header

- *Next Payload:* Type of the first payload in the message. The next payload types and their associated code values are shown in Table 10–2.
- *Major Version (MjVer):* Indicates the major version of the ISAKMP protocol in use.
- *Minor Version (MnVer):* Indicates the minor version of the ISAKMP protocol in use.

Table 10–2   ISAKMP Payload Types

Next Payload Type	Value
NONE	0
Security Association (SA)	1
Proposal (P)	2
Transform (T)	3
Key Exchange (KE)	4
Identification (ID)	5
Certificate (CERT)	6
Certificate Request (CR)	7
Hash (HASH)	8
Signature (SIG)	9
Nonce (NONCE)	10
Notification (N)	11
Delete (D)	12
Vendor ID (VID)	13
Reserved	14–127
Private Use	128–255

- *Exchange Type:* Type of exchange being used, which determines the message and payload orderings in the ISAKMP exchanges. The exchange types and their associated code values are shown in Table 10–3, and are explained later in this chapter.
- *Flags:* Identifies several options for the ISAKMP exchange. An encryption (E) bit is set to indicate all payload following the header is encrypted according to the algorithm defined in the ISAKMP SA (identified by the initiator and responder cookie). A commit (C) bit is used to ensure that the SA establishment is complete before encrypted material is exchanged. An authentication (A) bit allows the sending of information that is authenticated but not encrypted.
- *Message ID:* Unique message identifier to identify message.
- *Length:* The length of total message (header + payloads).

The Generic Header

Following the header just described is a generic payload header, shown in Figure 10–3. This header preceeds the payload. ISAKMP defines 13 different payloads, discussed next. The fields in this header perform the following functions.

Table 10–3   ISAKMP Exchange Types

Exchange Type	Value
NONE	0
Base	1
Identity protection	2
Authentication only	3
Aggressive	4
Informational	5
ISAKMP future use	6–31
DOI specific use	32–239
Private use	240–255

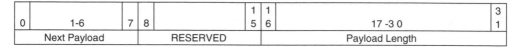

0	1-6	7	8		1 5	1 6	17 -3 0	3 1
	Next Payload			RESERVED			Payload Length	

Figure 10–3   The generic payload header

- *Next Payload:* Identifier for the payload type of the next payload in the message. This field provides a "chaining" capability: a payload can define another payload, which can define yet another payload, and so on. This approach provides a flexible, modular way to select appropriate "pieces" of security information to convey to a peer security node. Some of the payloads are dependent upon each other, and examples are cited shortly.
- *RESERVED:* Unused, set to 0.
- *Payload Length:* Length of the current payload, including the generic payload header.

Data Attributes

There are several instances within ISAKMP where it is necessary to represent data attributes. An example of this is the security association attributes contained in the transform payload. These data attributes are not an ISAKMP payload, but are contained within ISAKMP payloads. The format (not shown here) of data attributes provides the flexibility for representation of many different types of information. There can be multiple data attributes within a payload.

The Payloads

ISAKMP defines the following payloads, each of which is described in this part of the chapter:

- Security association payload
- Proposal payload
- Transform payload
- Key exchange payload
- Identification payload
- Certificate payload
- Certificate request payload
- Hash payload

- Signature payload
- Nonce payload
- Notification payload
- Delete payload
- Vendor ID payload

Some of these payloads are inter-dependent. For example, a transform payload is chained with a proposal payload.

Security Association Payload. This payload defines the SA, both for ISAKMP and other protocols such as IPSec, and indicates the DOI. It is used to negotiate the security attributes in relation to a DOI. Its contents are shown in Figure 10–4, and the fields in the payload perform the following functions.

- *Next Payload:* Identifier for the payload type of the next payload in the message.
- *RESERVED:* Unused, set to 0.
- *Payload Length:* Length in octets of the entire security association payload, including the SA payload.
- *Domain of Interpretation:* Identifies the DOI under which this negotiation is taking place, explained later in the chapter.
- *Situation:* A DOI-specific field that identifies the situation under which this negotiation is taking place.

Proposal Payload. This payload contains information used to negotiate the SA. Each proposal payload contains an SPI, and ensures the SPI is associated with the protocol ID. The proposal payload provides the initiating entity with the capability to present to the responding entity the security protocols and associated security mechanisms for use with the security association being negotiated. Figure 10–5 shows the format

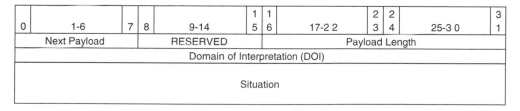

Figure 10–4   Security association (SA) payload

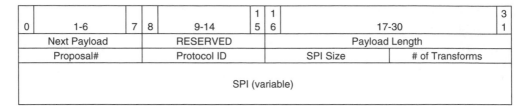

0	1-6	7	8	9-14	1 5	1 6	17-30	3 1
Next Payload				RESERVED			Payload Length	
Proposal#				Protocol ID			SPI Size	# of Transforms
SPI (variable)								

Figure 10–5   Proposal payload

for the proposal payload. The fields in the payload perform the following functions.

- *Next Payload:* Identifier for the payload type of the next payload in the message.
- *RESERVED:* Unused, set to 0.
- *Payload Length:* Length in octets of the entire proposal payload, including the proposal payload.
- *Proposal#:* Identifies the proposal number for the current payload.
- *Protocol ID:* Specifies the protocol identifier for the current negotiation. Examples include IPSec ESP and IPSec AH.
- *SPI Size:* Length of the SPI.
- *# of Transforms:* Specifies the number of transforms for the proposal. Each of these is contained in a transform payload, discussed shortly.
- *SPI:* The sending entity's SPI.

Transform Payload.   This payload contains the security mechanisms to be used with the designated protocol. See Figure 10–6. The payload provides the initiating entity with the capability to present to the responding entity multiple mechanisms or transforms for a given procedure. Each transform payload contains a set of attributes that are

0	1-6	7	8	9-14	1 5	1 6	17-30	3 1
Next Payload				RESERVED			Payload Length	
Transform #				Transform ID			RESERVED2	
SA Attributes								

Figure 10–6   Transform payload

pertinent to the transform, such as an encryption algorithm and shows the format for this payload. The fields in the payload perform the following functions.

- *Next Payload:* Identifier for the payload type of the next payload in the message.
- *RESERVED:* Unused, set to 0.
- *Payload Length:* Length of the current payload, including the generic payload header, transform values, and all SA attributes.
- *Transform #:* Identifies the transform number for the current payload. If there is more than one transform proposed for a specific protocol within the proposal payload, then each transform payload has a unique transform number.
- *Transform ID:* Specifies the transform identifier for the protocol within the current proposal. These transforms are defined by the DOI and are dependent on the protocol being negotiated.
- *RESERVED2:* Unused, set to 0.
- *SA Attributes:* Contains the security association attributes as defined for the transform given in the transform-ID field. The SA Attributes are represented using the data attributes format described earlier.

Key Exchange Payload.   The key exchange payload is used to support selected key exchange techniques such as Diffie-Hellman, RSA, Oakley, etc. Figure 10–7 shows the format for this payload, and the fields in the payload perform the following functions.

- *Next Payload:* Identifier for the payload type of the next payload in the message.
- *RESERVED:* Unused, set to 0.
- *Payload Length:* Length of the current payload, including the generic payload header.

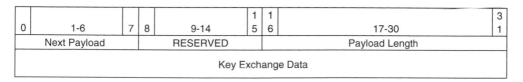

0	1-6	7	8	9-14	1 5	1 6	17-30	3 1
	Next Payload			RESERVED			Payload Length	
				Key Exchange Data				

Figure 10–7   The key exchange payload

- *Key Exchange Data:* Data required to generate a session key. The interpretation of this data is specified by the DOI and the associated key exchange algorithm.

Identification Payload.   The identification payload contains DOI-specific data used to exchange identification information. This information is used for determining the identities of communicating peers and may be used for determining authenticity of information. Figure 10–8 shows the format of the identification payload, and the fields in the payload perform the following functions.

- *Next Payload:* Identifier for the payload type of the next payload in the message.
- *RESERVED:* Unused, set to 0.
- *Payload Length:* Length of the current payload, including the generic payload header.
- *ID Type:* Specifies the type of identification being used.
- *DOI Specific:* Contains DOI-specific identification data.
- *Identification Data:* Contains identity information. The values for this field are DOI-specific.

Certificate Request Payload.   The certificate request payload provides a means to request certificates via ISAKMP. Certificate request payloads are included in an exchange whenever an appropriate directory service is not available to distribute certificates. The responder to the certificate request payload sends its certificate, if certificates are supported, based on the values contained in the payload. If multiple certificates are required, then multiple certificate request payloads are transmitted. Figure 10–9 shows the format of this payload. The fields in this payload perform the following functions.

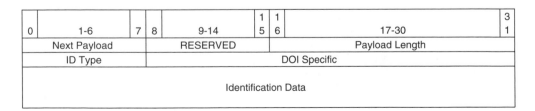

Figure 10–8   Identification payload

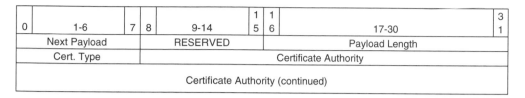

0	1-6	7	8	9-14	1 5	1 6	17-30	3 1
Next Payload			RESERVED			Payload Length		
Cert. Type			Certificate Authority					
Certificate Authority (continued)								

Figure 10–9   The certificate request payload

- *Next Payload:* Identifier for the payload type of the next payload in the message.
- *RESERVED:* Unused, set to 0.
- *Payload Length:* Length of the current payload, including the generic payload header.
- *Certificate (Cert.) Type:* Contains an encoding of the type of certificate requested, and available values are explained later.
- *Certificate Authority:* Contains an encoding of an acceptable certificate authority (such as Entrust) for the type of certificate requested. As an example, for an X.509 certificate this field would contain the X.500 Distinguished Name encoding of the Issuer Name of an X.509 certificate authority acceptable to the sender of this payload.

Certificate Payload.   The certificate payload provides a means to transport certificates or other certificate-related information via ISAKMP and can appear in any ISAKMP message. The certificate payload must be accepted at any point during an exchange. Figure 10–10 shows the format of this payload. The fields in the payload perform the following functions.

- *Next Payload:* Identifier for the payload type of the next payload in the message. If the current payload is the last in the message, then this field will be 0.
- *RESERVED:* Unused, set to 0.

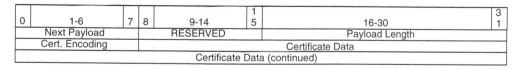

0	1-6	7	8	9-14	1 5	16-30	3 1
Next Payload			RESERVED		Payload Length		
Cert. Encoding			Certificate Data				
Certificate Data (continued)							

Figure 10–10   The certificate payload

- *Payload Length:* Length of the current payload, including the generic payload header.
- *Certificate (Cert.) Encoding:* This field indicates the type of certificate or certificate-related information contained in the Certificate Data field. As examples, it may contain a PGP certificate, a DSN signed key, an X.509 certificate, etc.
- *Certificate Data:* Actual encoding of certificate data. The type of certificate is indicated by the Certificate Encoding field.

Hash Payload. The hash payload contains data generated by the hash function (selected during the SA establishment exchange), over some part of the message and/or ISAKMP state. This payload may be used to verify the integrity of the data in an ISAKMP message or for authentication of the negotiating entities. Figure 10–11 shows the format of the hash payload, and the fields in the payload perform the following functions.

- *Next Payload:* Identifier for the payload type of the next payload in the message.
- *RESERVED:* Unused, set to 0.
- *Payload Length:* Length of the current payload, including the generic payload header.
- *Hash Data:* Data that results from applying the hash routine to the ISAKMP message and/or state.

Signature Payload. The signature payload contains data generated by the Digital Signature function (selected during the SA establishment exchange), over some part of the message and/or ISAKMP state. This payload is used to verify the integrity of the data in the ISAKMP message, and may be of use for non-repudiation services. Figure 10–12 shows the format of the signature payload.

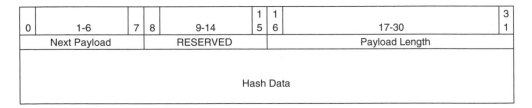

0	1-6	7	8	9-14	1 5	1 6	17-30	3 1
Next Payload			RESERVED			Payload Length		
Hash Data								

Figure 10–11   Hash payload

Figure 10–12 Signature payload

- *Next Payload:* Identifier for the payload type of the next payload in the message. If the current payload is the last in the message, then this field will be 0.
- *RESERVED:* Unused, set to 0.
- *Payload Length:* Length in octets of the current payload, including the generic payload header.
- *Signature Data:* Data that results from applying the Digital Signature function to the ISAKMP message and/or state.

Nonce Payload.   The nonce payload contains pseudo-random data used to guarantee liveness during an exchange and protect against replay attacks. Figure 10–13 shows the format of the nonce payload. If nonces are used by a particular key exchange, the use of the nonce payload will be dictated by the key exchange.

The nonce payload fields perform the following functions.

- *Next Payload:* Identifier for the payload type of the next payload in the message. If the current payload is the last in the message, then this field will be 0.
- *RESERVED:* Unused, set to 0.

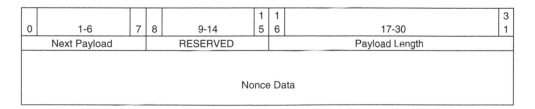

Figure 10–13 Nonce payload format

- *Payload Length:* Length in octets of the current payload, including the generic payload header.
- *Nonce Data:* Contains the random data generated by the transmitting entity.

Notification Payload.   The notification payload can contain both ISAKMP and DOI-specific data and is used to transmit informational data, such as error conditions. Figure 10–14 shows the format of the notification payload.

Notification, which occurs during or is concerned with a Phase-one negotiation, is identified by the initiator and responder cookie pair in the ISAKMP Header. The protocol identifier, in this case, is ISAKMP and the SPI value is 0 because the cookie pair in the ISAKMP header identifies the ISAKMP SA. If the notification takes place prior to the completed exchange of keying information, then the notification will be unprotected.

Notification, which occurs during or is concerned with a Phase-two negotiation, is identified by the initiator and responder cookie pair in the ISAKMP Header and the message ID and SPI associated with the current negotiation. One example for this type of notification is to indicate why a proposal was rejected.

The notification payload fields perform the following functions:

- *Next Payload:* Identifier for the payload type of the next payload in the message. If the current payload is the last in the message, then this field will be 0.
- *RESERVED:* Unused, set to 0.
- *Payload Length:* Length in octets of the current payload, including the generic payload header.

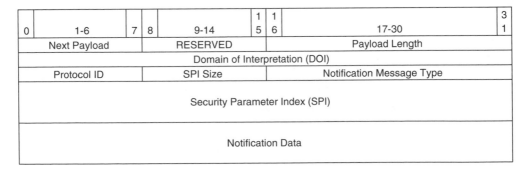

0	1-6	7	8	9-14	1 5	1 6	17-30	3 1
Next Payload			RESERVED			Payload Length		
Domain of Interpretation (DOI)								
Protocol ID			SPI Size			Notification Message Type		
Security Parameter Index (SPI)								
Notification Data								

Figure 10–14   Notification payload format

- *Domain of Interpretation:* Identifies the DOI under which this notification is taking place. For ISAKMP this value is 0 and for the IPSec DOI it is 1.
- *Protocol ID:* Specifies the protocol identifier for the current notification. Examples might include ISAKMP, IPSec ESP, IPSec AH, OSPF, TLS, etc.
- *SPI Size:* Length in octets of the SPI as defined by the Protocol-ID.
- *Notification Message Type:* Specifies the type of notification message. Additional text, if specified by the DOI, is placed in the Notification Data field.
- *SPI:* Security Parameter Index.
- *Notification Data:* Informational or error data transmitted in addition to the Notification Message Type.

Notification Message Types. Notification information can be error messages specifying why an SA could not be established. It can also be status data that a process managing an SA database wishes to communicate with a peer process. RFC 2408 (Section 3.14.1) explains these diagnostics, if you wish more detail.

Delete Payload. The delete payload contains a protocol-specific security association identifier that the sender has removed from its security association database and is, therefore, no longer valid. Figure 10–15 shows the format of the delete payload. It is possible to send multiple SPIs in a delete payload, however, each SPI must be for the same protocol. Mixing of protocol identifiers are not performed with the delete payload.

The delete payload fields are defined as follows:

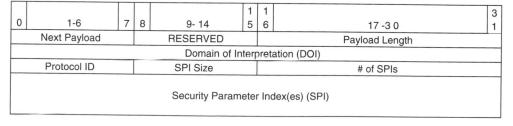

Figure 10–15   Delete payload format

- *Next Payload:* Identifier for the payload type of the next payload in the message. If the current payload is the last in the message, then this field will be 0.
- *RESERVED:* Unused, set to 0.
- *Payload Length:* Length in octets of the current payload, including the generic payload header.
- *Domain of Interpretation:* Identifies the DOI under which this deletion is taking place.
- *Protocol ID:* ISAKMP can establish security associations for various protocols, including ISAKMP and IPSec. This field identifies which security association database to apply the delete request.
- *SPI Size:* Length in octets of the SPI as defined by the Protocol-ID. In the case of ISAKMP, the initiator and responder cookie pair is the ISAKMP SPI.
- *# of SPIs:* The number of SPIs contained in the delete payload.
- *Security Parameter Index(es):* Identifies the specific security association(s) to delete. Values for this field are DOI and protocol specific.

Vendor ID Payload.   The vendor ID payload contains a vendor-defined constant. The constant is used by vendors to identify and recognize remote instances of their implementations. This mechanism allows a vendor to experiment with new features while maintaining backwards compatibility. This is not a general extension facility of ISAKMP. Figure 10–16 shows the format of the vendor ID payload.

The vendor ID Payload fields are defined as follows:

- *Next Payload:* Identifier for the payload type of the next payload in the message. If the current payload is the last in the message, then this field will be 0.
- *RESERVED:* Unused, set to 0.

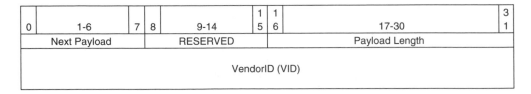

0	1-6	7	8	9-14	1 5	1 6	17-30	3 1
Next Payload			RESERVED			Payload Length		
VendorID (VID)								

Figure 10–16   Vendor ID payload format

- *Payload Length:* Length in octets of the current payload, including the generic payload header.
- *Vendor ID (VID):* Hash of the vendor string plus version (as described above).

OAKLEY and ISAKMP

The OAKLEY specification is described in Chapter 5. The mapping of OAKLEY fields to ISAKMP message structures are described here. All the OAKLEY message fields correspond to ISAKMP message payloads or payload components. The relevant payload fields are the SA payload, the AUTH payload, the certificate payload, the key exchange payload.

Table 10–4 indicates where each OAKLEY field appears in the ISAKMP message structure. These are recommended only, pending final resolution in other working groups.

EXAMPLES OF ISAKMP NEGOTIATIONS

The figures in this section of the chapter are examples [provided in RFC 2408 (Section 4.2)] of the messages exchanged to set up security associations between two machines. The examples are not exhaustive, but should give you a good idea of ISAPMP protocol flow. In all the examples,

Table 10–4   Mapping OAKLEY and ISAKMP Fields

CKY-I	ISAKMP header
CKY-R	ISAKMP header
MSGTYPE	Message Type in ISAKMP header
GRP	SA payload, Proposal section
g^x (or g^y)	Key Exchange payload, encoded as a variable precision integer
EHAO and EHAS	SA payload, Proposal section
IDP	A bit in the RESERVED field in the AUTH header
ID(I)	AUTH payload, Identity field
ID(R)	AUTH payload, Identity field
Ni	AUTH payload, Nonce Field
Nr	AUTH payload, Nonce Field
S{...}Kx	AUTH payload, Data Field
prf{K,...}	AUTH payload, Data Field

"HDR" means the header discussed earlier in this chapter. The abbreviations in the figures mean the following:

- *HDR:* An ISAKMP header containing the exchange type that defines the payload orderings.
- *SA:* An SA negotiation payload containing one or more proposal and transform payloads.
- *KE:* The key exchange payload.
- *Idx:* The identity payload for x. x can be: ii or ir for the ISAKMP initiator and responder, respectively, or x can be: ui, ur (when the ISAKMP daemon is a proxy negotiator), for the user initiator and responder, respectively.
- *HASH:* The hash payload.
- *SIG:* The signature payload.
- *AUTH:* A generic authentication mechanism, such as HASH or SIG.
- *NONCE:* The Nonce payload.
- *"*":* Signifies payload encryption after the ISAKMP header.
- *N/D:* A notify or delete payload

The Base Exchange

This exchange supports the key exchange and authentication information. The events making up this exchange are shown in Figure 10–17, and are summarized here:

- *Event 1:* The initiator begins the ISAKMP-SA negotiation by generating a proposal appropriate for protecting user traffic. The SA

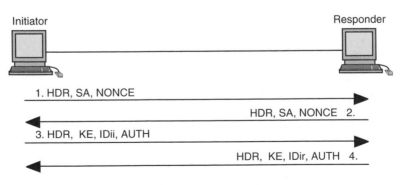

Figure 10–17   Base exchange

payload contains the SA, proposal and transform information, and the nonce payload is included to protect against replay attacks.

- *Event 2:* The responder sends back the SA, proposal, and transform payload (and Nonce), which conveys to the initiator that the basic SA has been accepted.
- *Events 3 and 4:* Initiator and responder exchange keying material used to arrive at a common shared secret and identification information. This information is transmitted under the protection of the agreed upon authentication function. The result is the establishment of the SA.

The Identity Protection Exchange

This exchange separates the key exchange information from the identity and authentication related information, in order to provide protection of the communicating identities. The identities are exchanged through the protection of a previously shared secret. The message exchanges are depicted in Figure 10–18, and are summarized here.

- *Event 1:* The initiator begins the ISAKMP-SA negotiation by generating a proposal appropriate for protecting user traffic. The SA payload contains SA, proposal and transform information, and the Nonce Payload is included to protect against replay attacks.
- *Event 2:* The responder indicates to the initiator the protection suite it has accepted.

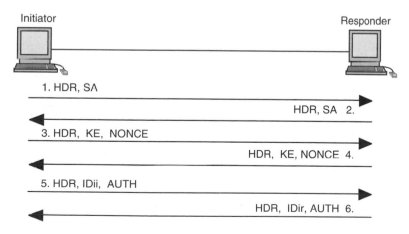

Figure 10–18   Identity protection exchange

- *Events 3 and 4:* The initiator and responder generate the key and exchange the keying material used for a shared common secret.
- *Events 5 and 6:* The initiator and responder exchange protected identification and the results of the agreed-upon authentication function. They have now verified identifiers.

Authentication Only Exchange

This exchange allows only authentication information to be exchanged between two security nodes if encryption services are not needed. No transmitted information is protected with this exchange. Figure 10–19 depicts the messages that are exchanged with this procedure, and these events are summarized here.

- *Event 1:* The initiator begins the ISAKMP-SA negotiation by generating a proposal appropriate for protecting user traffic. The SA payload contains SA, proposal and transform information, and the nonce payload is included to protect against replay attacks.
- *Event 2:* The responder indicates to the initiator the protection suite it has accepted. The responder also transmits identification information. This information is transmitted under the protection of the agreed upon authentication function.
- *Event 3:* The initiator sends its identification information, which is transmitted under the protection of the established authentication function.

The Aggressive Exchange

In order to reduce the number of messages exchanged to set up an SA, the aggressive exchange allows the security association, key ex-

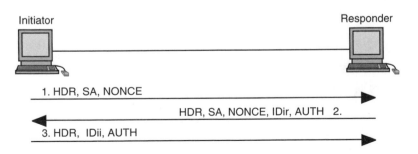

Figure 10–19   Authentication only exchange

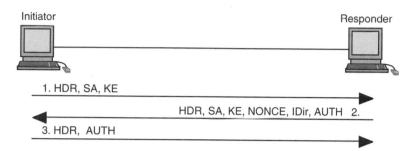

Figure 10–20   Aggressive exchange

change, and authentication payloads to be sent in one message. The trade-off of reducing the number of messages transmitted is that identity is not protected. Figure 10–20 depicts the messages that are exchanged with this procedure, and the message exchange events are summarized here.

- *Event 1:* The initiator begins the SAKMP-SA negotiation by generating a proposal appropriate for protecting user traffic. The SA payload contains SA, proposal and transform information.
- *Event 2:* The responder indicates to the initiator the protection suite it has accepted, including keying material used to arrive at a common agreement as well as shared secret and random information which is used to protect against replay attack.
- *Event 3:* The initiator sends the results of the agreed upon authentication function, which is protected by the common shared secret.

ISAKMP DOMAIN OF INTERPRETATION (DOI)

The ISAKMP Domain of Interpretation (DOI) is published as RFC 2407 [PIPE98],[2] and this section provides an overview of of ISAKMP DOI as defined in this RFC. A DOI defines payload formats, exchange types, and conventions for naming security-relevant information such as security policies or cryptographic algorithms and modes. A DOI identifier is used to interpret the payloads of ISAKMP payloads.

---

[2][PIPE98]. Piper, D. "The Internet IP Security Domain of Interpretation for ISAKMP," RFC 2407, November, 1998.

A DOI defines:

- *Situation:* A set of information that identifies the security services to be provided to an ISAKMP user.
- *Syntax:* A specific syntax for the proposed security services.
- *Naming:* A specific scheme for naming and identifying the security information, including CAs, security policy attributes, and key exchange algorithms.

Since ISAKMP is concerned with SAs, then SAs must be part of security and key management. ISAKMP then provides the protocol to establish and manage the SA in the following manner. A basic set of security attributes is negotiated to protect ISAKMP exchanges (including the authentication and key exchange that will be part of the ISAKMP protocol). These initial exchanges can be skipped if a set of security attributes is already in place. Anyway, after the set has been agreed upon, the established SA is used for subsequent entity that invoked ISAKMP.

IPSec/ISAKMP PAYLOADS

This section describes the IPSec/ISAKMP payloads: (a) the security association payload and (b) the identification payload. Figure 10–21 shows the security association payload. The fields in the payload perform

0	1-6	7	8	9-14	1 5	1 6	17-30	3 1
Next Payload			RESERVED				Payload Length	
Domain Interpretation (IP Sec)								
Situation (bitmap)								
Labeled Domain Identifier								
Secrecy Length (in octets)						RESERVED		
Secrecy Level								
Secrecy Cat Length (in bits)						RESERVED		
Secrecy Category Bitmap								
Integrity Length (in octets)						RESERVED		
Integrity Level								
Integ. Cat. Length (in bits)						RESERVED		
Interity Category Bitmap								

Figure 10–21   The Security Association Payload Format

the following functions (all reserved fields are set to 0 and all lengths are in octets):

- *Next Payload:* Identifies payload type of next payload in the message.
- *Payload Length:* Length of current payload, including generic header.
- *Domain of Interpretation:* Specifies the IPSec DOI, which has been assigned the value 1.
- *Situation:* Used to interpret the remainder of the security association payload. A situation (a set of information) is the basis for deciding how to protect a communications channel (published or unpublished encryption algorithms, for example). Both parties must understand the situation in order to establish a secure tunnel between them. The situation field is DOI-specific.
- *Labeled Domain Identifier:* IANA assigned number used to interpret the secrecy and integrity information.
- *Secrecy Level:* Specifies the mandatory secrecy level required.
- *Secrecy Category Length:* Length of the secrecy category (compartment) bitmap.
- *Secrecy Category Bitmap:* Used to designate secrecy categories (compartments) that are required.
- *Integrity Length:* Length of the integrity level identifier.
- *Integrity Level:* Specifies the mandatory integrity level required.
- *Integrity Category Length:* Length of the integrity category (compartment) bitmap.
- *Integrity Category Bitmap:* Used to designate integrity categories (compartments) that are required.

Figure 10–22 shows the format for the identification payload, which is used to identify the initiator of the security association. The receiver of this message uses the information to determine the correct host security policy for the association. As an example, the SA might stipulate that certain IP addresses, Protocol ID, and port numbers require authentication, and others need no authentication. The fields perform the following functions:

- *Next Payload:* Identifier for the payload type of the next payload in the message.
- *RESERVED:* Unused, set to 0.

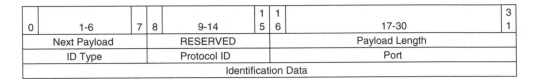

0	1-6	7	8	9-14	1 5	1 6	17-30	3 1
Next Payload			RESERVED			Payload Length		
ID Type			Protocol ID			Port		
Identification Data								

Figure 10–22   Identification payload format

- *Payload Length:* Length of the identification data, including the generic header.
- *Identification Type:* Value describing the identity information found in the Identification data field.
- *Protocol ID:* Value specifying an associated IP protocol ID (e.g., UDP/TCP). A value of 0 means that the Protocol ID field should be ignored.
- *Port:* Value specifying an associated port. A value of 0 means that the port field should be ignored.
- *Identification Data:* Value, as indicated by the identification type which is coded in accordance with the entries in Table 10–5. The next part of this section describes the identification type values.

Table 10–5   Identification Type Values

ID Type		Value
RESERVED	0	
ID_IPV4_ADDR	1	IPv4 address
ID_FQDN	2	Fully qualified domain name
ID_USER_FQDN	3	Fully qualified user name
ID_IPV4_ADDR_SUBNET	4	Range of IPv4 addresses and mask
ID_IPV6_ADDR	5	IPv6 address
ID_IPV6_ADDR_SUBNET	6	Range of IPv6 addresses and mask
ID_IPV4_ADDR_RANGE	7	Beginning and ending address range
ID_IPV6_ADDR_RANGE	8	Beginning and ending address range
ID_DER_ASN1_DN	9	X.500 Distinguished Name
ID_DER_ASN1_GN	10	X.500 General Name
ID_KEY_ID	11	Opaque byte stream (vendor-specific)

Table 10–6   Identification of Type Values

Protocol ID	Value
RESERVED	0
PROTO_ISAKMP	1
PROTO_IPSEC_AH	2
PROTO_IPSEC_ESP	3
PROTO_IPCOMP	4

Identification Type Values.   As the name implies, this field in the payload identifies the Internet reserved number for identifying operations, procedures or protocols.

Table 10–6 lists the values for the security protocol identifiers referenced in an ISAKMP proposal payload for the IPSEC DOI.

As part of an ISAKMP Phase I negotiation, the initiator's choice of key exchange offerings is made using some host system policy description. The actual selection of key exchange mechanism is made using the standard ISAKMP proposal payload. This list is the defined ISAKMP Phase I Transform Identifiers for the proposal payload for the IPSEC DOI.

Transform	*Value*
RESERVED	0
KEY_IKE	1

The authentication header protocol (AH) defines one mandatory and several optional transforms used to provide authentication, integrity, and replay detection. Table 10–7 lists the defined AH transform identifiers for the ISAKMP proposal payload for the IPSEC DOI.

The Encapsulating Security Payload (ESP) defines one mandatory and many optional transforms used to provide data confidentiality. Table

Table 10–7   AH Transforms

Transform ID	Value
RESERVED	0–1
AH_MD5	2
AH_SHA	3
AH_DES	4

Table 10–8   ESP Transforms

Transform ID	Value
RESERVED	0
ESP_DES_IV64	1
ESP_DES	2
ESP_3DES	3
ESP_RC5	4
ESP_IDEA	5
ESP_CAST	6
ESP_BLOWFISH	7
ESP_3IDEA	8
ESP_DES_IV32	9
ESP_RC4	10
ESP_NULL	11

10–8 lists the defined ESP transform identifiers for the ISAKMP proposal payload for the IPSEC DOI.

SUMMARY

ISAKMP defines the procedures to establish, negotiate, modify, and delete SAs, but does not define the procedures for how the key exchange itself occurs. This latter operation is defined in IKE. ISAKMP is a security association management protocol, and provides a framework for SA management, independent of the key generation, encryption, and authentication mechanisms.

11

Internet Key Exchange (IKE)

This chapter continues the discussion started in Chapter 10 about key exchange procedures. The focus is the Internet Key Exchange (IKE), published in RFC 2409. The approach to the examination of IKE is to highlight its major features and show examples of the IKE protocol flow between the two nodes to set up keys. The chapter concludes with an examination of two public key infrastructure (PKI) organizations, Entrust and VeriSign.

IKE BASICS

IKE describes a protocol using parts of (a) OAKLEY and (b) SKEME in conjunction with ISAKMP to exchange authenticated keying material between two parties, and to set up security associations such as AH and ESP for the IPSec DOI. Its purpose is to negotiate, and provide authenticated keying material for security associations (SAs) in a protected manner. IKE is generic enough to be used to define SAs other than those for IPSec. The SA that is established depends on the specific Domain of Interpretation (DOI). Currently there are DOIs for IPSec, RIPV2, and OSPF.

IKE is closely related to ISAKMP and uses the two phases of ISAKMP which were explained in Chapter 10. For IKE, the phases are:

- Phase one: Establishes the IKE security association
- Phase two: Uses the IKE security association to then negotiate an SA for IPSec, or another protocol

IKE defines two phase-one exchanges, one phase-two exchange and two "special" exchanges. Phase one relies on the identity protect and aggressive exchanges in ISAKMP and calls them main mode and aggressive mode, respectively. The full IKE exchanges are as follows:

- Phase-one exchange
    main mode
    aggressive mode
- Phase-two exchange
    quick mode
- Informational exchange
- New group exchange

As discussed in Chapter 10, IKE combines parts of OAKLEY and parts of SKEME with ISAKMP, to negotiate, and derive keying material for security associations in a secure and authenticated manner. Confidentiality is assured by the use of a negotiated encryption algorithm. Authentication is assured by the use of a negotiated method: a Digital Signature algorithm; a public key algorithm which supports encryption, or a pre-shared key.

DEFINITIONS

IKE is an extensive and complex protocol. Before we begin the analysis of its rules and procedures, several definitions of terms are needed, and listed below. These terms are fields or procedures used by IKE.

- *HDR:* An ISAKMP header whose exchange type is the mode. When written as HDR* it indicates payload encryption.
- *SA:* An SA negotiation payload with one or more proposals. An initiator may provide multiple proposals for negotiation; a responder replies with only one.

- *<P>_b:* Indicates the body of payload <P>—the ISAKMP generic payload is not included.
- *SAi_b:* The entire body of the SA payload (minus the ISAKMP generic header). That is, the DOI, situation, all proposals and all transforms offered by the initiator.
- *CKY-I* and *CKY-R:* The initiator's cookie and the responder's cookie, respectively, from the ISAKMP header.
- *g^xi* and *g^xr:* The Diffie-Hellman (DH) public values of the initiator and responder respectively.
- *g^xy:* The Diffie-Hellman shared secret.
- *KE:* The key exchange payload which contains the public information exchanged in a Diffie-Hellman exchange.
- *Nx:* The nonce payload; *x* can be: i or r for the ISAKMP initiator and responder, respectively.
- *IDx:* The identification payload for *x*. *x* can be: ii or ir for the ISAKMP initiator and responder, respectively, during phase-one negotiation; or ui or ur for the user initiator and responder, respectively, during phase two.
- *SIG:* The signature payload. The data to sign is exchange-specific.
- *CERT:* The certificate payload.
- *HASH:* (And any derivative such as HASH(2) or HASH_I) is the hash payload. The contents of the hash are specific to the authentication method.
- *prf(key, msg):* The keyed pseudo-random function—often a keyed hash function—used to generate a deterministic output that appears pseudo-random. The prfs are used both for key derivations and for authentication (i.e., as a keyed MAC).
- *SKEYID:* A string derived from secret material known only to the active players in the exchange.
- *SKEYID_e:* The keying material used by the ISAKMP SA to protect the confidentiality of its messages.
- *SKEYID_a:* The keying material used by the ISAKMP SA to authenticate its messages.
- *SKEYID_d:* The keying material used to derive keys for non-ISAKMP security associations.
- *<x>y:* Indicates that *x* is encrypted with the key *y*.
- *|:* Signifies concatenation of information—e.g., X | Y is the concatenation of X with Y.
- *[x]:* Indicates that x is optional.

PERFECT FORWARD SECRECY

Perfect Forward Secrecy (PFS) of both keying material and identities is provided by IKE. By specifying a Diffie-Hellman group, and passing public values in KE payloads, ISAKMP peers can establish PFS of keys. The identities are protected by SKEYID_e from the ISAKMP SA and therefore are not protected by PFS.

ASPECTS OF IKE AND ISAKMP

The following attributes are used by IKE and are negotiated as part of the ISAKMP security association: (a) encryption algorithm, (b) hash algorithm, (c) authentication method, (d) information about a Diffie-Hellman group.

MODES TO ESTABLISH AUTHENTICATED KEY EXCHANGE

As explained earlier, IKE defines two phase-one methods to establish an authenticated key exchange: main mode and aggressive mode. Each mode generates authenticated keying material from a Diffie-Hellman exchange. Main mode is required and aggressive mode is recommended.

In addition, the phase-two quick mode is implemented as a mechanism to generate fresh keying material and negotiate non-ISAKMP security services. Moreover, new group mode is recommended in RFC 1409 to be implemented as a mechanism to define private groups for Diffie-Hellman exchanges. Implementations are not supposed to switch exchange types in the middle of a key exchange operation.

All exchanges conform to standard ISAKMP payload syntax, attribute encoding, timeouts and retransmits of messages, and informational messages described in Chapter 10. The SA payload precedes all other payloads in a phase-one exchange.

Main mode and aggressive mode are both phase-one exchanges and are used to setup the IKE security association. Therefore, any other exchanges can take place only after the successful completion of one of these phases.

Main Mode

Main mode is an instantiation of the ISAKMP identity protect exchange and consists of the exchange of six messages. As shown later, the first two messages negotiate policy; the next two exchange Diffie-Hellman public values and ancillary data (e.g., nonces) necessary for the exchange; and the last two messages authenticate the Diffie-Hellman exchange.

Aggressive Mode

Aggressive mode is an instantiation of the ISAKMP aggressive exchange and consists of the exchange of three messages. The first two messages negotiate policy, exchange Diffie-Hellman public values and ancillary data necessary for the exchange. In addition, the second message authenticates the responder. The third message authenticates the initiator and provides a proof of participation in the exchange.

Security association negotiation is limited with aggressive mode. For example, the group in which the Diffie-Hellman exchange is performed cannot be negotiated. In addition, different authentication methods may further constrain attribute negotiation. If these restrictions are not acceptable, then main mode should be used.

Quick Mode and New Group Mode

Quick mode and new group mode have no corollary in ISAKMP. Main mode, aggressive mode, and quick mode perform security association negotiations. Security association offers take the form of transform payload(s) encapsulated in proposal payload(s) encapsulated in SA payload(s).

Four Methods Used with Main or Aggressive Mode

Four different authentication methods are used with main mode or aggressive mode: (a) a Digital Signature, (b and c) two forms of authentication with public key encryption, or (d) a pre-shared key. The value SKEYID is computed separately for each authentication method, and is therefore dependent upon each method, as shown below.

- For signatures: SKEYID = prf(Ni_b | Nr_b, g^xy)
- For public key encryption: SKEYID = prf(hash(Ni_b | Nr_b), CKY-I | CKY-R)
- For pre-shared keys: SKEYID = prf(pre-shared-key, Ni_b | Nr_b)

The result of either main mode or aggressive mode is three groups of authenticated keying material:

SKEYID_d = prf(SKEYID, g^xy | CKY-I | CKY-R | 0)
SKEYID_a = prf(SKEYID, SKEYID_d | g^xy | CKY-I | CKY-R | 1)
SKEYID_e = prf(SKEYID, SKEYID_a | g^xy | CKY-I | CKY-R | 2)

To authenticate phase-one exchanges, the initiator of the protocol generates HASH_I and the responder generates HASH_R. Recall that the hash function is very difficult to break and it is computationally infeasible to determine the input to the hash from its output. Therefore, the hash is used to authenticate each peer. The hashes for this operation are computed as follows:

HASH_I = prf(SKEYID, g^xi | g^xr | CKY-I | CKY-R | SAi_b | IDii_b)
HASH_R = prf(SKEYID, g^xr | g^xi | CKY-R | CKY-I | SAi_b | IDir_b)

For authentication with Digital Signatures, HASH_I and HASH_R are signed and verified; for authentication with either public key encryption or pre-shared keys, HASH_I and HASH_R directly authenticate the exchange. The entire ID payload (including ID type port, and protocol but excluding the generic header) is hashed into both HASH_I and HASH_R.

EXAMPLES OF IKE MESSAGE EXCHANGES

This section of the chapter provides examples of IKE message exchanges. Section 5 of RFC 2409 defines the following operations, and we examine them in the order shown below. I show selected examples of these operations and the RFC has considerably more details and several more examples, if you need them.

- Phase one: authenticated with signatures
- Phase one: authenticated with public key encryption
- Phase one: authenticated with a revised mode of public key encryption
- Phase one: authenticated with a pre-shared key

- Phase two: quick mode
- New group mode

Phase One: Authenticated with Signatures

As depicted in Figure 11–1, using signatures, the ancillary information exchanged during the second roundtrip are nonces; the exchange is authenticated by signing a mutually obtainable hash.

In events 1 and 2, the two peers negotiate the IKE SA and decide on the other parts of the exchange. Like ISAKMP, these events require that both parties place their cookies in the cookie field of the header.

In events 3 and 4, the peers exchange Diffie-Hellman keys (KE, which was set up in events 1 and 2), and pseudo-random nonces (Ni and Nr). Now, the peers can complete the Diffie-Hellman exchange, and protect their messages in events 5 and 6.

In events 5 and 6, the encrypted (by SKEYID_e) authenticating information is exchanged. SIG_I and SIG_R represent the signed data and are the result of the negotiated Digital Signature algorithm applied to HASH_I and HASH_R, respectively. IDii and IDir are the identifications of the payloads. As the [....] shows, the [CERT,] is the optional certificate for the exchange.

In Figure 11–2, aggressive mode with signatures in conjunction with ISAKMP is shown. Notice that half the number of messages are exchanged as main mode. The trade off is that in the aggressive mode there is a limitation on negotiation since the initiator must provide the Diffie-Helman

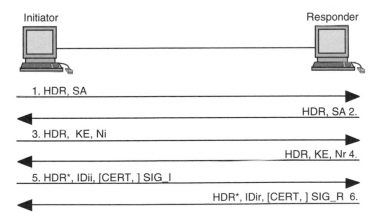

Figure 11–1   Phase one authenticated with signatures, main mode

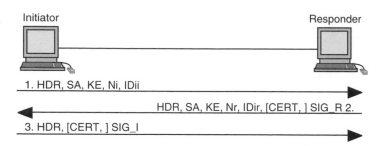

Figure 11-2 Phase one authenticated with signatures, main mode

value and the nonce in the first message. Therefore, the initiator cannot offer different Diffie-Hellman groups in different protection suites.

However, aggressive mode may be the only way to establish the IKE SA. For example, in a remote access dial-up situation, the address of the initiator is not known to the responder initially. In addition, if the initiator already knows about the responder, the aggressive mode is a more efficient exchange than the main mode.

In both modes, the signed data, SIG_I or SIG_R, is the result of the negotiated Digital Signature algorithm applied to HASH_I or HASH_R, respectively.

Phase One: Authenticated with Public Key Encryption

Using public key encryption to authenticate the exchange, the ancillary information exchanged between the peers is encrypted nonces. Each party's ability to reconstruct a hash (proving that the other party decrypted the nonce) authenticates the exchange. This operation requires that the initiator of the exchange must have the responder's public key.

If the responder has multiple public keys, a hash of the certificate the initiator is using to encrypt the ancillary information is passed as part of the third message. In this way the responder can determine which corresponding private key to use to decrypt the encrypted payloads and identity protection is retained. In addition to the nonce, the identities of the parties (IDii and IDir) are also encrypted with the other party's public key.

Figures 11-3 and 11-4 show main mode and aggressive mode respectively for phase one: authenticated with public key encryption. HASH(1) is a hash (using the negotiated hash function) of the certificate which the initiator is using to encrypt the nonce and identity. Unlike other authentication methods, authentication with public key encryption allows for identity protection with aggressive mode.

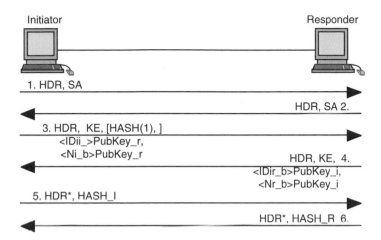

Figure 11–3   Phase one authenticated with public key encryption, main mode

In events 2 and 3, the identification payloads (IDii and IDir) and the nonces (Ni_b and Nr_b) are encrypted with each peer's public keys. The IDii and IDir are needed so each peer can use the appropriate public key for its response.

Phase One: Authenticated with a Revised Mode of Public Key Encryption

Authentication with public key encryption has advantages over authentication with signatures, but the operation entails four public key operations, two for encryption and two for decryption. The authentication

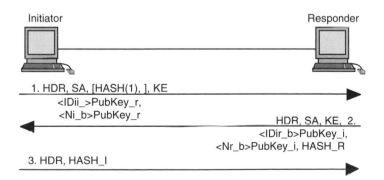

Figure 11–4   Phase one authenticated with public key encryption, aggressive mode

mode explained in this section retains the advantages of authentication
using public key encryption but uses only half the public key operations.

The nonce is still encrypted using the public key of the peer, however the peer's identity (and the certificate if it is sent) is encrypted using
the negotiated symmetric encryption algorithm (from the SA payload)
with a key derived from the nonce.

As with the public key encryption method of authentication, a
HASH payload may be sent to identify a certificate if the responder has
multiple certificates which contain a useable public key (e.g., if the certificate is not for signatures only, either due to certificate restrictions or
algorithmic restrictions). If the HASH payload is sent it is to be the first
payload of the second message exchange and is followed by the encrypted
nonce. If the HASH payload is not sent, the first payload of the second
message exchange is the encrypted nonce. In addition, the initiator may
optionally send a certificate payload to provide the responder with a public key with which to respond. Figure 11–5 shows this operation for main
mode (aggressive mode is not shown, and is available in RFC 2409).

HASH(1) is identical to its functions described earlier. Ke_i and
Ke_r are keys to the symmetric encryption algorithm negotiated in the
SA payload exchange. Only the body of the payloads are encrypted (in
both public key and symmetric operations), the generic payload headers

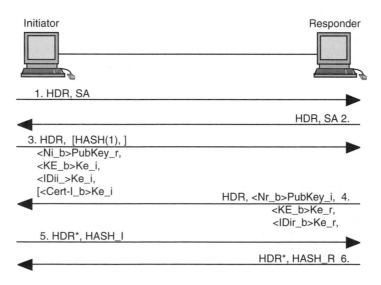

**Figure 11–5   Phase one with a revised mode of public key
encryption**

are left in the clear. The payload length includes that added to perform encryption.

Phase One: Authenticated With a Pre-Shared Key

When using pre-shared key authentication with main mode the key can only be identified by the IP address of the peers since HASH_I must be computed before the initiator has processed IDir. Aggressive mode allows for a wider range of identifiers of the pre-shared secret to be used. In addition, aggressive mode allows two parties to maintain multiple, different pre-shared keys and identify the correct one for a particular exchange.

Phase Two: Quick Mode

Quick mode is not a complete exchange itself. After main mode or aggressive mode is used to establish the IKE SA, quick mode can then be used to set up an IPSec SA. It is protected by the IKE SA, which was established (earlier).

The quick mode messages are authenticated with the prf (key, msg) function. The SKEYID is used to authenticate the message.

The information exchanged along with quick mode is protected by the ISAKMP SA—i.e., all payloads except the ISAKMP header are encrypted. In quick mode, a HASH payload immediately follows the ISAKMP header and an SA payload must immediately follow the HASH. This HASH authenticates the message and also provides liveliness proofs.

New Group Mode

New group mode is not to be used prior to establishment of an ISAKMP SA. The description of a new group only follows phase 1 negotiation. Figure 11–6 shows the exchange for this mode. This exchange is protected by the IKE SA. It allows peers to negotiate private groups, and a group identifier (for later use).

HASH(1) is the prf output, using SKEYID_a as the key, and the message-ID from the ISAKMP header concatenated with the entire SA proposal, body and header, as the data; HASH(2) is the prf output, using SKEYID_a as the key, and the message-ID from the ISAKMP header concatenated with the reply as the data. In other words, the hashes for the above exchange are:

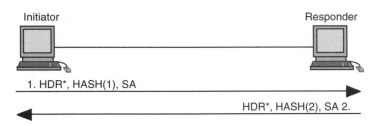

Figure 11–6   New group mode

$$HASH(1) = prf(SKEYID\_a, M\text{-}ID \mid SA)$$
$$HASH(2) = prf(SKEYID\_a, M\text{-}ID \mid SA)$$

ISAKMP Informational Exchanges

This protocol protects ISAKMP Informational Exchanges when possible. Once the ISAKMP security association has been established (and SKEYID_e and SKEYID_a have been generated), it is used by IKE peers to exchange status and error messages with each other.

OAKLEY GROUPS

With IKE, the group in which to do the Diffie-Hellman exchange is negotiated. Four groups—values 1 through 4—are defined. These groups originated with the OAKLEY protocol and are therefore called "OAKLEY Groups." The attribute class for "Group" is defined in Appendix A of RFC 2409.

MESSAGES FOR A COMPLETE IKE EXCHANGE

This section shows the messages exchanged to establish a secure channel between ISAKMP processes and generate key material, and then negotiate an IPSec SA. Figure 11–7 shows the payload exchanged between the two parties during the first round trip exchange, using main mode. The responder replies in kind but selects, and returns, one transform proposal (the ISAKMP SA attributes).

The second exchange consists of payloads in Figure 11–8(a) and (b). The shared keys, SKEYID_e and SKEYID_a, are now used to protect and authenticate all further communication. Note that both SKEYID_e and SKEYID_a are unauthenticated. The key exchange is authenticated over a signed hash. Once the signature has been verified using the authenti-

0	1-6	7	8		1 6	1 7	18-30	3 1
ISAKMP header with XCHG of main mode, and next payload of ISA_SA								
0		RESERVED				Payload length		
Domain of interpretation								
Situation								
0		RESERVED				Payload length		
Proposal #1		PROTO_ISAKMP			SPI size =0		# Transforms	
ISA_TRANS		RESERVED			Payload length			
Transform #1		KEY_OAKLEY			RESERVED2			
Preferred SA attributes								
0		RESERVED				Payload length		
Transform #2		KEY_OAKLEY			RESERVED2			
Alternate SA attributes								

Figure 11–7   The first exchange

cation algorithm negotiated as part of the ISAKMP SA, the shared keys, SKEYID_e and SKEYID_a can be marked as authenticated. In this example, certificate payloads are not exchanged.

Phase Two Using Quick Mode

The payloads in Figures 11–9(a) and (b) are exchanged in the first round of quick mode with ISAKMP SA negotiation. In this hypothetical exchange, the ISAKMP negotiators are proxies for other parties which have requested authentication.

The contents of the hash arc described in Figure 11–9(a). The responder replies with a similar message which only contains one transform—the selected AH transform. Upon receipt, the initiator can provide the key engine with the negotiated security association and the keying material. As a check against replay attacks, the responder waits until receipt of the message shown in Figure 11–9(b).

IPSEC, NAT, AND IKE

Previous chapters discussed IPSec, and Chapter 9 explains how IPSec and NAT are used at an IPSec node to provide both IPSec and NAT support, as defined in RFC 2709. This part of the chapter extends this discussion to the role of IKE in these operations.

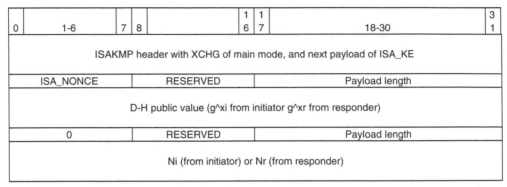

(a) Second exchange

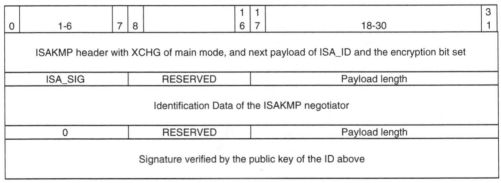

(b) Second exchange, continued

Figure 11–8   The second exchange (shared keys)

Figure 11–10 shows IKE operations with the IPC-NAT gateway. RFC 2709 does not require the IKE packets to be subjected to NAT processing. The IKE-ALG simply translates select portions of IKE payload as per the NAT map defined for the policy match.

Policies in quick mode are exchanged with a peer as a combination of IDci and IDcr payloads. The combination of IDs (policies) exchanged by each peer must match in order for the SA parameters on either end to be applied uniformly. If the IDs are not exchanged, the assumption would be that the quick mode negotiated SA parameters are applicable between the IP addresses assumed by the main mode.

Depending on the nature of security policies in place (e.g., end-to-end sessions between a pair of nodes vs. sessions with an address range),

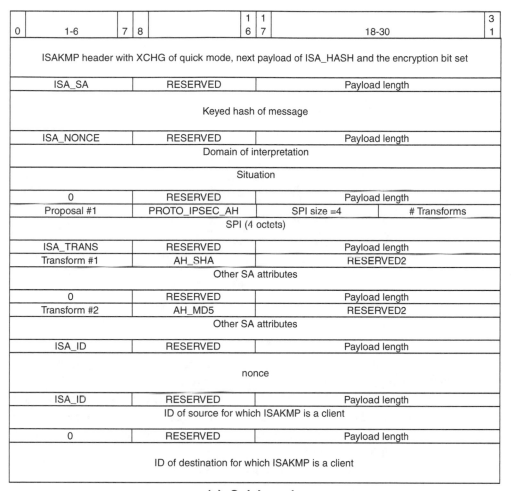

0	1-6	7	8		1 6	1 7	18-30	3 1
ISAKMP header with XCHG of quick mode, next payload of ISA_HASH and the encryption bit set							
ISA_SA		RESERVED		Payload length		
Keyed hash of message							
ISA_NONCE		RESERVED		Payload length		
Domain of interpretation							
Situation							
0		RESERVED		Payload length		
Proposal #1		PROTO_IPSEC_AH		SPI size =4		# Transforms	
SPI (4 octets)							
ISA_TRANS		RESERVED		Payload length		
Transform #1		AH_SHA		RESERVED2		
Other SA attributes							
0		RESERVED		Payload length		
Transform #2		AH_MD5		RESERVED2		
Other SA attributes							
ISA_ID		RESERVED		Payload length		
nonce							
ISA_ID		RESERVED		Payload length		
ID of source for which ISAKMP is a client							
0		RESERVED		Payload length		
ID of destination for which ISAKMP is a client							

(a) Quick mode

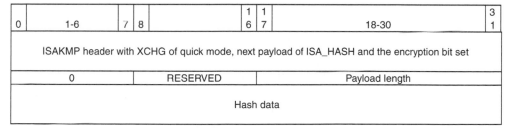

0	1-6	7	8		1 6	1 7	18-30	3 1
ISAKMP header with XCHG of quick mode, next payload of ISA_HASH and the encryption bit set							
0		RESERVED		Payload length		
Hash data							

(b) Quick mode, continued

Figure 11–9   Phase Two using quick mode

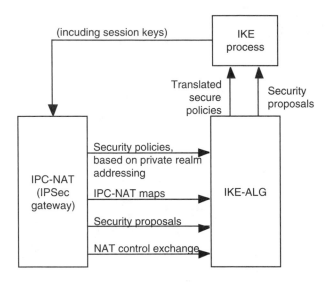

Figure 11–10   IKE-ALG translation of security policies, using NAT maps (RFC 2709)

IKE-ALG may need to request NAT to set up address bindings and/or transport bindings for the lifetime the sessions are negotiated. In the case where the ALG is unable to setup the necessary address bindings or transport bindings, IKE-ALG will not be able to translate security policies and that will result in IKE not pursuing phase-two negotiation for the effected policies.

When the negotiation is complete and successful, IKE will communicate the negotiated security parameters directly to the IPC-NAT gateway engine as described in Figure 11–10.

A NAT device that provides tunnel-mode IPSec security is required to administer security policies based on private realm addressing, and the security policies determine the IPSec tunnel end-point peer. As a result, a packet may be required to undergo different types of NAT translation depending upon the peer tunnel end-point. That is, IPC-NAT will need a unique set of NAT maps for each security policy configured. IPC-NAT will perform address translation in conjunction with IPSec processing differently with each peer, based on security policies. Figures 9–20 and 9–21 (in Chapter 9) depict the operation of IPSec tunneling in conjunction with NAT.

Operation of an IPC-NAT device may be distinguished from that of an IPSec gateway that does not support NAT as follows.

- IPC-NAT device has security policies administered using private realm addressing. A traditional IPSec gateway has its security policies administered using a single realm addressing.
- Elements fundamental to the security model of an IPC-NAT device includes IPC-NAT address mapping (and other NAT parameter definitions) in conjunction with security policies and SA attributes. Fundamental elements of a traditional IPSec gateway are limited only to security policies and SA attributes.

Traditional NAT is session oriented, allowing outbound-only sessions to be translated. All other flavors of NAT are bi-directional. Any and all flavors of NAT mapping may be used in conjunction with the security policies and secure processing on an IPC-NAT device.

However, a NAT device capable of providing security across IPSec tunnels can continue to support Normal-NAT for packets that do not require IPC-NAT. Address mapping and other NAT parameter definitions for Normal-NAT and IPC-NAT are distinct.

EXAMPLES OF PKI VENDORS

Entrust and VeriSign are two prominent companies that offer PKI products. Their approach is different in that Entrust offers a product that is purchased, installed, and maintained by a customer. VeriSign offers a full PKI service to a customer, in a sense an outsourced PKI service. This difference is important to a customer, and fortunately, these two alternatives are available. The Entrust approach is sometimes called "best-of-breed," in that security support is at the control of the customer. VeriSign offers a Web-based approach. One approach is appropriate for one company, but may not be appropriate for another one. For a detailed analysis of the cost-benefits of Entrust and VeriSign, I refer you to [MACH98],[1] from which I quote:

> The stark contrast between these two visions of managing security appeared again and again in our interviews. Entrust customers share a concern for best-of-breed security solutions that are under their control and managed by them. VeriSign's customers were content with the Web's de facto security model, as

---

[1][MACH98]. Machefsky, Ira. "A Total Economic Impact Analysis of Two PKI Vendors: Entrust and VeriSign," A White Paper from Giga Information Group, One Longwater Circle, Norwell, MA 02061.

being built by the browser vendors and VeriSign. In fact, they believe that only a general trust utility can achieve the global scale required for trust on the Web. As one of them put it: "VeriSign is a visionary. They have a public utility that works. They are a single, focused company. It takes a public utility to make a global impact." It is this faith in the public utility of trust that is being built on the Web, in contrast to a totally controlled best-of-breed security solution, that gives them the confidence to outsource their security management and trust model to VeriSign.

It seems that this position is as much a starting point as a conclusion with the customers we interviewed. It is a premise on the basis of which they make their decisions, a part of the enterprise's cultural DNA, rather than a conclusion they come to. It is tempered, we believe, by some of the flexibility they find, especially in the VeriSign solution (more on this topic in the "Flexibility" section). VeriSign's users seem to be taking more of an experimental and wait and see approach to the PKI. This makes them more willing to rent one and try it out rather than building a solution of their own. Entrust's customers seem to know exactly what they want, what they will do with it, and move aggressively to implement it.

We will have to see whether time and experience will modify these starkly opposed positions and allow movement from one side to the other of this security divide. However, even Entrust's most ardent supporters see the occasional use for VeriSign's trust model as a bootstrapping process to their own PKI. In order to use Entrust's managed PKI, special desktop software must be downloaded to the client. How can this be done in a trusted manner? One of Entrust's customers uses an SSL-enabled Web server using VeriSign server certificates for this purpose. Once the Entrust client software is installed, the Entrust PKI is established and supercedes the VeriSign PKI.

SUMMARY

IKE is an extension of ISAKMP. It is used to exchange authenticated keying material between two parties, and to set up security associations such as AH and ESP for the IPSec DOI. IKE is generic enough to be used to define SAs other than those for IPSec. The SA that is established depends on the specific domain of interpretation (DOI).

12

Security Operations in a Mobile Network

This chapter examines IS-41-C, a protocol that operates on the network side of North American mobile and wireless networks. The chapter begins with a description of the architecture of IS-41-C, followed by a description of its security services, principally with authenticating the mobile station user.

For the air interface operations in this chapter, I use IS-54-B examples, unless otherwise stated. Other air interfaces, such as IS-136, and IS-95, use similar procedures. Note that IS-41-C uses the following conventions: (a) a message shown in all upper case letters is a request message; (b) a message in all lower case letters is a response message.

THE IS-41-C SPECIFICATION

IS-41-C is published by the Telecommunications Industry Association (TIA). It permits the interworking of different vendor equipment (by placing the IS-41-C protocol suite in each vendor's product). IS-41-C was published originally in February, 1988, as Revision A. It has since undergone revisions A, B, and now C. With each revision, it has become more powerful and versatile. With the current release, it now supports the AMPS, IS-54-B, IS-136, and IS-95 air interfaces.

THE IS-41-C MODEL

IS-41-C exhibits a topology and model that is quite similar to GSM. Figure 12–1 depicts the functional entities of IS-41-C and the associated interfaces (reference points) between the functional entities. This figure represents a conceptual model only and a piece of physical equipment may have several functional entities and reference points internal to the equipment. That being the case, these components are not required to adhere to the IS-41-C standard.

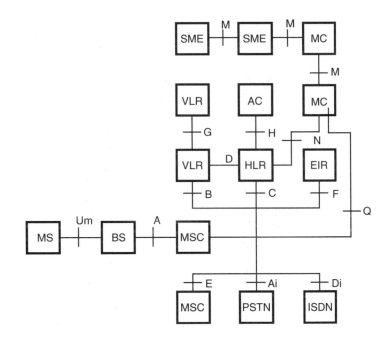

Where:

AC	Access control
BS	Base station
CSS	Cellular subscriber station
EIR	Equipment identity register
HLR	Home location register
ISDN	Integrated services digital network
MC	Message center
MSC	Mobile switching center
PSTN	Public switched telephone network
SME	Short message entity
VLR	Visitor location register

Figure 12–1   IS-41-C entities and reference points

The terms in this figure are listed at the bottom of the figure. The reference points in Figure 12–1 labeled Um, A, B, etc., are used to describe the interfaces and procedures (protocols) between the IS-41-C entities, such as mobile switching centers (MSCs). This chapter concentrates on the B, C, E, H, and Um interfaces. The A interface is not defined in IS-41-C.

THE FIVE SECURITY/PRIVACY OPERATIONS

The next sections of this chapter explain the operations employed by IS-41-C to support authentication and privacy operations. These operations have two key goals: (a) give the network assurance that the user's identifiers (and the user's account) are not being used by someone else (which could lead to incorrect billing to the user), and (b) ensure that the user's voice conversation or data transfer is not being "listened to" by an unauthorized party.

To make certain that a user is actually the valid user, IS-41-C defines five procedures for the authentication of the mobile station. Remember that IS-41-C is used for all the North American air interfaces, and the authentication operations are basically the same for all these interfaces. Some minor differences exist but are not significant enough to single out in this discussion.

The authentication operations entail the exchange of information between the network and the mobile station to ensure that the mobile station user is who the user *claims* to be. The idea is to use a shared secret key, called the SSD (for shared secret data), that is known only to the network and the mobile station. A successful authentication means the mobile station and the network: (a) have identical copies of the SSD stored in their internal memories, and (b) use the SSD to generate other values that are exchanged to verify (authenticate) the identity of the mobile station and the network, and encrypt the voice or data traffic.

This part of the chapter explains the five authentication and privacy operations used by IS-41-C in the order listed below. Each operation is described with (a) an explanation of the security and authentication parameters used, (b) examples of air side operations, and (c) examples of network side operations.

- Authentication of mobile station registration procedures
- Unique challenge-response procedures
- Authentication of mobile station originating a call

- Authentication of a call to a terminating mobile station
- Updating the shared secret data (SSD)

Authentication Parameters

Before we examine the five operations, let us take a look at the parameters that are used in the authentication operations. Refer to Figure 12–2. I mentioned the SSD parameter earlier. It is a 128-bit value stored in the mobile station and network. It is divided into two parts: SSD-A and SSD-B, as shown in Figure 12–2(a). SSD-A is used for authentication

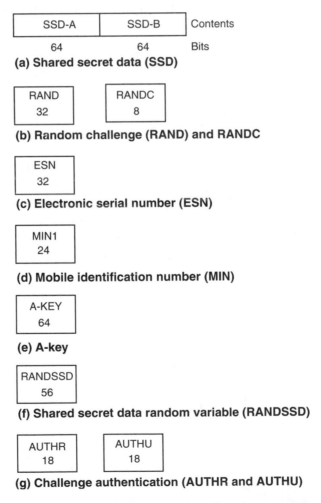

(a) Shared secret data (SSD)

(b) Random challenge (RAND) and RANDC

(c) Electronic serial number (ESN)

(d) Mobile identification number (MIN)

(e) A-key

(f) Shared secret data random variable (RANDSSD)

(g) Challenge authentication (AUTHR and AUTHU)

Figure 12–2   Security operations and parameters

procedures and SSD-B is used for encrypting voice traffic and selected messages. Later discussions explain how the SSD is created and managed.

The random challenge (RAND) variable shown in Figure 12–2(b) is a 32-bit random number that is issued periodically (broadcasted) by the network in two 16-bit parts: RAND1_A, and RAND1_B. RANDC is an 8-bit number used to confirm the last RAND received by the mobile station; it is the 8 most significant bits of RAND.

The electronic serial number (ESN) [Figure 12–2(c)] is the hardware identifier of the mobile station handset. The mobile identification number (MIN) [Figure 12–2(d)] is a 34-bit representation of the mobile station's 10-digit directory telephone number.

The A-key is a secret 64-bit value stored only at the mobile station and the authentication center (AC) [Figure12–2(e)]. If an AC does not exist, the key is stored at the user's HLR.

The shared secret data random variable (RANDSSD) [Figure 12–2(f)] is a 56-bit random number generated by the mobile station's home system. The unique challenge authentication response (AUTHR & AUTHU) [Figure 12–2(g)] is an 18-bit value generated by an authentication algorithm.

AUTHENTICATION OF MOBILE STATION REGISTRATION PROCEDURES

The Parameters

Registration Authentication is the first type of authentication operation supported by IS-41-C. The basic concept behind registration authentication is shown in Figure 12–3. Both the network and the handset execute a cellular authentication and voice encryption (CAVE) algorithm to create AUTHR.[1] As input to the CAVE algorithm, the mobile station and network use RAND, ESN, MIN1, and SSD-A. MIN1 is the Nxx-xxx part of the telephone number.

At the Air Interface

Registration operations at the air interface proceed in event 1 of Figure 12–4 by the network sending a Authenticate Directive message with

---

[1]The CAVE is not defined in IS-41-C. It is defined in other TIA specifications.

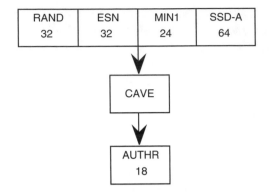

Where:
   AUTHR   Challenge authentication (response)
   CAVE   Cellular authentication and voice encryption
   ESN   Electronic serial number
   MIN   Mobile identification number
   RAND   Random value
   SSD   Shared secret data

Figure   12–3   Computation   of   AUTHR   for   registration challenge

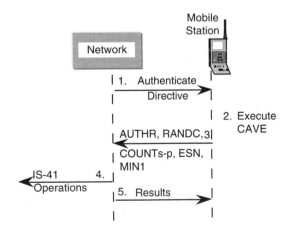

Where:
   AUTHR   Registration authentication key
   CAVE   Cellular authentication and voice encryption
   ESN   Electronic serial number
   MIN   Mobile identification number
   RANDC   Random value (part of RAND)

Figure 12–4   Authentication of mobile station registration on the air side

its contents indicating that the mobile station is to send a computed AUTHR to the network. In event 2, the mobile station executes the CAVE algorithm as shown in the previous figure and sends AUTHR and other parameters to the network, as shown in event 3. A count value (COUNT s-p) is also sent to the network, as is RANDC. The COUNT s-p parameter is explained later. The RANDC is used to confirm the last RAND received. This information is sent in (for IS-54-B) an RECC autonomous registration order message.

In event 4, the registration process is passed through to an authentication center. After the authentication process occurs in event 4, the mobile station is informed of its results (in event 5). The whole purpose of these procedures is to compare the AUTHR computed internally in the network to the value of AUTHR received from the mobile station.

On the Network Side

Figure 12–5 shows the registration authentication operations on the network side. The base station passes the mobile station's parameters to the serving MSC, which issues the IS-41-C AUTHREQ (Authorization Request) message to the VLR to initiate the authentication request operation (event 1). This information is passed to the mobile station's HLR (event 2) and then to authentication control (AC), event 3. The AC compares the received values for RANDC (and optionally COUNT s-p) with internally stored values associated with the received MIN1/ESN. If a match occurs, the AC executes the CAVE algorithm using the SSD-A value it has stored internally, as well as the other values shown for CAVE in Figure 12–3. The result of computation is AUTHR, which is

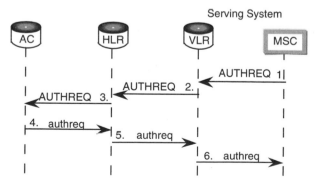

Figure 12–5   Registration authentication operations on the network side

compared to the mobile station's computed AUTHR. This result is returned to the HLR, MSC/VLR in the authreq message, shown in Figure 12–5 as events 4, 5, and 6.

The count value that was introduced earlier (COUNT s-p) is supplied by the mobile station and compared to a count variable at the AC. If they are equal, and the AUTHR values match, the AC accepts the authentication.

Encryption Capabilities.   Two other values can be returned to the mobile station by the AC. The signaling message encryption key (SMEKEY) is used to encrypt messages, and the voice privacy mask (VP-MASK) is used to encrypt voice traffic. The use of encryption capabilities is not a requirement in IS-41-C, nor in any of the air interfaces that are supported by IS-41-C.

UNIQUE CHALLENGE-RESPONSE PROCEDURES

The Parameters

The unique challenge is the second type of authentication supported by IS-41-C. Another parameter is computed for this operation. It is different from the authentication of mobile station registration just described because: (a) the network executes the CAVE algorithm first and sends a challenge (instead of the mobile station executing CAVE first), and (b) if the authentication of mobile station registration operation fails, this operation can be invoked, and (c) the RAND value used in the authentication of the mobile station registration is broadcast to all mobile stations in the cell, and updated periodically by the network. In contrast, the value used in the unique challenge is RANDU, which is 24-bit random pattern generated for a one-time unique challenge to a specific mobile station.

The network generates AUTHU as shown in Figure 12–6. It uses RANDU and the other parameters shown in the figure to compute AUTHU. As explained next, this value is sent to the mobile station as a unique challenge.

At the Air Interface

Figure 12–7 shows the operations for the unique challenge-response procedure for the air interface. It is similar to the authentication of mobile station registration procedure, discussed earlier, with the differences cited in the text associated with the previous figure.

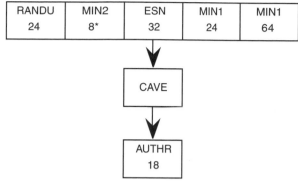

*8 least significant bits of MIN2

Where:
AUTHU   Unique challenge key
CAVE   Cellular authentication and voice encryption
ESN   Electronic serial number
MIN   Mobile identification number
RAND   Random value
SSD   Shared secret data

Figure 12–6   Computation of AUTHU for unique challenge

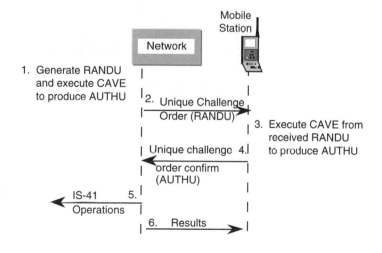

Where:
AUTHU   Unique challenge authentication
CAVE   Cellular authentication and voice encryption
ESN   Electronic serial number
MIN   Mobile identification number

Figure 12–7   Unique challenge-response procedure on the air side

In event 6, the network MSC informs the AC that the directive has been accepted, but not that authentication has been completed. In other words, event 6 is an acknowledgment of the AC operations that led to event 1. This operation is shown in Figure 12–8.

On the Network Side

Figure 12–8 shows the operations for the unique challenge-response procedure on the network side. It is similar to the authentication of mobile station registration procedure, discussed earlier. This example shows that the operation is initiated by the AC. It may also be initiated by the VLR if the VLR and AC are both sharing the SSD.

The parameters used in this operation (and originated by the AC) are: (a) served MS MIN, (b) served MS ESN, (c) RANDU number generated to produce AUTHU, and (d) AUTHU, which is the expected MS response to

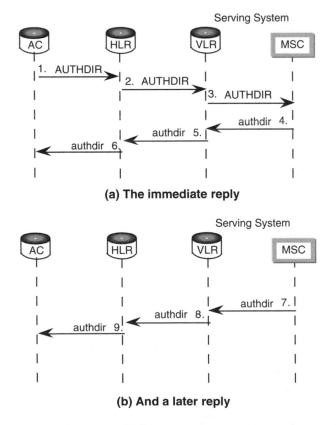

(a) The immediate reply

(b) And a later reply

Figure 12–8   Unique challenge-response procedure on the network side

this challenge. These parameters are passed to the HLR, then the VLR in events 1 and 2. The VLR adds the location area ID (LOCID) to the message, if it is available, then forwards the message to the MSC (in event 3).

In events 4, 5, and 6, an empty authdir message is returned to indicate the directive has been accepted. These operations are shown as event 5 in Figure 12–7. This empty authdir message is sent if the MSC is not able to initiate a unique challenge to the mobile station at this time.

IS-41-C does not explain how the subsequent message transfer occurs. It must be inferred that the MSC does return an authdir message later to indicate success or failure of the authentication.

AUTHENTICATION OF MOBILE STATION ORIGINATING A CALL

The Parameters

The third type of authentication is executed when the mobile station originates a call. For this operation, the mobile station generates AUTHR, as in the registration authentication procedure, described earlier, but the input to CAVE is slightly different; see Figure 12–9. In place of the MIN1 value, the last six digits of the dialed number is used. The mobile station sends AUTHR together with RANDC, and COUNT s-p to the network, and these operations are shown in Figure 12–10.

At the Air Interface

As just explained, when the mobile station is to originate a call, it must generate AUTHR from CAVE, with the input parameters of RAND, ESN, the last six digits of the dialed number, and SSD-A. This information is sent to the network in the authentication word C of the RECC origination message for IS-54-B. Figure 12–10 depicts this operation.

The network uses the received AUTHR to compare it against its own computation of AUTHR, once again using the same input to CAVE as the mobile station. If both computed AUTHRs are equal, channel assignment procedures begin.

On the Network Side

On the network side for call origination authentication, the MSC receives the authentication message from the mobile station. Its job is to compare the received values of RANDC (and optionally the count value) with values stored internally that are associated with the received MIN1/ESN. The network also computes AUTHR with the same input

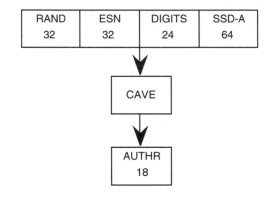

Where:
  AUTHR   Key for call origination
  CAVE   Cellular authentication and voice encryption
  ESN   Electronic serial number
  RAND   Random value
  SSD   Shared secret data

Figure 12–9   Computation of AUTHR for call origination

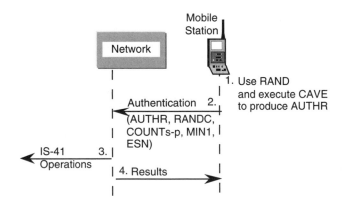

Where:
  AUTHR   Key for call origination
  CAVE   Cellular authentication and voice encryption
  RANDC   (8 most significant bits of RAND)

Figure 12–10   Authentication for call origination on the air side

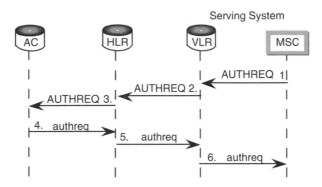

Figure 12–11   Authentication for call origination on the network side

described above, and compares the computed AUTHR with the mobile station's computed AUTHR. If they match, the mobile station is assigned the necessary resources to set up the call, as well as the resources for the originating call itself.

Figure 12–11 shows the operations on the network side for a successful authentication where the SSD is not shared (that is, the mobile station is attempting a call origination on a serving system that is not sharing an SSD with the AC).

The serving MSC sends the AUTHREQ message to the VLR, which contains the AUTHR, and the identity of the called party (the dialed digits). In events 1, 2, and 3, this information is forwarded to the AC, which determines that the mobile station is valid, and sends the authreq reply message back to the HLR, the VLR, and the MSC. This message may also contain a CDMA private long code mask (if the air interface is CDMA). It may also contain SMEKEY, and VPMASK, which were described earlier in this material. The authreq messages are shown in events 4, 5, and 6.

AUTHENTICATION OF CALL TO A TERMINATING MOBILE STATION

The Parameters

The authentication for terminating a call to the mobile station is the fourth type of authentication and is similar to other operations described in this material, but with some variations; see Figure 12–12. First, the

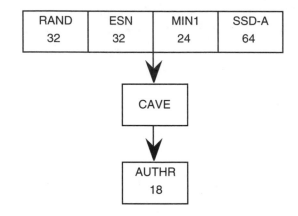

Where:

AUTHR	Key for call termination
CAVE	Cellular authentication and voice encryption
ESN	Electronic serial number
RAND	Random value
SSD	Shared secret data

Figure 12–12   Computation of AUTHR for call termination

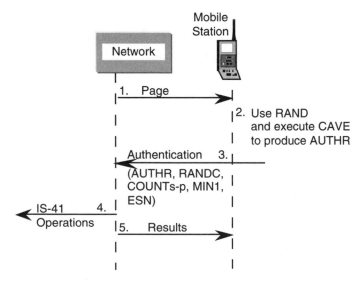

Figure 12–13   Authentication for call termination on the air side

computation of AUTHR is different in call termination than call origination: the MIN1 is used instead of dialed digits. Otherwise, everything else is the same.

At the Air Interface

As illustrated in Figure 12–13, for call termination, the mobile station receives a page message. In an IS-54-B system, this message is conveyed in the system parameter overhead message. The mobile station executes the CAVE algorithm to create AUTHR, and sends this value, along with RANDC, and COUNTs-p to the network in the (for IS-54-B) authentication word C of the RECC page response message.

The network receives this information and compares the received values of RANDC (and optionally COUNT) to those values associated with the MIN1 and ESN that were sent in the message. If the computed AUTHRs are equal, the station is assigned the necessary resources to manage the terminating setup of the call, as well as resources for the call itself.

On the Network Side

The message flow for IS-41-C for a call termination to a mobile station is the same as for call origination, but as just discussed, the AUTHR value is computed by CAVE with different input parameters. Figure 12–14 shows this operation.

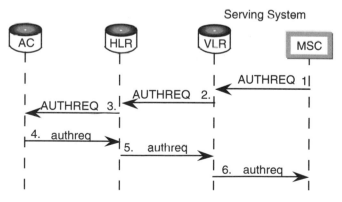

Figure 12–14   Authentication for call termination on the network side

UPDATING THE SHARED SECRET DATA (SSD)

The Parameters

Updating the SSD is the fifth major security/privacy operation defined in IS-41-C. The SSD is generated from a key stored in the handset and at the AC. This key is called the A-key. The SSD is generated using the A-key upon an order from the network. This concept is somewhat similar to the security measures in GSM, except that the North American systems do not define the use of the subscriber interface module (SIM) card. The AC generates a new SSD by executing the CAVE algorithm by using the subscriber's secret A-key, the ESN, and 56-bit RAND, which is called RANDSSD; see Figure 12–15(a).

Another value, called AUTHBS, is used in the SSD update procedures. It is generated with CAVE, and with the input parameters

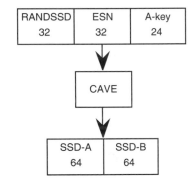

(a) Computation of Shared Secret Data (SSD)

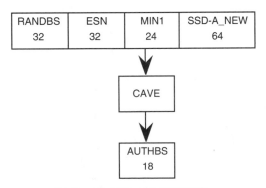

(b) Computation of AUTHBS

Figure 12–15   SSD Computations

RANDBS and SSD-A_NEW. This later value was a result of the calculation in the top figure, which is then used as input to the CAVE calculation in Figure 12–15(b).

At the Air Interface and on the Network Side

Figure 12–16 shows how the SSD values are updated. When the network creates the new SSD, it sends a message to the mobile station directing it to update the SSD by using the RANDSSD, shown as event 1.

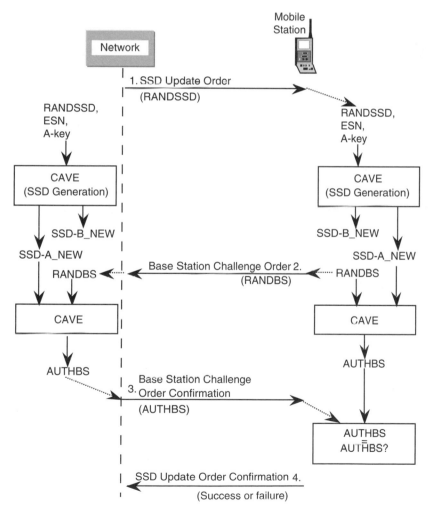

Figure 12–16 The shared secret data (SSD) update operations

In turn, the mobile station generates the new SSD using its secret A-key, the ESN, and the RANDSSD. Next, the mobile station sends to the network a challenge using a 32-bit random number called RANDBS, shown as event 2.

The mobile station generates an 18-bit AUTHBS value by once again executing the CAVE algorithm with input as RANDBS and the new SSD-A. The authentication center also performs the operation by executing CAVE with input of RANDBS and the new SSD-A. After this operation occurs, the network responds to the mobile station with the AUTHBS value, shown as event 3. If the two AUTHBS values match, the handset then accepts the new SSD and responds with an ACK to the network, shown as event 4.

One could ask, why all these operations just to update some security parameters? The answer is that these procedures allow the network to verify the mobile station, *and* they also allow the mobile station to verify the network. After all, the SSN Update Order in event 1 may not be from a legitimate party (the network). So, the mobile station verifies the network by the Base Station Challenge Order message in event 2. The RANDBS value, provided by the mobile station must be used by the network, in conjunction with SSD-A_NEW to compute AUTHBS, which is sent to the mobile station in event 3. The mobile station compares this AUTHBS with its own computed AUTHBS to determine if the network is legitimate.

SUMMARY

IS-41-C uses the information at the air interface to manage the network side of the cellular call. It uses the information from the telephone network to manage the network side of the cellular call. IS-41-C supports both privacy and authentication procedures, but network providers may not offer the privacy services.

13

Follow-ups to This Book

As you have likely surmised after reading this book, Internet security is a vast subject. As I stated in the preface, one goal of this book has been to introduce you to the subject of security in an internet and the Internet, and the protocols employed to obtain security services. One of my biggest challenges in writing this book was choosing what topics I included or did not include.

We only scratched the surface of the subject of Internet security. Several volumes of books can be written on the subject.

The intent of the Prentice Hall Advanced Communications Series (and this book) is to acquaint you with the basic principles, concepts, and ideas of the subject, and point you to more information, if you choose to pursue the subject further.

To that end, I recommend that you follow up on the information provided in this book with a visit to:

- General Discussion: ipsec@lists.tislabs.com
- To Subscribe: ipsec-request@lists.tislabs.com
- Archive: ftp://ftp.tis.com/pub/lists/ipsec or ftp.ans.net/pub/archive/ipsec

You may notice that I am recommending you concentrate on IPSec. I make this recommendation because of the importance this "protocol suite" is assuming in the industry. Notwithstanding, the references below provide information about Internet security specifications other than IPSec.

I have quoted many sources and references in this book, and a bibliography of these sources is included at the back of the book. I call your attention to four books that I recommend highly (and publisher information, etc., is in the bibliography):

- [SING99] Simon Singh, *The Code Book*
- [SMIT98] Michael Smith, *Station X*
- [STAL99] William Stallings, *Cryptography and Network Security*
- [DORA99] Naganand Dorawamy and Dan Harkins, *IPSec: The New Security Standard for the Internet, Intranets, and Virtual Private Networks*

The Internet security specifications (the drafts) are works in progress and some are changing frequently. Notwithstanding, the list of working drafts and RFCs shown below will provide you with essential information for taking your knowledge of Internet security to the next level.

I wish you good fortune (and much tenacity). These specifications make up hundreds of pages of text.

The lists below are from the IPSec Web page (enter IPSec in your general search window). Also, it is an easy task to retrieve these documents. Just go to *www.ietf.org,* and follow the directions.

Drafts:

The ESP Triple DES Transform
ESP with Cipher Block Chaining (CBC)
The ESP DES-XEX3-CBC Transform
The ISAKMP Configuration Method
The Use of HMAC-RIPEMD-160-96 within ESP and AH
A GSS-API Authentication Method for IKE
DHCP Configuration of IPSEC Tunnel Mode
Extended Authentication Within ISAKMP/Oakley (XAUTH)
A Hybrid Authentication Mode for IKE

A Framework for Group Key Management for Multicast Security
A PKIX Profile for IKE
Security Policy Specification Language
Intra-Domain Group Key Management Protocol
Security Policy System
IPSec Monitoring MIB
IPSec DOI Textual Conventions MIB
Policy Framework for IP Security
IPSec Interactions with ECN
ISAKMP & IKE Extensions Methods
IPSec Policy Schema
The Internet Key Exchange (IKE)
The ESP SKIPJACK-CBC Cipher Algorithm With Implicit IV
Additional ECC Groups For IKE
ISAKMP DOI-Independent Monitoring MIB
Content Requirements for ISAKMP Notify Messages
Security Policy Protocol
IKE Base Mode
IKE Monitoring MIB
IPSec Flow Monitoring MIB
Fixing IKE Phase 1 Authentication HASH

Request For Comments (RFCs):

IP Authentication using Keyed MD5 (RFC 1828)
The ESP DES-CBC Transform (RFC 1829)
HMAC: Keyed-Hashing for Message Authentication (RFC 2104)
MD5-HMAC IP Authentication with Replay Prevention (RFC 2085)
Security Architecture for the Internet Protocol (RFC 2401)
The NULL Encryption Algorithm and Its Use With IPSec (RFC 2410)
IP Security Document Roadmap (RFC 2411)
IP Authentication Header (RFC 2402)
The OAKLEY Key Determination Protocol (RFC 2412)
The ESP CBC-Mode Cipher Algorithms (RFC 2451)
The Use of MD5-HMAC-96 within ESP and AH (RFC 2403)

The Use of HMAC-SHA-1-96 within ESP and AH (RFC 2404)

The ESP DES-CBC Cipher Algorithm With Explicit IV (RFC 2405)

IP Encapsulating Security Payload (ESP) (RFC 2406)

The Internet IP Security Domain of Interpretation for ISAKMP (RFC 2407)

Internet Security Association and Key Management Protocol (ISAKMP) (RFC 2408)

The Internet Key Exchange (IKE) (RFC 2409)

Appendix A

Coding for Prominent Security Functions

This appendix contains examples of code written for several prominent security functions used by Internet security protocols. The background information for this code is described in the main body of this book. Notwithstanding, it is recommended you read the RFC in which the code is provided, because the RFC author usually has additional comments about the code, as well as other ideas for implementing the functions that are beyond the scope of this book.

The following examples are provided in this appendix:

- MD5, Update algorithm
- MD5, Step 4
- HMAC, keyed-hashing for message authentication
- Generation and retrieval of ciphertext in DESE-bis

Please note the copyright notations about RFCs in the front matter of this book. For the MD5 RFC, the following copyright notations apply:

granted to make and use derivative works provided that such works are identified as "derived from the RSA Data Security, Inc. MD5 Message-Digest Algorithm" in all material mentioning or referencing the derived work.

RSA Data Security, Inc. makes no representations concerning either the merchantability of this software or the suitability of this software for any particular purpose. It is provided "as is" without express or implied warranty of any kind.

These notices must be retained in any copies of any part of this documentation and/or software.

MD5 UPDATE ALGORITHM (SOURCE: RFC 1321 [APPENDIX A], AUTHOR RON RIVEST)

This code is from Appendix A for MD5 and RFC 1321.

This code contains the following files taken from RSAREF: A Cryptographic Toolkit for Privacy-Enhanced Mail:

    global.h — global header file

    md5.h — header file for MD5

    md5c.c — source code for MD5

For more information on RSAREF, send email to <rsaref@rsa.com>.

The appendix also includes the following file:

    mddriver.c — test driver for MD2, MD4 and MD5

The driver compiles for MD5 by default but can compile for MD2 or MD4 if the symbol MD is defined on the C compiler command line as 2 or 4.

The implementation is portable and should work on many different plaforms. However, it is not difficult to optimize the implementation on particular platforms, an exercise left to the reader. For example, on "little-endian" platforms where the lowest-addressed byte in a 32-bit word is the least significant and there are no alignment restrictions, the call to Decode in MD5Transform can be replaced with a typecast.

A.1 global.h

```
/* GLOBAL.H - RSAREF types and constants
 */


/* PROTOTYPES should be set to one if and only if the compiler sup-
   ports function argument prototyping.
The following makes PROTOTYPES default to 0 if it has not already
been defined with C compiler flags.
 */
#ifndef PROTOTYPES
#define PROTOTYPES 0
#endif


/* POINTER defines a generic pointer type */
typedef unsigned char *POINTER;


/* UINT2 defines a two byte word */
typedef unsigned short int UINT2;


/* UINT4 defines a four byte word */
typedef unsigned long int UINT4;


/* PROTO_LIST is defined depending on how PROTOTYPES is defined above.
If using PROTOTYPES, then PROTO_LIST returns the list, otherwise it
  returns an empty list.
 */
#if PROTOTYPES
#define PROTO_LIST(list) list
#else
#define PROTO_LIST(list) ()
#endif
```

A.2 md5.h

```
/* MD5.H - header file for MD5C.C
 */


/* MD5 context. */
typedef struct {
  UINT4 state[4];                            /* state (ABCD) */
  UINT4 count[2];       /* number of bits, modulo 2^64 (lsb first) */
  unsigned char buffer[64];                    /* input buffer */
} MD5_CTX;
```

```
void MD5Init PROTO_LIST ((MD5_CTX *));
void MD5Update PROTO_LIST
  ((MD5_CTX *, unsigned char *, unsigned int));
void MD5Final PROTO_LIST ((unsigned char [16], MD5_CTX *));
```

A.3 md5c.c

```
#include "global.h"
#include "md5.h"

/* Constants for MD5Transform routine.
 */

#define S11 7
#define S12 12
#define S13 17
#define S14 22
#define S21 5
#define S22 9
#define S23 14
#define S24 20
#define S31 4
#define S32 11
#define S33 16
#define S34 23
#define S41 6
#define S42 10
#define S43 15
#define S44 21


static void MD5Transform PROTO_LIST ((UINT4 [4], unsigned char [64]));
static void Encode PROTO_LIST
  ((unsigned char *, UINT4 *, unsigned int));
static void Decode PROTO_LIST
  ((UINT4 *, unsigned char *, unsigned int));
static void MD5_memcpy PROTO_LIST ((POINTER, POINTER, unsigned int));
static void MD5_memset PROTO_LIST ((POINTER, int, unsigned int));

static unsigned char PADDING[64] = {
  0x80, 0, 0, 0, 0, 0, 0, 0, 0, 0, 0, 0, 0, 0, 0, 0, 0, 0, 0, 0, 0, 0,
  0, 0, 0, 0, 0, 0, 0, 0, 0, 0, 0, 0, 0, 0, 0, 0, 0, 0, 0, 0, 0, 0,
  0, 0, 0, 0, 0, 0, 0, 0, 0, 0, 0, 0, 0, 0, 0, 0, 0, 0
};


/* F, G, H and I are basic MD5 functions.
```

```
*/
#define F(x, y, z) (((x) & (y)) | ((~x) & (z)))
#define G(x, y, z) (((x) & (z)) | ((y) & (~z)))
#define H(x, y, z) ((x) ^ (y) ^ (z))
#define I(x, y, z) ((y) ^ ((x) | (~z)))


/* ROTATE_LEFT rotates x left n bits.
 */
#define ROTATE_LEFT(x, n) (((x) << (n)) | ((x) >> (32-(n))))


/* FF, GG, HH, and II transformations for rounds 1, 2, 3, and 4.
Rotation is separate from addition to prevent recomputation.
 */
#define FF(a, b, c, d, x, s, ac) { \
  (a) += F ((b), (c), (d)) + (x) + (UINT4)(ac); \
  (a) = ROTATE_LEFT ((a), (s)); \
  (a) += (b); \
  }
#define GG(a, b, c, d, x, s, ac) { \
  (a) += G ((b), (c), (d)) + (x) + (UINT4)(ac); \
  (a) = ROTATE_LEFT ((a), (s)); \
  (a) += (b); \
  }
#define HH(a, b, c, d, x, s, ac) { \
  (a) += H ((b), (c), (d)) + (x) + (UINT4)(ac); \
  (a) = ROTATE_LEFT ((a), (s)); \
  (a) += (b); \
  }
#define II(a, b, c, d, x, s, ac) { \
  (a) += I ((b), (c), (d)) + (x) + (UINT4)(ac); \
  (a) = ROTATE_LEFT ((a), (s)); \
  (a) += (b); \
  }


/* MD5 initialization. Begins an MD5 operation, writing a new context.
 */
void MD5Init (context)
MD5_CTX *context;                                        /* context */
{
  context->count[0] = context->count[1] = 0;
  /* Load magic initialization constants.
*/
  context->state[0] = 0x67452301;
  context->state[1] = 0xefcdab89;
  context->state[2] = 0x98badcfe;
  context->state[3] = 0x10325476;
}
```

```
/* MD5 block update operation. Continues an MD5 message-digest
   operation, processing another message block, and updating the
   context.
 */
void MD5Update (context, input, inputLen)
MD5_CTX *context;                                              /* context */
unsigned char *input;                                     /* input block */
unsigned int inputLen;                          /* length of input block */
{
  unsigned int i, index, partLen;

  /* Compute number of bytes mod 64 */
  index = (unsigned int)((context->count[0] >> 3) & 0x3F);

  /* Update number of bits */
  if ((context->count[0] += ((UINT4)inputLen << 3))
 < ((UINT4)inputLen << 3))
 context->count[1]++;
  context->count[1] += ((UINT4)inputLen >> 29);

  partLen = 64 - index;

  /* Transform as many times as possible.
*/
  if (inputLen >= partLen) {
 MD5_memcpy
   ((POINTER)&context->buffer[index], (POINTER)input, partLen);
 MD5Transform (context->state, context->buffer);

 for (i = partLen; i + 63 < inputLen; i += 64)
   MD5Transform (context->state, &input[i]);

 index = 0;
  }
  else
 i = 0;

  /* Buffer remaining input */
  MD5_memcpy
 ((POINTER)&context->buffer[index], (POINTER)&input[i],
  inputLen-i);
}

/* MD5 finalization. Ends an MD5 message-digest operation, writing the
   message digest and zeroizing the context.
 */
void MD5Final (digest, context)
```

```
unsigned char digest[16];                          /* message digest */
MD5_CTX *context;                                         /* context */
{
  unsigned char bits[8];
  unsigned int index, padLen;

  /* Save number of bits */
  Encode (bits, context->count, 8);

  /* Pad out to 56 mod 64.
*/
  index = (unsigned int)((context->count[0] >> 3) & 0x3f);
  padLen = (index < 56) ? (56 - index) : (120 - index);
  MD5Update (context, PADDING, padLen);

  /* Append length (before padding) */
  MD5Update (context, bits, 8);
  /* Store state in digest */
  Encode (digest, context->state, 16);

  /* Zeroize sensitive information.
*/
  MD5_memset ((POINTER)context, 0, sizeof (*context));
}
/* MD5 basic transformation. Transforms state based on block.
 */
static void MD5Transform (state, block)
UINT4 state[4];
unsigned char block[64];
{
  UINT4 a = state[0], b = state[1], c = state[2], d = state[3], x[16];

  Decode (x, block, 64);

  /* Round 1 */
  FF (a, b, c, d, x[ 0], S11, 0xd76aa478); /* 1 */
  FF (d, a, b, c, x[ 1], S12, 0xe8c7b756); /* 2 */
  FF (c, d, a, b, x[ 2], S13, 0x242070db); /* 3 */
  FF (b, c, d, a, x[ 3], S14, 0xc1bdceee); /* 4 */
  FF (a, b, c, d, x[ 4], S11, 0xf57c0faf); /* 5 */
  FF (d, a, b, c, x[ 5], S12, 0x4787c62a); /* 6 */
  FF (c, d, a, b, x[ 6], S13, 0xa8304613); /* 7 */
  FF (b, c, d, a, x[ 7], S14, 0xfd469501); /* 8 */
  FF (a, b, c, d, x[ 8], S11, 0x698098d8); /* 9 */
  FF (d, a, b, c, x[ 9], S12, 0x8b44f7af); /* 10 */
  FF (c, d, a, b, x[10], S13, 0xffff5bb1); /* 11 */
```

```
FF (b, c, d, a, x[11], S14, 0x895cd7be); /* 12 */
FF (a, b, c, d, x[12], S11, 0x6b901122); /* 13 */
FF (d, a, b, c, x[13], S12, 0xfd987193); /* 14 */
FF (c, d, a, b, x[14], S13, 0xa679438e); /* 15 */
FF (b, c, d, a, x[15], S14, 0x49b40821); /* 16 */


/* Round 2 */
GG (a, b, c, d, x[ 1], S21, 0xf61e2562); /* 17 */
GG (d, a, b, c, x[ 6], S22, 0xc040b340); /* 18 */
GG (c, d, a, b, x[11], S23, 0x265e5a51); /* 19 */
GG (b, c, d, a, x[ 0], S24, 0xe9b6c7aa); /* 20 */
GG (a, b, c, d, x[ 5], S21, 0xd62f105d); /* 21 */
GG (d, a, b, c, x[10], S22,  0x2441453); /* 22 */
GG (c, d, a, b, x[15], S23, 0xd8a1e681); /* 23 */
GG (b, c, d, a, x[ 4], S24, 0xe7d3fbc8); /* 24 */
GG (a, b, c, d, x[ 9], S21, 0x21e1cde6); /* 25 */
GG (d, a, b, c, x[14], S22, 0xc33707d6); /* 26 */
GG (c, d, a, b, x[ 3], S23, 0xf4d50d87); /* 27 */
GG (b, c, d, a, x[ 8], S24, 0x455a14ed); /* 28 */
GG (a, b, c, d, x[13], S21, 0xa9e3e905); /* 29 */
GG (d, a, b, c, x[ 2], S22, 0xfcefa3f8); /* 30 */
GG (c, d, a, b, x[ 7], S23, 0x676f02d9); /* 31 */
GG (b, c, d, a, x[12], S24, 0x8d2a4c8a); /* 32 */


/* Round 3 */
HH (a, b, c, d, x[ 5], S31, 0xfffa3942); /* 33 */
HH (d, a, b, c, x[ 8], S32, 0x8771f681); /* 34 */
HH (c, d, a, b, x[11], S33, 0x6d9d6122); /* 35 */
HH (b, c, d, a, x[14], S34, 0xfde5380c); /* 36 */
HH (a, b, c, d, x[ 1], S31, 0xa4beea44); /* 37 */
HH (d, a, b, c, x[ 4], S32, 0x4bdecfa9); /* 38 */
HH (c, d, a, b, x[ 7], S33, 0xf6bb4b60); /* 39 */
HH (b, c, d, a, x[10], S34, 0xbebfbc70); /* 40 */
HH (a, b, c, d, x[13], S31, 0x289b7ec6); /* 41 */
HH (d, a, b, c, x[ 0], S32, 0xeaa127fa); /* 42 */
HH (c, d, a, b, x[ 3], S33, 0xd4ef3085); /* 43 */
HH (b, c, d, a, x[ 6], S34,  0x4881d05); /* 44 */
HH (a, b, c, d, x[ 9], S31, 0xd9d4d039); /* 45 */
HH (d, a, b, c, x[12], S32, 0xe6db99e5); /* 46 */
HH (c, d, a, b, x[15], S33, 0x1fa27cf8); /* 47 */
HH (b, c, d, a, x[ 2], S34, 0xc4ac5665); /* 48 */


/* Round 4 */
II (a, b, c, d, x[ 0], S41, 0xf4292244); /* 49 */
II (d, a, b, c, x[ 7], S42, 0x432aff97); /* 50 */
II (c, d, a, b, x[14], S43, 0xab9423a7); /* 51 */
II (b, c, d, a, x[ 5], S44, 0xfc93a039); /* 52 */
```

```
  II (a, b, c, d, x[12], S41, 0x655b59c3); /* 53 */
  II (d, a, b, c, x[ 3], S42, 0x8f0ccc92); /* 54 */
  II (c, d, a, b, x[10], S43, 0xffeff47d); /* 55 */
  II (b, c, d, a, x[ 1], S44, 0x85845dd1); /* 56 */
  II (a, b, c, d, x[ 8], S41, 0x6fa87e4f); /* 57 */
  II (d, a, b, c, x[15], S42, 0xfe2ce6e0); /* 58 */
  II (c, d, a, b, x[ 6], S43, 0xa3014314); /* 59 */
  II (b, c, d, a, x[13], S44, 0x4e0811a1); /* 60 */
  II (a, b, c, d, x[ 4], S41, 0xf7537e82); /* 61 */
  II (d, a, b, c, x[11], S42, 0xbd3af235); /* 62 */
  II (c, d, a, b, x[ 2], S43, 0x2ad7d2bb); /* 63 */
  II (b, c, d, a, x[ 9], S44, 0xeb86d391); /* 64 */


  state[0] += a;
  state[1] += b;
  state[2] += c;
  state[3] += d;

  /* Zeroize sensitive information.
*/
  MD5_memset ((POINTER)x, 0, sizeof (x));
}


/* Encodes input (UINT4) into output (unsigned char). Assumes len is
  a multiple of 4.
 */
static void Encode (output, input, len)
unsigned char *output;
UINT4 *input;
unsigned int len;
{
  unsigned int i, j;

  for (i = 0, j = 0; j < len; i++, j += 4) {
 output[j] = (unsigned char)(input[i] & 0xff);
 output[j+1] = (unsigned char)((input[i] >> 8) & 0xff);
 output[j+2] = (unsigned char)((input[i] >> 16) & 0xff);
 output[j+3] = (unsigned char)((input[i] >> 24) & 0xff);
  }
}


/* Decodes input (unsigned char) into output (UINT4). Assumes len is
  a multiple of 4.
 */
static void Decode (output, input, len)
UINT4 *output;
```

```
unsigned char *input;
unsigned int len;
{
  unsigned int i, j;

  for (i = 0, j = 0; j < len; i++, j += 4)
 output[i] = ((UINT4)input[j]) | (((UINT4)input[j+1]) << 8) |
   (((UINT4)input[j+2]) << 16) | (((UINT4)input[j+3]) << 24);
}


/* Note: Replace "for loop" with standard memcpy if possible.
 */


static void MD5_memcpy (output, input, len)
POINTER output;
POINTER input;
unsigned int len;
{
  unsigned int i;

  for (i = 0; i < len; i++)
  output[i] = input[i];
}


/* Note: Replace "for loop" with standard memset if possible.
 */
static void MD5_memset (output, value, len)
POINTER output;
int value;
unsigned int len;
{
  unsigned int i;

  for (i = 0; i < len; i++)
 ((char *)output)[i] = (char)value;
}
```

A.4 mddriver.c

```
/* MDDRIVER.C - test driver for MD2, MD4 and MD5
 */


/* The following makes MD default to MD5 if it has not already been
   defined with C compiler flags.
 */
#ifndef MD
```

```c
#define MD MD5
#endif


#include <stdio.h>
#include <time.h>
#include <string.h>
#include "global.h"
#if MD == 2
#include "md2.h"
#endif
#if MD == 4
#include "md4.h"
#endif
#if MD == 5
#include "md5.h"
#endif


/* Length of test block, number of test blocks.
 */
#define TEST_BLOCK_LEN 1000
#define TEST_BLOCK_COUNT 1000


static void MDString PROTO_LIST ((char *));
static void MDTimeTrial PROTO_LIST ((void));
static void MDTestSuite PROTO_LIST ((void));
static void MDFile PROTO_LIST ((char *));
static void MDFilter PROTO_LIST ((void));
static void MDPrint PROTO_LIST ((unsigned char [16]));


#if MD == 2
#define MD_CTX MD2_CTX
#define MDInit MD2Init
#define MDUpdate MD2Update
#define MDFinal MD2Final
#endif
#if MD == 4
#define MD_CTX MD4_CTX
#define MDInit MD4Init
#define MDUpdate MD4Update
#define MDFinal MD4Final
#endif
#if MD == 5
#define MD_CTX MD5_CTX
#define MDInit MD5Init
#define MDUpdate MD5Update
#define MDFinal MD5Final
#endif
```

```
/* Main driver.

Arguments (may be any combination):
  -sstring - digests string
  -t       - runs time trial
  -x       - runs test script
  filename - digests file
  (none)   - digests standard input
 */
int main (argc, argv)
int argc;
char *argv[];
{
  int i;

  if (argc > 1)
 for (i = 1; i < argc; i++)
   if (argv[i][0] == '-' && argv[i][1] == 's')
     MDString (argv[i] + 2);
   else if (strcmp (argv[i], "-t") == 0)
     MDTimeTrial ();
   else if (strcmp (argv[i], "-x") == 0)
     MDTestSuite ();
   else
     MDFile (argv[i]);
  else
 MDFilter ();

  return (0);
}

/* Digests a string and prints the result.
 */
static void MDString (string)
char *string;
{
  MD_CTX context;
  unsigned char digest[16];
  unsigned int len = strlen (string);

  MDInit (&context);
  MDUpdate (&context, string, len);
  MDFinal (digest, &context);

  printf ("MD%d (\"%s\") = ", MD, string);
  MDPrint (digest);
```

```
  printf ("\n");
}


/* Measures the time to digest TEST_BLOCK_COUNT TEST_BLOCK_LEN-byte
  blocks.
 */
static void MDTimeTrial ()
{
  MD_CTX context;
  time_t endTime, startTime;
  unsigned char block[TEST_BLOCK_LEN], digest[16];
  unsigned int i;
  printf
("MD%d time trial. Digesting %d %d-byte blocks ...", MD,
  TEST_BLOCK LEN, TEST_BLOCK_COUNT);

  /* Initialize block */
  for (i = 0; i < TEST_BLOCK_LEN; i++)
 block[i] = (unsigned char)(i & 0xff);

  /* Start timer */
  time (&startTime);

  /* Digest blocks */
  MDInit (&context);
  for (i = 0; i < TEST_BLOCK_COUNT; i++)
 MDUpdate (&context, block, TEST_BLOCK_LEN);
  MDFinal (digest, &context);

  /* Stop timer */
  time (&endTime);

  printf (" done\n");
  printf ("Digest = ");
  MDPrint (digest);
  printf ("\nTime = %ld seconds\n", (long)(endTime-startTime));
  printf
("Speed = %ld bytes/second\n",
  (long)TEST_BLOCK_LEN * (long)TEST_BLOCK_COUNT/(endTime-startTime));
}


/* Digests a reference suite of strings and prints the results.
 */
static void MDTestSuite ()
{
  printf ("MD%d test suite:\n", MD);
```

```
  MDString ("");
  MDString ("a");
  MDString ("abc");
  MDString ("message digest");
  MDString ("abcdefghijklmnopqrstuvwxyz");
  MDString
 ("ABCDEFGHIJKLMNOPQRSTUVWXYZabcdefghijklmnopqrstuvwxyz0123456789");
  MDString
 ("1234567890123456789012345678901234567890\
123456789012345678901234567890123456789012");
}


/* Digests a file and prints the result.
 */
static void MDFile (filename)
char *filename;
{
  FILE *file;
  MD_CTX context;
  int len;
  unsigned char buffer[1024], digest[16];


  if ((file = fopen (filename, "rb")) == NULL)
 printf ("%s can't be opened\n", filename);


  else {
 MDInit (&context);
 while (len = fread (buffer, 1, 1024, file))
   MDUpdate (&context, buffer, len);
 MDFinal (digest, &context);


 fclose (file);


 printf ("MD%d (%s) = ", MD, filename);
 MDPrint (digest);
 printf ("\n");
  }
}


/* Digests the standard input and prints the result.
 */
static void MDFilter ()
{
  MD_CTX context;
  int len;
  unsigned char buffer[16], digest[16];
```

```
  MDInit (&context);
  while (len = fread (buffer, 1, 16, stdin))
 MDUpdate (&context, buffer, len);
  MDFinal (digest, &context);

  MDPrint (digest);
  printf ("\n");
}

/* Prints a message digest in hexadecimal.
 */
static void MDPrint (digest)
unsigned char digest[16];
{
 unsigned int i;

  for (i = 0; i < 16; i++)
 printf ("%02x", digest[i]);
}
```

A.5 Test suite

   The MD5 test suite (driver option "-x") should print the following
   results:
```
MD5 test suite:
MD5 ("") = d41d8cd98f00b204e9800998ecf8427e
MD5 ("a") = 0cc175b9c0f1b6a831c399e269772661
MD5 ("abc") = 900150983cd24fb0d6963f7d28e17f72
MD5 ("message digest") = f96b697d7cb7938d525a2f31aaf161d0
MD5 ("abcdefghijklmnopqrstuvwxyz") = c3fcd3d76192e4007dfb496cca67e13b
MD5 ("ABCDEFGHIJKLMNOPQRSTUVWXYZabcdefghijklmnopqrstu-
vwxyz0123456789") =
d174ab98d277d9f5a5611c2c9f419d9f
MD5
("12345678901234567890123456789012345678901234567890123456
78901234567890") = 57edf4a22be3c955ac49da2e2107b67a
```

MD5 UPDATE ALGORITHM (SOURCE: RFC 1321 [SECTION 3.4], AUTHOR RON RIVEST)

   This code is part of step 4 of the MD5 operations, introduced in
Chapter 5.

```
/* Process each 16-word block. */
```

```
For i = 0 to N/16-1 do

  /* Copy block i into X. */
  For j = 0 to 15 do
    Set X[j] to M[i*16+j].
  end /* of loop on j */


  /* Save A as AA, B as BB, C as CC, and D as DD. */
  AA = A
  BB = B
  CC = C
  DD = D


  /* Round 1. */
  /* Let [abcd k s i] denote the operation
      a = b + ((a + F(b,c,d) + X[k] + T[i]) <<< s). */
  /* Do the following 16 operations. */
  [ABCD  0  7  1]  [DABC  1 12   2]  [CDAB  2 17   3]  [BCDA  3 22   4]
  [ABCD  4  7  5]  [DABC  5 12   6]  [CDAB  6 17   7]  [BCDA  7 22   8]
  [ABCD  8  7  9]  [DABC  9 12  10]  [CDAB 10 17  11]  [BCDA 11 22  12]
  [ABCD 12  7 13]  [DABC 13 12  14]  [CDAB 14 17  15]  [BCDA 15 22  16]


  /* Round 2. */
  /* Let [abcd k s i] denote the operation
      a = b + ((a + G(b,c,d) + X[k] + T[i]) <<< s). */
  /* Do the following 16 operations. */
  [ABCD  1  5 17]  [DABC  6  9  18]  [CDAB 11 14  19]  [BCDA  0 20  20]
  [ABCD  5  5 21]  [DABC 10  9  22]  [CDAB 15 14  23]  [BCDA  4 20  24]
  [ABCD  9  5 25]  [DABC 14  9  26]  [CDAB  3 14  27]  [BCDA  8 20  28]
  [ABCD 13  5 29]  [DABC  2  9  30]  [CDAB  7 14  31]  [BCDA 12 20  32]


  /* Round 3. */
  /* Let [abcd k s t] denote the operation
      a = b + ((a + H(b,c,d) + X[k] + T[i]) <<< s). */
  /* Do the following 16 operations. */
  [ABCD  5  4 33]  [DABC  8 11  34]  [CDAB 11 16  35]  [BCDA 14 23  36]
  [ABCD  1  4 37]  [DABC  4 11  38]  [CDAB  7 16  39]  [BCDA 10 23  40]
  [ABCD 13  4 41]  [DABC  0 11  42]  [CDAB  3 16  43]  [BCDA  6 23  44]
  [ABCD  9  4 45]  [DABC 12 11  46]  [CDAB 15 16  47]  [BCDA  2 23  48]


  /* Round 4. */
  /* Let [abcd k s t] denote the operation
      a = b + ((a + I(b,c,d) + X[k] + T[i]) <<< s). */
  /* Do the following 16 operations. */
  [ABCD  0  6 49]  [DABC  7 10  50]  [CDAB 14 15  51]  [BCDA  5 21  52]
  [ABCD 12  6 53]  [DABC  3 10  54]  [CDAB 10 15  55]  [BCDA  1 21  56]
```

```
[ABCD  8  6 57]  [DABC 15 10 58]  [CDAB  6 15 59]  [BCDA 13 21 60]
[ABCD  4  6 61]  [DABC 11 10 62]  [CDAB  2 15 63]  [BCDA  9 21 64]


/* Then perform the following additions. (That is increment each
   of the four registers by the value it had before this block
   was started.) */
A = A + AA
B = B + BB
C = C + CC
D = D + DD


end /* of loop on i */
```

HMAC: KEYED-HASHING FOR MESSAGE AUTHENTICATION (SOURCE: RFC 2104 [APPENDIX], AUTHORS: HUGO KRAWCZYK, MIHIR BELLARE, AND RAN CANETTI)

For the sake of illustration we provide the following sample code for the implementation of HMAC-MD5 as well as some corresponding test vectors (the code is based on MD5 code as described in [MD5]).

```
/*
** Function: hmac_md5
*/

void
hmac_md5(text, text_len, key, key_len, digest)
unsigned char*  text;           /* pointer to data stream */
int           text_len;         /* length of data stream */
unsigned char*  key;            /* pointer to authentication key */
int           key_len;          /* length of authentication key */
caddr_t         digest;         /* caller digest to be filled in */

{
      MD5_CTX context;
      unsigned char k_ipad[65];   /* inner padding -
                                   * key XORd with ipad
                                   */
      unsigned char k_opad[65];   /* outer padding -
                                   * key XORd with opad
                                   */
      unsigned char tk[16];
      int i;
      /* if key is longer than 64 bytes reset it to key=MD5(key) */
```

```
if (key_len > 64) {

        MD5_CTX        tctx;

        MD5Init(&tctx);
        MD5Update(&tctx, key, key_len);
        MD5Final(tk, &tctx);

        key = tk;
        key_len = 16;
}


/*
 * the HMAC_MD5 transform looks like:
 *
 * MD5(K XOR opad, MD5(K XOR ipad, text))
 *
 * where K is an n byte key
 * ipad is the byte 0x36 repeated 64 times

 * opad is the byte 0x5c repeated 64 times
 * and text is the data being protected
 */


/* start out by storing key in pads */
bzero( k_ipad, sizeof k_ipad);
bzero( k_opad, sizeof k_opad);
bcopy( key, k_ipad, key_len);
bcopy( key, k_opad, key_len);

/* XOR key with ipad and opad values */
for (i=0; i<64; i++) {
        k_ipad[i] ^= 0x36;
        k_opad[i] ^= 0x5c;
}
/*
 * perform inner MD5
 */
MD5Init(&context);                          /* init context for 1st
                                             * pass */
MD5Update(&context, k_ipad, 64)    /* start with inner pad */
MD5Update(&context, text, text_len);/* then text of datagram */
MD5Final(digest, &context);        /* finish up 1st pass */
/*
 * perform outer MD5
 */
```

```
        MD5Init(&context);                  /* init context for 2nd
                                             * pass */
        MD5Update(&context, k_opad, 64);    /* start with outer pad */
        MD5Update(&context, digest, 16);    /* then results of 1st
                                             * hash */
        MD5Final(digest, &context);         /* finish up 2nd pass */
}
```

Test Vectors (Trailing '\0' of a character string not included in test):

```
  key =           0x0b0b0b0b0b0b0b0b0b0b0b0b0b0b0b0b
  key_len =       16 bytes
  data =          "Hi There"
  data_len =      8  bytes
  digest =        0x9294727a3638bb1c13f48ef8158bfc9d


  key =           "Jefe"
  data =          "what do ya want for nothing?"
  data_len =      28 bytes
  digest =        0x750c783e6ab0b503eaa86e310a5db738


  key =           0xAAAAAAAAAAAAAAAAAAAAAAAAAAAAAAAA
  key_len =       16 bytes
  data =          0xDDDDDDDDDDDDDDDDDDDD...
                  ..DDDDDDDDDDDDDDDDDDDD...
                  ..DDDDDDDDDDDDDDDDDDDD...
                  ..DDDDDDDDDDDDDDDDDDDD...
                  ..DDDDDDDDDDDDDDDDDDDD
  data_len =      50 bytes
  digest =        0x56be34521d144c88dbb8c733f0e8b3f6
```

GENERATION OF AND RETRIEVAL OF CIPHERTEXT IN RFC 1969: PPP DES ENCRYPTION PROTOCOL (DESE-bis). (AUTHORS: KEITH SKLOWER, AND GERRY M. MEYER).

Generation of the Ciphertext

In this discussion, E[k] will denote the basic DES cipher deter-mined by a 56-bit key k acting on 64 bit blocks. and D[k] will de-note the corresponding decryption mechanism. The padded plaintext described in the previous section then becomes a sequence of 64 bit blocks P[i] (where i ranges from 1 to n). The circumflex character (^) represents the bit-wise exclusive-or operation applied to 64-bit blocks.

When encrypting the first packet to be transmitted in the opened
state let C[0] be the result of applying E[k] to the Initial Nonce
received in the peer's ECP DESE option; otherwise let C[0] be the
final block of the previously transmitted packet.

The ciphertext for the packet is generated by the iterative

$$C[i] = E[k](P[i] \char`\^ C[i-1])$$

process for i running between 1 and n.

6.3. Retrieval of the Plaintext

When decrypting the first packet received in the opened state,
let C[0] be the result of applying E[k] to the Initial Nonce transmitted in the ECP DESE option. The first packet will have sequence
number zero. For subsequent packets, let C[0] be the final block of
the previous packet in sequence space. Decryption is then accomplished by

$$P[i] = C[i-1] \char`\^ D[k](C[i]),$$

for i running between 1 and n.

Recovery after Packet Loss

Packet loss is detected when there is a discontinuity in the sequence numbers of consecutive packets. Suppose packet number N - 1
has an unrecoverable error or is otherwise lost, but packets N and
N + 1 are received correctly.

Since the algorithm in the previous section requires C[0] for
packet N to be C[last] for packet N - 1, it will be impossible to
decode packet N. However, all packets N + 1 and following can be
decoded in the usual way, since all that is required is the last
block of ciphertext of the previous packet (in this case packet N,
which WAS received).

Appendix B

Network Address Translation (NAT)

The Network Address Translation (NAT) allows an organization to use private, non-registered IP addresses (non-globally routable addresses) within its own routing domain. If traffic is to be sent out of this domain, NAT translates these addresses to globally routable addresses. The reverse process occurs at the router for traffic received by the domain. NAT thus allows an organization to use its own private addresses. It also supports a process called the TCP load distribution feature that allows the mapping of a single global address to multiple non-global addresses. This feature is used to conserve addresses, and is explained shortly. NAT is described in RFC 1631, and examples used in this discussion are sourced from this RFC and [CISC98].

Figure B–1 is used to introduce the basic concepts of NAT. First, a couple of definitions are in order. An *inside local IP address* is a non-global address that is assigned to a host. This host resides on an inside network—one that uses non-global addresses. An *inside global IP address* is a global address and represents the inside address to the outside networks (global addressing networks). Router A in this figure houses a NAT table that correlates these addresses.

The bottom part of Figure B–1 shows how NAT is used to map addresses between the inside and outside networks. In event 1, host B sends an IP datagram to Host D, through router A. Router A checks the address in the datagram and knows that source address (SA) 176.16.1.1 is an inside address. If an entry in the NAT table does not exist, the router dynamically selects an available global address from a pool of addresses, and creates an entry in the table. In event 2, the router replaces the inside SA with the corresponding outside SA, and forwards the datagram.

In event 3, host D replies, and uses its SA of 191.1.1.3, and the NAT global address for the destination address (DA) of 191.1.1.1. This datagram is received by router A, which performs the mapping of the global DA of 191.1.1.1 to the inside DA of 176.16.1.1, depicted as event 4 in the figure.

NAT is a straightforward configuration; essentially the local IP and global IP addresses are entered into the table during the configuration, along with the inside and outside interfaces on the router.

NAT allows the reuse of inside global addresses by mapping one of these addresses to more than one local address. This operation is called

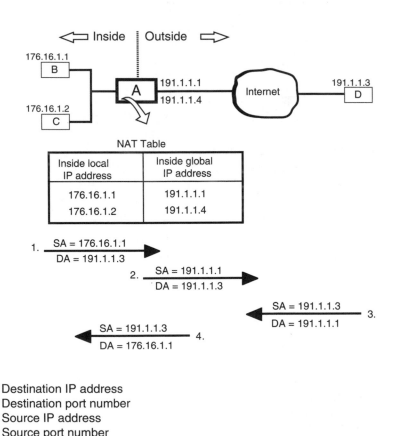

Where:
   DA   Destination IP address
   DP   Destination port number
   SA   Source IP address
   SP   Source port number

Figure B–1   Network Address Translation (NAT)

overloading an inside global address. The ability to maintain unambiguous identification of all user sessions is through the inside local address, the inside global address, plus the port numbers that are carried in the TCP or UDP segment header.

NAT defines another address; it is called the *outside global IP address,* and it is a conventional IP address assigned to a host on the globally addressable outside network.

Figure B–2 shows how this part of NAT works. In event 1, host B sends a datagram to host D, through router A. The figure shows the

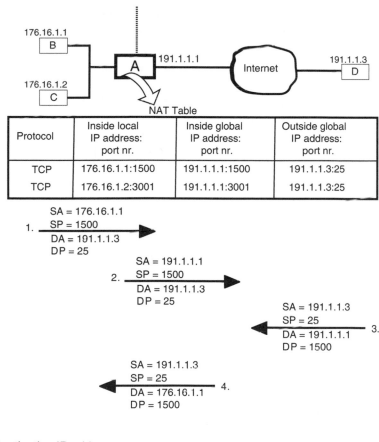

Figure B–2   Overloading inside global addresses

source address (SA), source port (SP), destination address (DA), and destination port (DP). The router intercepts the datagram, and performs either static or dynamic translation of the inside local IP address (176.16.1.1) to a shared inside global IP address (191.1.1.1).

In event 2, the router forwards the datagram toward the destination host D. In event 3, host D replies. The host simply exchanges the destination address and port number with the source address and port number.

Router A receives this datagram, and looks at the NAT table to determine what it is to do. It uses the socket pair shown in event 3 as a key to the table.

In event 4, the translation is made back to host B's inside local IP address and the datagram is delivered to host B in the inside network.

The same operation can be performed for host C, using the second entry in the NAT table.

The configuration at the router entails the allocation of a pool of global addresses as needed, and then correlating them with the inside addresses and the associated input and output interfaces.

Abbreviations

3DESE   Triple-DES Encryption Protocol
ACK   acknowledgment
ARP   Address Resolution Protocol
AUC   authentication control center
BITC   bump-in-the-code
BITS   bump-in-the-stack
BITW   bump-in-the-wire
CA   certification authorities
CEK   content-encryption key
CHAP   Challenge-Handshake Authentication Protocol
CLNP   Connectionless Network Protocol
CM   ciphered message
DA   destination address
DESE-bis   DES Encryption Protocol version 2
D-H   Diffie-Hellman algorithm
DLC   data link control
DNS   domain name server
DOD   Department of Defense
DOI   domain of interpretation
DSP   digital service processor
DSU   data service unit
EAP   Extensible Authentication Protocol
ECP   Encryption Control Protocol
ESP   Encapsulated Security Protocol
FTP   File Transfer Protocol

GSM   Global System for Mobile Communications
HDLC   high-level data link control
HMAC   hashing for message authentication
HTML   Hypertext Markup Language
HTTP   Hypertext Transfer Protocol
IANA   Internet Assigned Numbers Authority
ICMP   Internet Control Management Protocol
ICMP   Internet Control Message Protocol
ICV   integrity check value
IETF   Internet Engineering Task Force
IGP   Internal Gateway Protocol
IKE   internet key exchange
IMEI   international mobile equipment identity
IMSI   international mobile subscriber identity
INSI   intranetwork switching interface
IP   Internet Protocol
IPCP   Internet Protocol Control Protocol
IPSec   Internet Security Protocol
IPv4   Internet Protocol version 4
IPv6   Internet Protocol version 6
IPv6CP   IPv6 Control Protocol

ISAKMP   Internet Security Association and Key Management Protocol
ISO   Internet Standards Organization
ISOC   Internet Society
ISP   internet service provider
KEK   key-encryption key
LAN   local access network
LCP   Link Control Protocol
LLC   logical link control
MAC   message authentication code
MD   message digest
MFWS   managed firewall service
MGCP   Media Gateway Control Protocol
MTU   maximum transmission unit
NAK   negative acknowledgment
NAS   network access server
NAT   network address translation
NCP   Network Control Protocol
NIC   network interface card
NIST   National Institute of Standards and Technology
OS   operating system
OSI   open systems interconnection
OSPF   open shortest path first
OTK   one-time key
PAP   Password Authentication Protocol
PAD   packet assembler/disassembler
PARC   Palo Alto Research Center
PCI   Protocol Control Information
PDU   protocol data unit
PFS   perfect forward security
PGP   pretty good privacy
PKI   public-key infrastructure
PPP   Point-To-Point Protocol
QOS   quality of service
RA   request authenticator
RADIUS   Remote Authentication Dial-In Service

RARP   Reverse Address Resolution Protocol
RD   receive delay
RFC   Request for Comments
RIPE   RACE Integrity Primatives Evaluation
RPC   remote procedure call
RR   resource record
RSA   Rivest-Shamir-Adelman
RSVP   Resource Reservation Protocol
RTT   round trip time
SA   security association
SAD   security association database
SAP   service access point
SD   send delay
SDLC   synchronous data link control
SGNC   signaling gateway/NAS controller
SHA   secure hash algorithm
SIM   subscriber identity module
SLA   service level agreement
SMTP   Simple Mail Transfer Protocol
SNA   systems network architecture
SNMP   Simple Network Management Protocol
SPD   security policy database
SPI   security parameter index
SRES   signed response
TCP   Transmission Control Protocol
TFTP   Trivial FTP
TLS   transport level security
TOS   type of service
TTL   time-to-live
UDP   User Data Protocol
URL   Uniform Resource Locator
VoIP   Voice over IP
VPN   virtual private network
WAN   wide area network

Index